GW00726970

Communities
of Reconciliation

Living faith in the public place

Johnston McMaster
Cathy Higgins

All rights reserved. No part of this publication may
be reproduced, stored in a retrieval system or
transmitted in any form or by any means,
electronic, mechanical, photocopying, scanning,
recording or otherwise, without the prior written
permission of the copyright owners and publisher
of this book.

6 5 4 3 2 1

© McMaster and Higgins
   2002

Designed by Colourpoint Books,
Newtownards
Printed by Nicholson & Bass

ISBN 1 904242 04 9

**Colourpoint gratefully
acknowledge the generous
assistance given by the Irish
School of Ecumenics towards
the publication of this book.**

Colourpoint Books
Unit D5, Ards Business Centre
Jubilee Road
NEWTOWNARDS
County Down
Northern Ireland
BT23 4YH
Tel: 028 9182 0505
Fax: 028 9182 1900
E-mail: info@colourpoint.co.uk
Web-site: www.colourpoint.co.uk

Cathy Higgins   Johnston McMaster

About the Authors

Cathy Higgins is a native of Portstewart. She is a lecturer on
the Irish School of Ecumenics Education for Reconciliation
Programme in Northern Ireland and the Border Counties. A
Masters graduate of ISE in Ecumenics, she has been accepted
for a doctoral programme in International Feminist Theology
with San Francisco Theological Seminary. Cathy has a
particular interest in women's theology and ecumenical
spirituality. She has published in this field and co-authored
with Johnston McMaster *Churches Working Together: A
Practical Resource.*

Johnston McMaster is a native of Portavogie. He is lecturer
and coordinator of the Irish School of Ecumenics Education
for Reconciliation Programme. His doctorate is from Garrett-
Evangelical Theological Seminary, Evanston, Illinois, with a
thesis on Methodist Stewardship in Irish Politics 1886–1989.
His interests are in political theology and Celtic spirituality.
His publications include *A Strategy for Peace: Training in Cross
Community Skills and Issues; The Future Returns: A Journey
with Columba and Augustine of Canterbury;* and *Churches on
the Edge: Responding Creatively To A Changing Time.*

Cover image
The cross depicted on the cover is the symbol used by the
cross-community chaplaincy in the University of Ulster at
Jordanstown, and is reproduced with kind permission.

Contents

Dreaming dreams, creating pathways
The challenge of being church in the twenty-first century

**Living faith at the edge
The Bible in the public square**

Course Three Outline

**Being authentic community for the twenty-first century
Exploring the biblical tension between institutional
religion and community**

Course Four Outline

4 **Journey towards communities of integrity
Exploring nationalism, identity and violence from
a biblical perspective**

Course Five Outline

5 **The politics of faith
Exploring the Bible as a political text** **5**

Bibliography

Acknowledgements

Our profound gratitude goes to all those who participated in the Education for Reconciliation programme, locally and globally. They tested, refined and enabled the content to reach its present form. Their enthusiasm, commitment and involvement have been invaluable; they were the teachers and practical theologians of reconciliation.

Our thanks also to Karen Nicholson whose word processing skills and critical commentary have made a significant contribution to the final text.

We dedicate these courses to those committed to peace-making and community building in Northern Ireland and throughout our global network.

Johnston McMaster

Cathy Higgins

Irish School of Ecumenics
Trinity College Dublin

Mission statement

The Irish School of Ecumenics is an international academic institute, Christian in its inspiration and ethos, interdenominational in structure and personnel. It exists to promote through research, teaching and outreach activities; the unity of Christians; dialogue between religions; and work for peace and justice in Ireland and abroad. Its resources are available to churches and other appropriate bodies committed to unity, dialogue and peace.

Learning together
Education for Reconciliation programme

General course objectives

1 To develop greater understanding between people from the different traditions in local communities.

2 To raise awareness of and explore key community, religious, cultural, political, social and reconciliation issues.

3 To empower participants to be actively involved in the practice of reconciliation within local communities.

4 To promote the practice of equity, diversity and interdependence between the traditions.

5 To enable participation in the building of an integrated and inclusive civic society through the practice of active citizenship.

Introduction

Education for Reconciliation is a series of courses developed with people from local communities for local communities. The focus is on social reconciliation and as such is broad based, covering a diverse range of issues, all of which are involved in a reconciliation process.

The facilitation process for each session is clearly laid out and the session worksheets and OHP contents are also included. For course facilitators, the OHP contents are available for purchase separately to allow them to be photocopied onto acetates. Each theme has extensive background notes, which should provide facilitators with enough information to give a confident delivery of the session. Each session is planned to last for two hours and timings for each component of the session are indicated. It is possible to be flexible with the timings.

The process uses various methods. There is input usually around an OHP. Interactive group work is a central feature because participants are engaged in learning from each other rather than from the facilitators. Role play or 'bibliodrama' is used and is an effective, imaginative way of getting inside a biblical story, scenario or contemporary issue. In some sessions creative writing or art work – the drawing of symbols – is used.

The Bible is used as a shared norm for all Christians and a particular approach is developed in understanding and applying the text. This is described in chapter 2 as 'A socio-political reading of Scripture'. It is important for facilitators to read this introduction to the reading strategy which is dealt with again in the opening session of the course, 'The politics of faith: exploring the Bible as a political text'. All biblical quotations are from the New Revised Standard Version (NRSV), Oxford Press, 1995.

Facilitators will also find it helpful to spend some time on chapter 1, 'Methods in Education for Reconciliation'. This will provide insights into the underlying methodologies used in the Education for Reconciliation programme and also help facilitators to appreciate the processes used.

The third chapter deals with 'The art of theological reflection' which is considered to be an important process in developing theologies of reconciliation for the public place. Theological reflection is taking place during course sessions and the concluding chapter attempts to articulate the art through diagrams and commentary. Beyond courses, participants need to continue with theological reflection which is ultimately about doing theology as practical action in local communities.

The Education for Reconciliation team at the Irish School of Ecumenics (Belfast) offers this course manual as a resource to local congregations or local inter-church groups: the aim is to enable them to engage with the reconciling process that is needed in a society emerging from conflict though still living within contested space. The team is confident that local facilitators will be able to use this material in helpful ways. Team members are available for consultation, which will enable courses to be undertaken.

The Education for Reconciliation programme is about people in local communities doing theology, engaging with explorations of reconciliation and engaging with initiatives and actions towards reconciliation.

Whoever we are, and wherever we are, God has given us a ministry of reconciliation.

Chapter 1

Methods in Education for Reconciliation

The changing context and the peace process provide the challenge to educate for reconciliation. A key question facing educators in this area is what shall we teach and how shall we teach it?

Reconciliation can easily become a buzzword with a soft edge. Within faith communities it is sometimes only understood as a vertical relationship between God and the individual or, at the very most, a one-to-one personal reconciliation. Reconciliation, which is hard edged, needs to be community orientated and take the political and social context seriously.

The reality is that Northern Ireland is a contested society with identities often defined in opposition to each other. The community and structural divisions run deep, with roots in centuries of history. Privatised or pietistic reconciliation have nothing to say to such a society.

Reconciliation needs to be understood and developed as social reconciliation. The word originally came from the world of politics and economics. It is these political and economic origins that lie behind the two particular words for reconciliation used in the New Testament. The word derived from economics means 'to give and take', 'to exchange'; the word derived from politics means 'to bring together into a new form of community'. We might then say that reconciliation is about taking initiatives and actions that make enemies into friends through give and take and by building new and different forms of community. This kind of reconciliation is about transforming relationships and structures through lengthy processes requiring courage, risk and commitment.

The Education for Reconciliation courses of the Irish School of Ecumenics are attempting to take seriously this kind of social reconciliation. It is for this reason that they cover a wide spectrum of themes and issues from civic responsibility to creating a non-violent culture, from religion and nationalism to creating a just economic ethics and gender equality.

The Education for Reconciliation courses follow particular methodologies that have been developed over the last six years by staff in consultation with course participants from local communities. As part of our strategic development process, Education for Reconciliation courses take place in all nine Ulster counties, plus Louth and Leitrim.

A number of significant factors shape the Education for Reconciliation programme:

1. It is grass roots based.

The courses take seriously the local context. Through networking and dialogue, people come together in a given area to explore the type of course that would address their particular needs. The initial meeting may be the result of a local initiative to bring people from the different churches together, or it may be in response to a local conversation begun by the Education for Reconciliation team.

It may take a few months for a future course to emerge, as individuals share their concerns and discuss issues and themes they would like to address. As conversations develop so do relations within the group.

The local group essentially designs the programme, deciding on its style and content. Staff, then, take the course outline away to unpack it and give it shape.

2. It is locally owned.

Local ownership of the course is an important part of the reconciliation process. Staff, therefore, try to involve local people as much as possible. When they first come together, most groups admit their ignorance of the various Christian traditions. This is not just Protestant–Catholic ignorance, as those from the various Protestant traditions often have little understanding of each other. Local ministers are invited in to describe their traditions and participants learn about local churches that they may have driven past but never entered. This often paves the way for those in the group to visit each other's churches and experience each other's worship. Local people, one Catholic and the other Protestant, usually facilitate this journey of understanding. The reconciliation process becomes more embedded through a real sense of local ownership.

3. It crosses boundaries.

As Northern Ireland is a divided society with much of life segregated, from formal education to social, educational and religious life, crossing the boundaries is an important step. Space is provided on the courses to begin boundary crossings. Participants, aware of the risks in sharing perceptions, fears and suspicions, nevertheless commit to the process, aware that it is only through meaningful encounter that 'the other' is rehumanised. As distances are crossed, and sometimes painful journeys undertaken, new relational possibilities open up.

Victims and perpetrators hear each other's stories and aid each other in the healing of raw wounds and excruciating memories. People who have lived in the shadow of a 'peace wall', fearing those on the other side, realise what they share in common. Members of other world faiths voice their experiences and perspectives, adding diversity and richness to the encounter. The realisation dawns that the seemingly huge effort involved in crossing boundaries reaps a fruitful bounty.

4. It is contextual.

No one lives or believes in a vacuum. Life is always lived, and authentic faith is shaped, in a particular context. Furthermore, there is no reconciliation without addressing the context, in all its pain, complexity and ambiguity. Participants on courses are encouraged to engage with Northern Ireland issues; this involves taking account of the totality of relationships, north–south as well as east–west. Local contexts are also addressed. This may involve developing a profile of the local community in terms of social, economic, political and religious concerns. Paying attention to context emphasises the fact that the horizons of reconciliation include all aspects of life, from people to institutions, from God to the created world.

5. It is relational.

Education for Reconciliation courses are concerned to build community, based on friendship, trust, equality and respect. Courses offer safe spaces for people to meet and encounter each other through interactive sharing and activities. As these encounters deepen and develop, strangers become friends.

In the courses reconciliation themes and issues are approached from a relational perspective. Theological doctrines, like justification by faith, the priesthood of all believers, Scripture and tradition, and Eucharist, are re-examined in their original context to recover their relational understanding of God, people and the world. The session on 'Tolerance' in the 'Living Faith At The Edge' course illustrates how Paul's letter to the Romans can be read relationally.

6. It aims to transcend painful histories.

We have often been selective in our reading of history, focusing exclusively on our chosen traumas. Fresh pain and new traumas have been created over the last 30 years. One thing we can be sure of is that neither the Protestant nor the Catholic community have a monopoly on suffering. If Education for Reconciliation is to be effective it needs to include opportunities for the telling of stories, the sharing of pain, the healing of memories and the creative, redemptive, transcending of painful histories. Only then will a new, inclusive narrative and understanding of our shared history emerge out of the pain-filled compassionate encounters of those on the journey toward reconciliation.

7. It uses the right brain.

A good deal of educational and theological method is left-brained. The analytical, rational, logical and verbal approach has its place, but by itself it stifles our capacity for fresh ideas. It has little appeal to imagination and, therefore, lacks real transformative potential. When the imagination is fired, alternative possibilities are created. It is through the imagination and the poetic that alternative or fresh social and relational vision emerges. The vision of a reconciled society requires an activated imagination.

The right side of the brain is artistic, imaginative, intuitive and poetic. It is also the side of the brain in touch with feelings and emotions. The classical Western rationalist paradigm is too limited. All of the right brain needs to be engaged in Education for Reconciliation. How else can there be a transformation of the fear, grief, anger, even frozen anger and the opening up of compassion to the suffering on the other side? At the heart of the conflict and community division is an emotional matrix. This is where the use of creative and artistic media is highly significant.

So Education for Reconciliation courses make use of role play, bibliodrama and poetry as ways of exploring issues and as a means of getting in touch with feelings. The creativity of participants is amazing as they enter imaginatively into characters or situations. There is humour and pain and a much more in-depth engagement with issues than would be possible through a left-brain approach. Art is now also being developed as a way of exploring deep feelings. Use of the right brain is essential if Education for Reconciliation is to have a good emotional foundation.

8. It is an empowering process.

Programmes of Education for Reconciliation seek to engage people in a process or a journey which empowers for action within church and society. The purpose is to enable people to be reconcilers. This means helping people develop reflective skills that will assist them in reflecting on personal and community experience, and help them to connect the encounters and challenges of everyday life with faith perspectives. Ongoing reflection, and making the connections, shape deeper faith perspectives and practical responses. Participants talk of having greater confidence to contribute to discussions in the public place and to challenge stereotypes and prejudices, as well as engage in respectful dialogue.

9. It is rooted in Scripture.

Education for Reconciliation courses recognise the Bible as a key resource and shared norm for all

Christians. Courses have been developed using scriptural texts as a way in to exploring socio-political and economic issues. This approach encourages participants to consider emerging contemporary themes in the light of biblical perspectives. Key to reading and interpreting Scripture is taking seriously its social and political contexts. The next chapter, 'A socio-political reading of Scripture', will unpack this innovative methodology more fully. Participants on courses have responded with enthusiasm and excitement to this approach, claiming it sheds light on the ongoing relevance of the Bible for the contemporary context.

10. It is team-taught.

The experience of teaching these courses has reaffirmed for us the value and necessity of a team-teaching approach. The content explored and the issues that arise are too complex and demanding for one person to deal with adequately. It requires the combined skills and insights of two people, allowing for one of the team to be actively listening while the other is responding. The balance of Catholic/Protestant, male/female has enriched the course dynamic and provided a living model of reconciliation. This approach has not been lost on course participants. Where possible, it is strongly recommended that a team-teaching approach be used.

The methodologies described above have been developed in the ongoing process of teaching and learning, which is a two-way process between course facilitators and participants. These methodologies have, therefore, been tried and tested in local communities. However, they are by no means final and remain open to development.

The course methodologies and contents have been shared with international groups, especially those engaged in peace education and reconciliation work in various world conflict situations, including Latin America, the Middle East, Eastern Europe and Asia Pacific. The approach has resonated with educators and activists from these conflict regions and there is recognition that the Education for Reconciliation model is one that can be used and/or adapted elsewhere.

Education for Reconciliation offers a strategic model of reconciliation for the public place and it is also a practical model of local community theology. This programme enables people to make the journey toward social reconciliation:

"Working toward that
    all-inclusive
        justice-filled,
            peace-abiding
                reign and realm of the One
                    who is 'I AM'."

(Linda J Vogel, *Teaching And Learning In Communities Of Faith: Empowering Adults Through Religious Education*, Jossey-Bass Publishers, 1991, p 174.)

Chapter 2

A socio-political reading of Scripture

Education for Reconciliation is about social reconciliation. It is about reconciliation in the socio-political square. A more popular understanding of reconciliation tends to privatise it and deal with the vertical relationship between God and the individual. It may have a horizontal dimension but usually only at the level of personal relationships. The interpretation of the faith tradition and a reading of the Bible tends to be confined to the private and at most one-to-one relationships.

The courses offered in this manual attempt to approach reconciliation through a range of social and political issues. Reconciliation is about community and the public relationships within community. This calls for a re-reading of faith and biblical traditions. In all of the courses the Bible has a central role. It is used as the primary norm for the Christian community – its foundational document – and the invitation, whether through input, interactive group work or role play/bibliodrama, is to engage with the biblical world and the contemporary world. Put simply, the Bible is being read as a public text in the public context. This approach calls for a different reading of the text than readings with which people may be more familiar. The approach to Scripture used widely in the Education for Reconciliation courses is a socio-political reading of the text. As with the Education for Reconciliation methodologies, so too this approach to reading Scripture has been tested and developed in the group process. If hermeneutics is about the methods and principles of interpretation, then these courses, piloted and tested in a number of places, are about people having fun with hermeneutics. This socio-political reading of the biblical text has been 'turning the lights on' for many – exciting participants and enabling them to connect faith to public life in creative and meaningful ways. The method has become key to doing community theology and putting reconciliation where it originally belonged, in the public square and market place.

To read the Bible in the public square and as a public text does require a different reading strategy. It is useful to recognise at the outset that there are no neutral readings of Scripture and there is no politically neutral reading of the text. Not a little biblical study in the world of academia has deluded, and in some cases still deludes, itself with the thought that it is engaged with objective, scientific, value-free scholarship. It never has been! Pietism in its various forms also deludes itself that its readings declare the pure revelation of God. It never does! To equate scholarly readings with objective truth and pietistic readings with the revelation of God is to live in a pretend world and a very dangerous one since, far from being politically neutral, all readings and interpretations have political consequences.

We do not read the biblical text without interpretation and all who interpret bring their presuppositions and biases. We are always reading and interpreting Scripture through lenses, often heavily tinted. We read as people confessionally traditioned from social, class, ethnic, age and gender perspectives. Much of this is inevitable. I am middle-aged, middle class, white and male and apart from age the rest is not likely to change! But I do need to realise that my reading lens do not provide pure objectivity or pure truth. I always need other perspectives beyond my social location and in the twenty-first century that means global perspectives.

Over the last three decades political readings of the biblical text have been developed. To describe this approach as new would be to misjudge and misread history. Political readings have been around for as long as the text has existed. What has emerged since the 1970s is a "return to normality" (Richard Bauckham, *The Bible in Politics: How to Read the Bible Politically*, SPCK, 1989, p 1).

We are now recognising that all our knowledge is socially situated; that when we read any text, including the Bible, we are profoundly influenced by the society in which we live and our particular place within that society. We already, therefore, bring political commitments to the text and these commitments, even unconsciously, are shaping our reading. The use of a text from John's Gospel illustrates a widespread political use, some might say abuse, of the text: "Greater love hath no man than this, to lay down his life for his friends." The text is inscribed on war memorials and spoken on Remembrance Sunday and it was frequently used about the republican hunger strikers in 1981. None of these uses of the text has anything to do with its original context: it had nothing to do with war or death by hunger strike. The readings are political and out of context, yet the use has embedded itself deeply in mindsets.

Not all political readings are constructive. An analysis can be made of the usage of many biblical texts to test the political implications and consequences. There are readings which support the abuse of power, legitimise systems of domination, political, economic and gendered, and give support to a social or political status quo that is sectarian, racist or ethno-centred. So-called neutral, value-free or spiritualised readings of the Bible have been quite good at this. Political readings with integrity are those which challenge domination and violence and help liberate people and communities for justice, reconciliation and public well-being.

To contribute towards social reconciliation in Northern Ireland the faith community needs an intentional and constructive socio-political reading of Scripture. How does such a reading strategy work?

Diagram 1 models a way of doing theology, engaging with theological and ethical reflection in the public place.

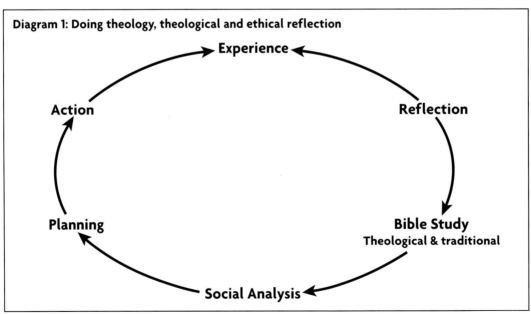

Diagram 1: Doing theology, theological and ethical reflection

Experience — Reflection — Bible Study (Theological & traditional) — Social Analysis — Planning — Action

The process begins with our social, communal and political experience leading to reflection. The next chapter deals with 'The art of theological reflection'. The reflection on experience engages with study of the Bible and theological tradition. To enhance this interaction between social experience and text, some social and political analysis is required. We need to know our world, which in its most immediate form is our local community, but always the local set in more global contexts. Just to ask Northern Ireland questions is much too narrow and confined and will lead to narrow theology and practice.

Doing theology is more than an intellectual exercise or talking, even if it is deeply reflective. Theology is for doing and ethics are for living. Beyond the social analysis and biblical, theological and experiential reflection lies planning, including developing strategies for action, reconciliation or whatever. Concrete action is an important and necessary part of the process of doing theology. This leads again to social experience and once more on to reflection.

Diagram 2 deals with the process involved in a socio-political reading of Scripture.

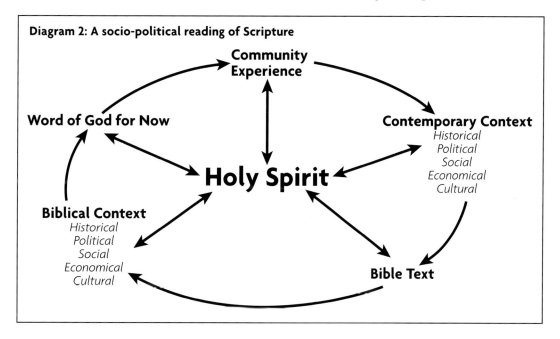

Since this is a reading of a public text in a public context, community experience is a good starting point. Personal experience is important and is always set in a community context. Community experience taps into a wider, more collective experience and includes the experience of social, communal and political events within the local, regional, national or international arenas.

This leads to reflection on the contemporary context. Context has both width and depth and includes the historical dynamics as well as political, social, economic and cultural dimensions. This is the world we live in, be it local or global, and these are the dynamics at work.

From this very public world we engage the biblical text. Within the public context, or standing in the public square, we read Scripture. But Scripture is never purely text. All of Scripture is set in a plurality of contexts. There is not a biblical world but biblical worlds. Yet these worlds and contexts have the same basic dimensions as our own. Behind every biblical text is a historical, political, social, economic and cultural context. Every book, gospel, letter is historically, politically, socially, economically and culturally situated. These are both context and foreground to the text. The entire Bible has public contexts. The biblical story of faith is set in history, in a world of power politics and economic exploitation. Faith itself takes shape in these socio-political and economic struggles. We may well plunder, rob and abuse the text if we do not read the Bible in its public contexts.

The following framework of questions may help us to know what we are looking for as we try to enter the biblical worlds and contexts.

◆ When was the text written?

◆ Who was the author of the text?

◆ What important historical events and developments were taking place at the time of the text?

◆ What forms of social organisation are reflected in the text?

◆ To whom is the text addressed?

(David Lockhead in *The Bible and Liberation*, edited by Norman K Gottwald and Richard A Horsley, Orbis, SPCK, 1993, p 135.)

It also needs to be kept in mind that the biblical text as we now have it took its final shape long after an event happened or a prophet spoke. The book of Exodus reached its final form in the sixth-century Babylonian exile and is therefore addressed to another particular context and community experience. The Gospel of Matthew was written some 50 years after Jesus walked in Galilee and is shaped by the Gospel writer(s) to address the issues and challenges facing a Christian community, probably in Antioch in the mid-80s of the first century. It may be appropriate to engage with layers of context when interpreting the text.

In the diagram, the contemporary context, text and biblical context are in an interactive process, impinging on each other. It is out of this creative, interactive process that a word of God is heard for now. Again the word of God for now is not a private word but out of this contextual process it is a word in and for the public place. It is not, however, the final word. There is no final word, but only a word for now. It may be inadequate or insufficient for another time, so the interpretative circle continues and the word for now feeds into community experience and through the circle again of reflective process.

At the heart of the interactive process between contemporary contexts and worlds and those of the Bible is the Holy Spirit. As the faith community reflects on its public contexts with the biblical contexts, the Spirit is present in the openness and dialogue, leading us to insights, perspectives and actions which can enable the practice of justice, reconciliation, love and peace in the public world of our time. The Spirit as the presence and activity of God is already there in the public square.

It is this socio-political reading of the Bible that is central to exploring the public themes and issues in the Education for Reconciliation courses. Through input, interactive group work, artwork, creative writing or role play/bibliodrama, this socio-political reading is the key interpretative approach. It is proving to be both fun and liberating in local communities.

Chapter 3

The art of theological reflection

Theological reflection is an art and a necessary one. Without reflection in any field we cannot ide
new truth, insight and meaning. This is no less true of theological reflection. A key task for the Chr
community is to reflect theologically.

Theology has too often been left to professional theologians. Too often professional theologians h
produced academic theology, which does not filter down to, or connect with, people on the ground
is not to disparage academic theology but to acknowledge that some important connections have be
broken. Theology is the reflective faith of the church or faith community. A gap between the acader
and the church has been allowed to open up. It is not often realised that for the first centuries of th
Christian faith the great theologians were hard working bishops and pastors. John Calvin and John
Wesley were significant theologians of the sixteenth and eighteenth centuries and they were hard-wo
parish clergy. Living theology is pastoral theology earthed in the lives of people and communities. V
need to be found to build a bridge between the academy and the local community.

Another considerable gap has developed between theology and spirituality. This may be due to th
models of theology that have evolved. Theology has become a cerebral activity rooted in the myth o
scientific objectivity and social and political neutrality. Theological systems have been created that,
claiming neutrality, have legitimised systems of political domination or patriarchal control. Theolo;
not divorced from power relations.

Disconnected from spirituality, theology lacks a heartbeat, a dynamic inner coherence and ethos
Without spirituality, theology fails to be empowering, liberating and transforming. Theology need:
rooted in the liturgy, worship and prayer of the faith community. At its best doing theology is a fo
prayer and a liturgical act. It also needs to be rooted in DIAKONIA, the concrete action and servi
the faith community in the public place.

People do theology. Theology is the task of local people doing theology at the coalface or the
grassroots. Market square theology is the calling of all God's people – not just professional theolo;
bishops, priests and clergy. Theologies of reconciliation in a contested society will not be produce

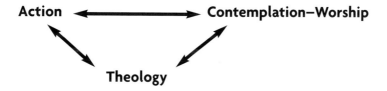

places removed from the deep divisions and messiness of a contested, conflictual society. Theolog
reconciliation will be local, grassroots theologies. To construct such theologies will require the art
theological reflection.

The methodologies used in the Education for Reconciliation courses lend themselves to such
reflection. The courses have developed in local communities. The issues and themes explored are

national and global issues with which people struggle. There is no single-track approach to reconciliation but a multi-track one, all intersecting at different points. What is emerging is a significant theology of reconciliation, which may be described as 'Clapham Junction theology'. Clapham Junction is the largest and busiest railway junction in Britain with lines converging from all directions, intersecting and criss-crossing in a way that at first sight is bewildering but nonetheless has purpose and direction. Such are grassroots or local theologies of reconciliation.

People are doing theology and are already engaged with the art of theological reflection. How can this reflection be enhanced?

Theological reflection is exploration which is connected to and interacts with the wisdom of the biblical and theological heritage. Theological reflection has been defined as:

> . . . the discipline of exploring our individual and corporate experience in conversation with the wisdom of a religious heritage. The conversation is a genuine dialogue that seeks to hear from our own beliefs, actions, and perspectives, as well as from those of the tradition. It respects the integrity of both. Theological reflection therefore may confirm, challenge, clarify, and expand how we understand our own experience and how we understand the religious tradition. The outcome is new truth and meaning for living.

(Patricia O'Connell Killen and John De Beer, *The Art of Theological Reflection*, Crossroad, 1998, p 51.)

In the chapter dealing with 'A socio-political reading of Scripture' a reflective process (**Diagram 1**) shows how such theological reflection might take place.

In **Diagram 1** below another perspective on the reflective process is offered.

The process begins with local community experience, which includes projects and programmes. The story needs to be told and heard publicly. Feelings need to be engaged. Too often we work out of our

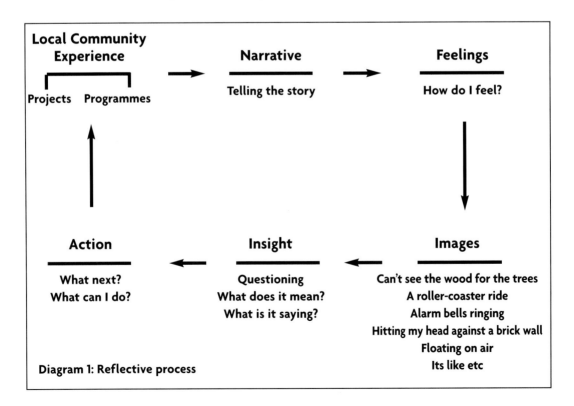

Diagram 1: Reflective process

heads, rationalising and intellectualising. There is a place for hard thinking but also for getting in touch with feelings. That may often be where the real issues are. Feelings are important for theological reflection.

It is often when people are in touch with feelings that images arise. Those images need to be described because they may well take us to the heart of the matter (see **Diagram 3**). When the images are considered and questioned, insights may emerge. If there is willingness and readiness the insights can lead to action.

This reflection process may be used in any setting, which may not necessarily be religious. It has been used with effect by a group of professional youth workers. The process from images to insight needs to be connected to resources and in the Christian context these are the biblical and theological traditions, described in **Diagrams 2** and **3** as the received wisdom.

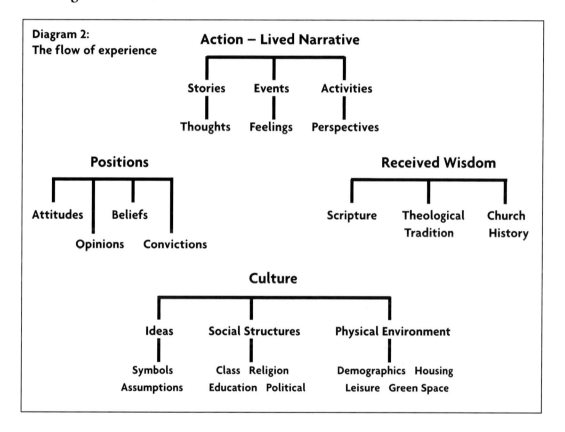

Diagram 2: The flow of experience

Our community experience flows in and out of four broad streams. These are:

◆ Action – Lived Narrative
◆ Received Wisdom
◆ Culture
◆ Positions

None of the four streams exist in isolation. Our stories, events and feelings are interacting with the received wisdom, the theological traditions of our church communities and the biblical insights that come to us from the past, along with the new insights gained from a socio-political reading of the text. This also includes the global insights shared by those from other cultures and historical experiences. Our experience is always within a cultural context where various realities impinge upon and shape our lives. It is through the interaction of all these that we form attitudes, opinions, beliefs and convictions. Described as our positions, these need to be constantly tested through the action, be clarified, modified or changed in interaction with the received wisdom, and live in creative tension with the whole cultural environment which is our public living space.

Diagram 3: Reflective Framework

◆ Focus on local community experience

◆ Narrate the experience

◆ Identify the heart of the matter

◆ Conversation between heart of the matter and received wisdom

◆ Identify new truth, insight, meaning, theory

◆ Commit to enhanced or new action

　The **heart of the matter** always needs exploration and interpretation.

　The **heart of the matter** is the:

◆ central question;

◆ tension;

◆ issue;

◆ theme;

◆ problem;

◆ challenge;

◆ opportunity.

This diagram offers a 'hands on' experience of theological reflection. It can and has been used as a reflective exercise.

The heart of the matter is important and always needs exploration and interpretation. The seven dimensions in the diagram may help to identify with some precision what the heart of the matter is for us. The conversation then needs to continue with the received wisdom of the biblical and theological traditions. Here we allow the central issue to interact with the biblical text using, in particular, a socio-political reading strategy. Interactive reflection on and exploration of theologies of Incarnation, Trinity or the Holy Spirit, to name a few key aspects of the theological wisdom, can lead us to "confirm, challenge, clarify, and expand how we understand our own experience and how we understand the religious tradition. The outcome is new truth and meaning for living" (Killen and John De Beer, p 51).

Since truth in the Bible is for doing, the theological reflection leads us to enhanced or new commitments to action in the community. The art of theological reflection then is necessary if local people are to construct theologies of reconciliation that can be applied to the public place. Such theological reflection is about doing theology that ultimately is about doing reconciliation. It is the practice of theology, which is the public practice of reconciliation. Education for Reconciliation is about no less.

Course One Outline

Dreaming dreams, creating pathways
The challenge of being church in the twenty-first century

Course description

This introductory course provides an opportunity to explore Christian traditions and the role of the churches in society. Given the changing nature of society, there are challenges for churches in the different models of being church. A particular challenge is to connect biblical insights to community and to dream about what church and society might look like 25 years from now.

Course outline

Session 1   Who are we? Where do we belong?

Exploring our Christian traditions

Session 2   Do our churches have a conscience?

The churches and social responsibility

Session 3.   Called to be church

Exploring the connection between church and public issues

Session 4   What we may be!

Reflecting on the changing face of church and society

Session 5   The church yesterday, today, tomorrow

Exploring different models of church

Session 6   A new faith for a new time

Connecting biblical insights to community

Session 7   Walking together on common ground

Exploring what we share

Session 8   Dreaming dreams!

Formulating a twenty-first-century vision for church

Session 1 Introduction

Who are we? Where do we belong? Exploring the Christian traditions

If knowledge is a dangerous thing, not knowing is much worse. Ignorance breeds prejudice, which in turn can become bigotry. Beyond these lie stereotypical images, which easily become demonised. At the extreme, the enemy may be 'taken out' just because he or she is different. After 30 years of conflict and violence in Northern Ireland, rooted in centuries of history, many will recognise the process that leads from ignorance. There are serious levels of misunderstanding and even misrepresentation. This is not just an issue between Catholics and Protestants. There are deep levels of ignorance and prejudice between people from the Protestant traditions. Knowing the Christian traditions may not only deal with prejudice but fear as well. There is much trust building to be done.

At times some traditional theological formulations do not help. To retain theological formulations in which the Pope is described as anti-Christ is a serious contribution to sectarian division. To keep insisting that Protestant churches are not really or fully churches or that Protestant celebrations of the Eucharist are somehow defective also perpetuates sectarian divisions. The self-sufficiency of churches has sometimes led to insensitivity in the use of language. The confidence in the absoluteness of 'truth claims' has too often been heard as arrogance and experienced as exclusion. To insist that Catholics are not really Christian or that Protestant churches are not really churches is both arrogant and excluding. If relationships are at the heart of the gospel, then dogmatic reticence may be in order. If all language and theological formulations are relative to culture and social context, then the practice of mitigation in relation to forms and means of expression is necessary. If God is ultimately unknowable and the ultimate mystery, then a spirit of humility is called for which might lead all of us together to a deeper sense of knowing.

To know where Christian traditions have come from is also necessary. History provides perspectives, which can also lead to humility and sometimes repentance. There is a tendency to tell the story of our respective traditions in a highly spiritual way. Every church story is spiritual. The church is a divine creation. At the same time in its history and contemporary expression it is a sociological reality. It is even part of the story of human sinfulness. There have been and are abuses of power. Churches have blessed wars and legitimised violence against Jews, Muslims, women, the poor and those with a different sexual orientation. Church history makes messy and often embarrassing reading. Exploring our Christian traditions requires critical openness and honesty. Truth claims often need to be replaced with truth telling.

Political dynamics and power are never far away from each of the traditions. No Irish church has been politically neutral and the roots of all our traditions are in political power relations and events including conquest, invasion or domination. It is important, therefore, to know where the traditions came from. The participants time lines may have significant gaps. Ignorance or selectivity of memory may be at work.

The Roman Catholic Church, as we know it today, took shape in Ireland in the twelfth century involving the political dynamics of Anglo-Norman invasion and Irish power relations. The Celtic model of almost 700 years gave way to a much more Romanised and centralised model.

The first model of the Protestant Reformation arrived in the form of Anglicanism in the sixteenth century on the back of the Tudor invasion. Soon after, the Anglican church became the established or state church and remained as such until 1869. This resulted in the emergence of the ruling Protestant ascendancy and the systematic introduction of penal laws against the majority population.

Presbyterianism arrived a century later with the Plantation of Ulster and introduced the reformed model of Reformation. The first Irish presbytery was created in 1642 by officers in the Covenanting army sent to crush the 1641 Catholic Rebellion.

Methodism took root in Ireland in the mid-eighteenth century at the height of the Protestant ascendancy and with John Wesley supportive of the penal laws.

The four larger traditions have roots in major political events and were shaped by the political experiences. In exploring the Irish Christian traditions the past needs to be owned, not least because of sectarian roots which have fed contemporary sectarian expressions and relationships.

At the same time the good stories also need to be told and what is best in each tradition affirmed. The time line exercise itself will do that. At the conclusion participants should have a better understanding of their own tradition as well as greater appreciation of others. It is possible for ignorance and prejudice to be reduced.

Session 1 Plan

Welcome and introduction (15 minutes)

Group members are asked to find someone they do not know at all or well, introduce themselves and share their hopes and expectations for the course. (Circulate 2 or 3 times.)

Introduction to programme and developing a group contract for the course (10 minutes)

Facilitators might find it useful to consult the Community Relations Council publication Churches Working Together: A Practical Resource (Johnston McMaster and Cathy Higgins, 2000).

Single identity group work (35 minutes)

Each group creates its own denominational time line, which will include significant moments and people in the story of its denomination from the beginning to the present.

Feedback from each group (30 minutes)

After each group reports back, create a small group 'buzz session' to identify and then collate a list of questions and issues that arise from the group's timelines.

Plenary discussion (30 minutes)

Explore the questions and issues that have been raised.

Session 2 · Introduction

Do our churches have a conscience?
The churches and social responsibility

Churches are themselves social institutions. They are part of civic society and as such share some responsibility for the common good of the community. The church exists in a social context and the faith which it proclaims ought to have a visible social meaning. Irish churches have found various ways of expressing their social faith.

There are church-related agencies working in regions of famine, poverty and development. There are church-based homes for the elderly and centres for the rehabilitation of offenders or those involved with substance abuse. Hostels provide shelter for the homeless and drop-in centres offer food and space for meeting. In Northern Ireland churches provide about 75% of youth work provision. All of the larger churches have made public statements on a range of social issues from abortion to policing and political dialogue.

Local congregations often provide drop-in centres, crèche facilities and play schools. In more recent years there has been an increase in various forms of community involvement. In some areas the model of community church has been developed.

The concept of public church is also developing. Public church is a faith community with a social mission, which ought to be characterised by:

◆ respect for the legitimate autonomy of other social institutions, ie public church cannot be the hegemonic institution of Christendom but must respect the reality of secularisation;

◆ acceptance of some responsibility for the well-being of the wider society, ie the public church cannot be sectarian, focused solely on the spiritual well-being of its membership;

◆ commitment to work with other social institutions in shaping the common good of the society, ie the public church must be broadly ecumenical, working not only with other Christian believers but with all people of good will – believers of all types and non-believers as well. (Michael J Himes and Kenneth R Himes, *Fullness of Faith: The Public Significance of Theology*, Paulist Press, 1993, p 2.)

A growing part of today's social context is secularisation. This means that churches are no longer connected to the structures of power as they once were. Many areas of social life have been removed from the control of religious bodies. That is no bad thing for communities of faith. The privatisation that often accompanies secularisation is different and ought to be opposed by believers of all kinds. Relegating faith to the private sphere is a contradiction of the social nature of faith and the social vision of God in the Trinity. The church needs to be engaged with society but not seek to control it. Many community development groups do not want church involvement because of a history of control. Secularisation has changed and is changing the church's role in society. The church needs to adapt to this new social context and develop appropriate strategies for social engagement and partnership.

DIAKONIA is the New Testament word for service. One of its key New Testament uses is to refer to:

activities such as serving at table, providing hospitality to guests (Matthew 8 v 15; Luke 4 v 39; 8 v 3), supplying the necessities of life or ministering to (Matthew 25:44; 27:55; Mark 15:41), or acting on behalf of the poor (Romans 15:31).

(Maria Harris, *Fashion Me a People: Curriculum in the Church*, Westminster/John Knox Press, 1989, p 144.)

DIAKONIA is an essential part of the church's purpose and in every societal context it needs to develop and renew its curriculum of service. Maria Harris lists four forms of DIAKONIA (ibid, pp 148–55).

◆ Social care – caring action to the whole person.

◆ Social ritual – vigils, petitions, silent protests.

◆ Social empowerment – helping others help themselves and eliminating dependence.

◆ Social legislation – address the systems and structures that perpetuate unjust conditions.

The latter may include advocacy. All the forms of DIAKONIA require some level of community audit, mapping and analysis. Profiling a local area in terms of community needs and gaps is an important exercise. The response from the faith community may be personal and public and accomplished in many ways. But it does require concrete, practical responses. When the congregation is gathered for worship the social context is not ignored. If it is, the church is being sectarian. Worship takes place in the social context and ought to sensitise consciences, providing an alternative vision of what society might be and, above all, birth compassion which hears the cry of the suffering and acts compassionately and concretely.

Session 2 Plan

Welcome and introduction (10 minutes)

Reminder of ground rules

Single identity group work exercise 1 (30 minutes)

Identify the social/community issues that:

your denomination is involved in;

your local church is involved in.

Feedback (20 minutes)

Group work exercise 2 (30 minutes)

In mixed groups, compile a profile of your area in terms of community needs and gaps.

Plenary discussion (30 minutes)

Why should the church be involved in these issues?

In the light of the discussion, what are the churches not doing within the community?

Session 2, Handout 1

Group work exercise 1

Identify the social/community issues that:

1. your denomination is involved in;

2. your local church is involved in.

Group work exercise 2

In mixed groups, compile a profile of your area in terms of community needs and gaps.

Session 3   Introduction

Called to be church
Exploring the connection between church and public issues

In this age of individualism and privatisation the notions of 'public church' are somewhat alien. While religion may be considered an important element in many people's lives, its role in the wider society – to work alongside other social institutions for the common good – is generally ignored. An obvious downside to this separation of church and society is the overlooking of the social context and meaning of faith, and a fragmentation of religious concerns from the political, civic and economic activities of life. The challenge to our churches, then, is to engage with our secularised context without attempting to control the encounter. Public church has an important role in the society:

> to provide with alternative visions of what is desirable and possible, to stimulate deliberation about them, provide a re-evaluation of premises and values and aims to broaden the range of potential responses and deepen society's understanding of itself.

(Robert Reich in Himes and Himes, *Fullness of Faith: The Public Significance of Theology*, Paulist Press, 1993, p 23.)

Public church, while grounded in the Bible and tradition, welcomes diversity within its community. It nurtures openness, recognising God's image and presence in people outside the institutional structures and in unexpected places. Living a public faith entails commitment to the building of a society based on compassion, economic and political justice, diversity and interdependence. It takes seriously our partnership with God in bringing "light to the nations" (Isaiah 42:7), using a language which resonates with our society and a process that honours the life experiences, insights and contributions of new dialogue partners. This approach is not a new one; it has its roots in the early Christian church and finds an advocate in Paul. Paul's first letter to the Corinthians is primarily concerned with the manner in which the Christian church in Corinth can create an alternative community that is not separate from Corinthian society, but public and co-existing in the market place.

To understand the radical nature of Paul's vision for the church, some understanding of Corinthian society is necessary. Corinth was the commercial centre of Greece as well as being the centre for government administration. It was a highly stratified society and the minority of wealthy élites made their money from trade. Like other Roman colonies its wealthy citizens recognised the economic advantages of cultivating loyalty to the empire. They built a temple in honour of the emperor which had pride of place in the city centre and organised city-wide festivals and the Caesarean games to promote social cohesion. The Corinthian Christians were a microcosm of Corinthian society and mirrored socio-economic and cultural divisions, with the wealthy members being in the minority and the majority membership representing the lower socio-economic strata (I Corinthians 1:26).

The Eucharist had become an expression of the economic division in the society, where the wealthy expected to be served the superior food, depriving the poor of their most substantial meal of the week. To maintain their status and cultivate social and business relationships, wealthy Christians participated in civic meals, thereby eating meat consecrated to idols and took part in civic religious festivals with temple prostitutes, which caused offence to poorer members of the church. Finally, the privileged élite operated the law and courts to their own advantage and wealthy Christians, who participated in this practice, were thereby injuring the poor and vulnerable in the society.

Paul's primary concern is with the survival of the Christian church as an alternative public church in Corinthian society. He opposes the practices of the wealthy members in the church and encourages the Christian community to embody the just social relations that are lacking in the surrounding environment, which includes abandoning litigation in the courts and handling their own disputes.

Paul uses the metaphor of 'the body' to describe the type of alternative community he envisages (I Corinthians 12:12–13). He is aware the term 'body' is also a well-established political metaphor to describe 'the body politic', the citizen body of a city state. He sets out to show how incompatible the values of privilege and power, that mark the civic society, are with the self-giving values of Christ. Paul envisages a public faith and church that will be independent and over against the value system in the dominant society, modelling instead God's design for the whole 'body politic'. He endorses an inclusive church, where everyone is welcomed, where differences are celebrated and co-operation and solidarity are encouraged, and where economic resources are shared. Church for Paul exists where violence is not tolerated, oppressive systems and structures are critiqued, and where equitable and just relations make for peaceful co-existence.

Paul's vision for public church and faith is as relevant in our context as it was in first-century Corinth. It challenges us to ask the questions: what sort of public church are we trying to create? What values go to the heart of it? And is it possible to build a civic society based on compassion, economic and political justice, diversity and interdependence?

Session 3 Plan

Welcome and introduction (5 minutes)

Buzz session (10 minutes)

  What do you understand by public faith/church?

Feedback (10 minutes)

Overheads (5 minutes)

  Corinth – the socio-political context.

God's alternative society (10 minutes)

  Questions for clarification

Single identity group work exercise 1 (30 minutes)

  What is your denomination's response to:

  lone parent families;

  paramilitaries/culture of violence;

  building the peace.

Feedback (15 minutes)

Mixed group work exercise 2 (20 minutes)

In three groups, take one of the issues and come up with a biblical story/text that connects with the issue and be prepared to state why.

Feedback (15 minutes)

Overhead 1

Corinth – the socio-political context

Social structure of the city

◆ Caesar refounded Corinth – 44 BCE

◆ Settled freedmen – Roman citizens

◆ Eight of seventeen Christian names – Latin, Greeks, Jews

Rapid economic upturn

◆ Handsomely built houses

◆ Resumption of Isthmian games

◆ Wealth based mainly on trade

◆ Great and wealthy city – Greece's commercial centre

◆ Centre of government administration

Sharp division between rich and poor

◆ "Sordidness of the rich and the misery of the poor"
(Contemporary Greek writer)

Corinthian Christians

◆ Diverse ethnic origins

◆ Different social strata – mainly poor/slaves

◆ Theological/cultural divisions

◆ Lord's Supper

◆ Eating meat sacrificed to idols

◆ Support of itinerant missionaries

◆ Support of Paul

◆ Corinthian church is a microcosm of Corinthian society.

Overhead 2

God's alternative society

Corinth

◆ Network of cells – spreading into the province of Achaia

◆ Social movement

◆ Paul urges group solidarity

◆ Community of saints – opposed to the 'world'

◆ Conduct its life in complete independence of the world

◆ Church lives under the radical freedom of the gospel

◆ Paul's 'body' metaphor – the body of Christ

◆ Well-established political metaphor

◆ Citizen body of the city state

◆ 'Body politic'

Corinthian Church

◆ Independent communities over against dominant society

◆ Social-economic solidarity which is international and different from the empire model

◆ The language of politics highlights the unity, harmony and mutual cooperation of the faith community

◆ Model a community of interdependence

◆ Corinthian churches form an alternative society

◆ Model God's design for the whole 'body politic'

Session 3, Handout 1

Paul's community model: 1 Corinthians 12:13–26

[13] For in the one Spirit we were all baptised into one body – Jews or Greeks, slaves or free – and we were all made to drink of one Spirit. [14] Indeed, the body does not consist of one member but of many. [15] If the foot were to say, 'Because I am not a hand, I do not belong to the body,' that would not make it any less a part of the body. [16] And if the ear were to say, 'Because I am not an eye, I do not belong to the body,' that would not make it any less a part of the body. [17] If the whole body were an eye, where would the hearing be? If the whole body were hearing, where would the sense of smell be? [18] But as it is, God arranged the members in the body, each one of them, as he chose. [19] If all were a single member, where would the body be? [20] As it is, there are many members, yet one body. [21] The eye cannot say to the hand, 'I have no need of you,' nor again the head to the feet, 'I have no need of you.' [22] On the contrary; the members of the body that seem to be weaker are indispensable, [23] and those members of the body that we think less honourable we clothe with greater honour, and our less respectable members are treated with greater respect; [24] whereas our more respectable members do not need this. But God has so arranged the body, giving the greater honour to the inferior member, [25] that there may be no dissension within the body, but the members may have the same care for one another. [26] If one member suffers, all suffer together with it; if one member is honoured, all rejoice together with it.

NRSV Bible

Session 3, Handout 2

Single identity group work exercise 1

What is your denomination's response to:

1. lone parent families;

2. paramilitaries/culture of violence;

3. building the peace.

Mixed group work exercise 2

In three groups, take one of the issues outlined above and come up with a biblical story/text that connects with the issue. Be prepared to state why.

Session 4 Introduction

What we may be!
Reflecting on the changing face of church and society

One thing we can be sure of in life is the inevitability of change, whether it be physical, emotional or spiritual. Sometimes change brings a welcome release from a difficult oppressive situation or mindset; at other times it can cause unspeakable pain with the death of a loved one, the break-up of a marriage or the loss of a job. Then there are the occasions when change occurs in the wider society, impacting the social, economic or political institutions and processes as in times of war or economic depression or the development of new, more powerful technologies requiring the learning of appropriate skills and attitudes. Faith has a role to play in helping us meet and cope with change and in the encounter, faith itself changes and evolves. What shape do these faith changes take? It usually means "changes in the ways one holds, understands and takes responsibility for living one's faith" (James Fowler, *Faithful Change: The Personal and Public Challenges of Postmodern Life*, Abingdon Press, 1996, p 67). As we arrive at a different understanding of ourselves in relationship with others and the society in which we live, we often need to find new ways of living or making sense of the world. This process is an uncomfortable one for the individual concerned and for those directly affected by the individual's questions and choices.

The stages one moves through in coping with and adapting to change are the same for individuals and institutions. As the latter involves a diverse range of people, the process is often more difficult and protracted. Reflection on the individual's response to change at the level of faith development can shed light on the church's institutional reaction to change. Change in the nature of the person's relationship to church may come about because of a realisation that institutional structures are stifling growth or attempting to block change. It may equally result from a disenchantment with the belief world and the perspectives on God and the Scriptures adhered to within the particular tradition.

Faced with having to leave the familiar and previously 'safe' religious context behind, in order to retain personal integrity, an individual often finds him or herself feeling lost and confused and generally lacking a sense of future direction. This period of uncertainty continues until a new and more adequate meaning for one's life emerges with the possibilities of different and more appropriate experiences of religious practice. The processes involved in change are such that it is necessary to experience the feelings of loss, confusion and restlessness before the person is able to glimpse signposts pointing up a new more life-giving direction.

Not everyone is able to make this transition. Some stay with the familiar and suppress feelings of anger or frustration creating difficulties for themselves and for those around them; others who choose to stay cope by ignoring their dissatisfaction, numbing that inner critical voice through endless activity. For those who use their energy avoiding change the possibility of a hope filled joyful future is bleak. What of churches faced with the need to change? The church does not exist in a vacuum but always in a social context. Given that society on a global scale is undergoing rapid and radical change, the church does not remain unaffected. It too is caught up in the maelstrom of the change dynamic.

The advances in technology and communications make possible the creation of global networks on a scale never imagined. We are becoming increasingly aware of our connectedness with other people and places, as our TV screens and newspapers report on simple advances, territorial wars, cultural events or political manoeuvrings in countries we may not even have heard of. Recent acts of terrorism have not only reminded us of our vulnerability but raised difficult questions about foreign policy legislation and its impact on the ground. There is a growing awareness of a need for responsible action and accountability on a global scale. Another consequence of media coverage of wars or natural disasters in the southern hemisphere is to bring to public attention the extreme poverty, suffering and alienation of large numbers of people. At the same time images of lavish living, obscene consumerism and increasing competitiveness send a very different message that encourages the drive towards individualism.

Numerous other issues confront us on a daily basis – mounting evidence of ecological disaster, increased racial or sectarian tension and domestic violence. Reflection on the national or international scene leaves many confounded and uncertain as to how best to respond.

The churches have a role in empowering people to respond in a compassionate and just way, not by telling them what to do but by educating people to understand the liberating message in the Scriptures and traditions. The teaching of Jesus and the prophets before him took seriously the realities of socio-economic and political oppression. They advocated a reversal of the system in favour of economic redistribution, compassionate justice, solidarity with the poor and marginalised and development of a community ethic of care and responsibility. The churches can help people to reflect on how their present practice and choices connect with God's promised future.

The churches themselves, if they are to remain credible authentic witness, need to practice that openness and vulnerability to God's spirit in the world. Only then will they be in a position to support people struggling to change and give prophetic leadership in the direction of God's promised kingdom of liberation and reconciliation for all.

The church proclaims a God who "has come out for freedom and justice against slavery and oppression . . . for life against death" (Walter Brueggemann, *Peace*, Chalice Press, 2001, p 136). The church believes those promises have begun to be fulfilled in Jesus Christ. If the church is to challenge those who do not believe in this promised newness and those who out of self interest want to maintain the status quo, then it needs to model new ways of being and living.

Letting go of old and tired models and structures, allowing the wind of the spirit to blow newness and freshness into formulas, practices and perspectives is at once frightening and liberating. As with individual change, institutional change is often painful, shocking, confusing and lonely. The God of the Exodus and the cross is familiar with these experiences. Yet God offers the promise of new life, fresh hope and joy, at the other side. Society may take seriously churches which proclaim and follow the God of Moses and Jesus into the twenty-first century.

Session 4 Plan

Welcome and introduction (5 minutes)

Single identity group work exercise 1 (20 minutes)

Reflect denominationally on:

1. How your church has changed over the last two decades.

2. The changes that have affected your local congregation in that time.

Feedback and discussion (25 minutes)

In the discussion include some of the following questions:

Why have changes occurred?

Are they good changes?

In what way are the changes going on in the church mirroring the changes going on in society?

Role-play (20 minutes preparation, 20 minutes role-play)

'Exploring attitudes to change'

The Worship Development Group has been given the task of outlining a service. There are three different approaches within the group.

1. Those against the traditional who want to experiment and innovate.

2. Those who are set against all change and newness. Everything is to be done as it always has been.

3. Those who want the best of the traditional with some new approaches.

Create the three groups to represent each of these approaches and together meet to plan the service of worship.

Reflection (30 minutes)

Invite each of the groups to reflect on how they felt in their role.

What group dynamics were taking place?

What were the real issues?

How might things have been done differently?

How do we respond to change within a group, which has a diversity of attitudes and opinions?

Session 4, Handout 1

Group work exercise 1

Working within your own denomination consider:

1. How has your church changed over the last two decades?

2. What changes have occurred in your local congregation in that time?

Ask a representative from your group to feedback your responses to both questions.

Session 4, Handout 2

What we may be! – reflecting on the changing face of church and society

Role-play

'Exploring attitudes to change'

The Worship Development Group has been given the task of outlining a service. There are three different approaches within the group.

• Those against the traditional who want to experiment and innovate.

• Those who are set against all change and newness. Everything is to be done as it always has been.

• Those who want the best of the traditional with some new approaches.

Task:

Create the three groups to represent each of these approaches. Spend some time with those who agree with your approach, clarifying what you want to see in this service.

Finally meet with other members of the Development Group to plan the service of worship.

Session 5 Introduction

The church, yesterday, today, tomorrow
Exploring different models of church

There is no one model of church. Sometimes church communities make claims to represent the true church, which usually includes practice and structure. The claim is often made at particular moments in history when renewal is experienced. A 'new' church emerges claiming to have rediscovered the pristine New Testament church. Every renewal model has claimed to have recovered the original. But which original? The New Testament has a plurality of models, not just of ways of being church but also structures and worship practice. Diversity is a rich part of the New Testament documents.

The truth itself can be diverse. Claims to have rediscovered the authentic New Testament church are often also about absolute truth claims. Even in the renewal there can be not a little arrogance, even sinfulness! Such claims usually ignore contexts which, as always, shape the models and the expressions of truth. The house churches of the New Testament were shaped and formed in a variety of cultural, social and political contexts. They were always the church in the world and the 'world' was a place of many worlds.

Paul's activity was urban-based and crossed the boundaries of many worlds. A close reading of his letters reveals a creative ability to use vocabulary, metaphors and symbols, in particular contexts to communicate his pastoral concerns to localised situations. His 'body' image in 1 Corinthians has picked up a commonly used political buzz word in Corinthian society. Not only Christians but anyone in Corinth would have grasped his 'body' metaphor. In Philippi he again borrowed a key civic word and made creative use of the familiar Philippean experience of double citizenship.

When Matthew's Gospel was written around the 80s of the first century it was written for a faith community probably in Antioch. In a larger community where Christians were experiencing antagonism, conflict and even violence, the Sermon on the Mount and the Beatitudes in particular called the Matthean community to be a church of the merciful, peacemakers and justice seekers. Context shaped the emphases.

The first letter of Peter was written probably to a displaced, even homeless, group of people. They certainly were in a situation of suffering and in need of a hopeful sense of who they were. The key pilgrim people theme made a lot of experiential sense. In more ways than one this church could not stand still.

Wherever the church exists it does so "in the conflict between the lordship of Christ and the powers and forces of society" (Jurgen Moltmann, *The Power of the Powerless*, SCM Press, 1983, p 157). In this sense the church's context is always one of conflict. That may be easier to recognise in the New Testament where the churches are always minorities in a frequently antagonistic world. In the Western world where churches have been part of the Christendom model and therefore often majorities, the conflict may be more difficult to realise. Yet there is always a conflict between Christ and Caesar and in a post-Christendom situation that may become more obvious. The task of the church then and now is to live "with Christ's text in this world's context" (Ibid, p 157).

In the Western world there are at least three recognisable models of church. The established church is a national, state church often tied closely to government and power. Or the church may live out of a model of cultural establishment where there is again a close alignment between the institution and the dominant political and power structures.

The free churches have no official political links and probably have a history of nonconformity. However, in some situations they have lost their nonconformist emphasis by becoming culturally captive.

The 'bourgeois' church offers 'cheap grace'. It has been described as the 'service church', which aims to offer everyone whatever they want. It is a 'comfort zone' church characterised by individualism and uncommitted middle-class religion.

Jurgen Moltmann highlights three more dynamic models of church. The confessing church acknowledges Christ as its only Lord.

> And that means confessing him as lord of its whole life – not merely personal life, but public life as well; not simply religious life, but political life too. And in this way it declares that it is prepared for resistance against everything that contradicts Christ's promise and his claim.
>
> (Ibid, p 164.)

The church as liberating community is involved in solidarity with the weak, vulnerable and marginalised of society. It is a church open to the suffering and the poor. This church can provide "the experience of a liberating, healing community at the breaking points of our divided society" (Ibid, p 165).

The church as prophetic community not only overcomes the limitations of bourgeois religion; it also overcomes all narrow provincialism, and that means Irish as well as European provincialism. The prophetic community is a global, ecumenical community in which the whole world is our family. The prophetic church will live on a global map speaking with the voices of the oppressed world, voicing the demand for justice and peace. It is the church where we can:

> . . . find ourselves and the meaning of our lives in the community which confesses Christ, liberates men and women who have been debased and humiliated, and makes itself one with people all over the world.
>
> (Ibid, p 166.)

The three New Testament models of being church used in this study need to be read within the context of their own worlds and also in the global contexts of today. In the end we reflect on the texts in the contemporary world's contexts.

Session 5 Plan

Welcome and introduction (5 minutes)

Over the last four sessions we have been considering how our churches responded to different issues. In the discussion we may have realised that our churches have different styles. We are expressing in the life of our congregations different ways of being church. That we live and walk along different pathways is positive.

Group work exercise 1 (15 minutes)

Draw a symbol to represent the church

Draw the worldview of the church

Feedback (10 minutes)

In the New Testament there is a rich diversity of ways of being church. It has been suggested that there are 65 different models within the New Testament. So God obviously believes in diversity. In this session we are only going to look at three of these models.

Group work exercise 2 (30 minutes)

The group will be divided into three mixed groups and each group will be given one of the following three texts, along with background information:

1 Corinthians 12:4–27 – Body of Christ Model
Matthew 5:1–12 – Community of the Reign of God
1 Peter 2:9–11 – Pilgrim People

For background information to Scripture texts see handouts.

Task (20 minutes):

In an open forum, present your model of church using any medium you wish.

Feedback (20 minutes)

After each group reports back there will be space for the others to ask questions of that group.

Plenary discussion (20 minutes)

The following questions will be teased out in an open discussion.

1. What does it mean to be any of these models in today's world?

2. What shape would your congregational life take if modelled on any one of these?

Session 5, Handout 1

Group work exercise 1

- Draw a symbol to represent the church.
- Draw the worldview of the church.

Session 5, Handout 2

Group work exercise 2

The group will be divided into three mixed groups and each group will be given a text along with background information to consider. In an open forum, present your model of church using any medium you wish. After each group reports back there will be space for the others to ask questions of that group.

A) Matthew 5:1–12 – Community of the reign of God

◆ The Beatitudes are the heart of the Sermon on the Mount, which express the core values that belong to the reign of God in the world.

◆ This is how the people who belong to the reign of God live in society.

◆ The reign of God is always something more than the church, yet the church is called by God to be a sign of this reign.

◆ Read the Beatitudes and reflect on what model of church they represent.

Text – Matthew 5:1–12

[1] When Jesus saw the crowds, he went up the mountain; and after he sat down, his disciples came to him. [2] Then he began to speak, and taught them, saying: [3] Blessed are the poor in spirit, for theirs is the kingdom of heaven. [4] Blessed are those who mourn, for they will be comforted. [5] Blessed are the meek, for they will inherit the earth. [6] Blessed are those who hunger and thirst for righteousness, for they will be filled. [7] Blessed are the merciful, for they will receive mercy. [8] Blessed are the pure in heart, for they will see God. [9] Blessed are the peacemakers, for they will be called children of God. [10] Blessed are those who are persecuted for righteousness' sake, for theirs is the kingdom of heaven. [11] Blessed are you when people revile you and persecute you and utter all kinds of evil against you falsely on my account. [12] Rejoice and be glad, for your reward is great in heaven, for in the same way they persecuted the prophets who were before you.

NRSV Bible

Session 5, Handout 3

B) 1 Peter 2:9–10 (Pilgrim People)

The first letter of Peter was written to a scattered Christian community who were being maligned and were suffering at the hands of the political power of the empire.

The letter was written to affirm an apprehensive people of their identity (verse 9) and in the strength of that identity to help them see that in this world they would always be a people on the move and on a journey (verse 11).

Read the text and explore what it means to be a model of church as people on pilgrimage.

Text – 1 Peter 2:9–10

9 But you are a chosen race, a royal priesthood, a consecrated nation, a people set apart to sing the praises of God who called you out of the darkness into his wonderful light. 10 Once you were not a people at all and now you are the People of God; once you were outside the mercy and now you have been given mercy.

Jerusalem Bible

Session 5, Handout 4

C) 1 Corinthians 12:4–27 – Body of Christ Model

◆ In session 3 we noted Paul's use of the metaphor 'the body' and saw that it was a very public political word in first-century Corinth.

◆ Now we focus on the imagery of the human body with its many parts.

◆ A major problem Paul faced in the Corinthian churches was a group of people insisting everyone fit into a single mould. In other words they wanted a one-dimensional model of church. Paul believed that God had other ideas.

◆ Read the text and explore the model of church presented by Paul and what this means for being church in the present time.

Text – 1 Corinthians 12:4–27

4 'Now there are varieties of gifts, but the same Spirit; 5 and there are varieties of services, but the same Lord; 6 and there are varieties of activities, but it is the same God who activates all of them in everyone. 7 To each is given the manifestation of the Spirit for the common good. 8 To one is given through the Spirit the utterance of wisdom, and to another the utterance of knowledge according to the same Spirit, 9 to another faith by the same Spirit, to another gifts of healing by the one Spirit, 10 to another the working of miracles, to another prophecy, to another the discernment of spirits, to another various kinds of tongues, to another the interpretation of tongues. 11 All these are activated by one and the same Spirit, who allots to each one

individually just as the Spirit chooses. [12] For just as the one body is one and has many members, and all the members of the body, though many, are one body, so it is with Christ. [13] For in the one Spirit we were all baptised into one body – Jews or Greeks, slaves or free – and we were all made to drink of one Spirit. [14] Indeed the body does not consist of one member but of many. [15] If the foot were to say, 'Because I am not a hand, I do not belong to the body,' that would not make it any less a part of the body. [16] And if the ear were to say, 'Because I am not an eye, I do not belong to the body', that would not make it any less a part of the body. [17] If the whole body were an eye, where would the hearing be? If the whole body were hearing, where would the sense of smell be? [18] But as it is, God arranged the members in the body, each one of them, as he chose. [19] If all were a single member, where would the body be? [20] As it is, there are many members, yet one body. [21] The eye cannot say to the hand 'I have no need of you', nor again the head to the feet, 'I have no need of you.' [22] On the contrary, the members of the body that seem to be weaker are indispensable, [23] and those members of the body that we think less honourable we clothe with greater honour, and our less respectable members are treated with greater respect; [24] whereas our more respectable members do not need this. But God has so arranged the body, giving the greater honour to the inferior member, [25] that there may be no dissension within the body, but the members may have the same care for one another. 26 If one member suffers, all suffer together with it; if one member is honoured, all rejoice together with it. [27] Now you are the body of Christ and individually members of it.

NRSV Bible

Session 5, Handout 5

The church yesterday, today, tomorrow

Exploring different pathways to being church

Questions for plenary discussion

1. What does it mean to be any of these models in today's world?

2. What shape would your congregational life take if modelled on anyone of these?

Session 6 **Introduction**

A new faith for a new time
Connecting biblical insights to community

What type of Christian faith is possible, even necessary, in what some are calling a post-Christian, increasingly secularised context? How can Christians meet the challenges, embrace the possibilities and engage even more creatively with the desires for peace and security, economic and ecological sustainability and an authentic, engaged spirituality at local and global levels? Often the task to live the 'good news' of God's kingdom with enthusiasm and compassion can seem a daunting one. Recognising the difficulties inherent in faithfully living the gospel vision, Christ promised to send the Holy Spirit (Acts 1:8) to enable the disciples to witness effectively in the world. The Acts of the Apostles shows the Spirit of God at work crossing boundaries, enabling communication between peoples from different social, cultural and ethnic communities, and creating new structures to ensure equality of treatment and opportunity. The Spirit enhanced the early Christian church to preach an alternative vision of community and practice a counter-cultural, communal lifestyle.

The story of Peter and Cornelius shows the Spirit redrawing the boundaries of the Christian community toward greater inclusivity (Acts 10:44). The early Christians recognised that baptism, the sacrament of initiation into the Christian community, was the radical sacrament of equality. In baptising Cornelius and his household Peter was breaking down the divisions between Jews and Gentiles, affirming, like Paul, in the letter to the Galatians, "All . . . are one in Christ Jesus" (Galatians 3:28b). Peter affirmed that it is our common faith in Jesus Christ, which unites us and overcomes all boundaries.

In the first declaration made by Peter to the Christian community in Acts we are told the gifts of the Spirit are entrusted to women and men alike (Acts 2:17–18). In the male-dominated, patriarchal culture of the Greco-Roman world, women were recognised only in relation to men. They had no honour of their own and their role was to safeguard the honour of their male sponsor, whether it be father, husband, brother or son. Without the protection and economic provision afforded by her male sponsor, women in general were left destitute. Jewish culture and law forbade women the opportunity to work outside of the home or to own property. Roman law and Hellenistic culture differed in this respect and it was possible for women to follow a trade, own property and accumulate wealth. Within the early Christian movement women were treated as equal members and emerged as initiators and leaders of the movement. Lydia, referred to in Acts 16, was a wealthy Christian woman from the Greco-Roman world. Her economic independence meant that she was in a position to make available her home for a house church to meet in Philippi; what is more, she became leader of that house church. This practice of fostering the radical discipleship of equals began to lose ground in the church at the end of the first century as is apparent in the pastoral epistles of Timothy and Titus. The shift occurred from spirit-filled, communal authority to an authority vested in local male officers who take on the prophetic role of teaching authority and the decision-making power of the community. In this context women's leadership was marginalised and restricted to a circle of women (1 Timothy 2:11–12).

Paul's encounter with the Athenians recorded in Acts 17 reveals someone who is at ease in the multi-cultural diversity of the market place, where competing and current ideas and questions are being energetically discussed. Paul does not shy away from learning about, and engaging with, the plurality of perspectives. He recognises the advantage of familiarising himself with the buzzwords and 'market speak' of his time. Believing that the Spirit of God is available in all places (17:23), his concern is to show how the God that Jesus reveals is the creator and sustainer of the world, and the answer to and fulfiller of the deepest longings of the human heart. Paul, in engaging with the local context and speaking in terms that people connected with, models how the twenty-first-century church can engage with those in the churches, on its fringes and on the outside. Paul is prepared to use whatever means and vehicles are necessary to introduce people to the God of Jesus Christ. In so doing, he brings the current insights and rich perspectives from the market place to bear on the gospel 'God-talk' in order to transmit the faith he has received.

The Holy Spirit is amongst us creating the space for us to risk new boundary crossings, to create a truly inclusive, egalitarian society and to find new ways of languaging the faith, to sustain and nourish the whole household of God. Peter and Paul often met with failure in seeking to live out the Christian faith, yet continued in the direction of greater risk-taking. This is encouragement indeed to strive after the realisation of the radical, liberating and relevant vision of Christian living that has been gifted to us by the faithful witness of our predecessors. Like them we, too, can take comfort from the fact that the Spirit of God continues to lead the way.

Session 6 Plan

Welcome and introduction (10 minutes)

In the last session we explored three ways of being church in the New Testament. The different models of church in the New Testament were not nice spiritual groups but rather lived in real-life situations and in a real world. Often they had to face social, cultural and political problems and they had to struggle to respond to them. In this session we will look at three particular problems and challenges that faced the earliest Christian communities, as reflected in the story of the church in the Acts of the Apostles.

Group work exercise 1 (45 minutes)

The group is divided into three mixed groups and each group is given one of the following three texts, along with background information and questions for consideration:

Acts 10 – The Story of Peter and Cornelius.

Acts 16:14–15, 40 – The Story of Lydia

Acts 17:16–31 – Paul at Athens

Task:

In these texts the group is to consider real-life situations, exploring how they were dealt with and making connections with their own particular situations.

Feedback (30 minutes)

After each presentation the other participants are invited to ask questions of the group giving feedback. (15 minutes)

Plenary discussion (20 minutes)

The group is asked to consider the following question.

In what ways do these responses to first-century social and cultural challenges help us as church to respond to contemporary social and cultural issues?

Session 6, Handout 1

Group work exercise 1

The group is divided into three mixed groups and each group will be given one of the following three texts, along with background information and questions for consideration.

◆ Acts 10 – The Story of Peter and Cornelius

◆ Acts 15:14–15,40 – The Story of Lydia

◆ Acts 17:16–31 – Paul at Athens

Task:

In these texts consider the real-life situations, exploring how they were dealt with and how you can make connections with your own particular situations.

Session 6, Handout 2

A.) Acts 10 – God has no favourites!

◆ Cornelius was a Roman Army officer of the Italian cohort stationed in Caesarea.

◆ This is the first alleged case of a Gentile seeking entry into the Christian church.

◆ No one in the Jerusalem church seemed to be ready and willing to receive Gentiles, nor were they aware Christ had intended the gospel to be preached to all the nations.

◆ The desire of Cornelius, prompted by a dream, to join the church created a terrible dilemma for Peter and his colleagues. Could they permit a Gentile to become a member of a Jewish Christian community without the candidate first embracing Judaism? Since the most important expression of church membership was 'the breaking of the bread' at a common meal, how could a pagan be accepted as one of their table companions? Could they, Jewish Christians, enter the house and share the food, presumed to be unclean, of a non-Jew?

The author of Acts offers a twofold supernatural solution:

1. A vision enjoining Peter to discard the Jewish dietary law. Peter's protest that he had never eaten "anything that is common" is countered by a voice from on high: "What God has cleansed you must not call common" (10:14–15).

2. The decisive proof of the acceptability of Gentiles came when the Holy Spirit 'fell' on Cornelius and his household and they burst out in glossolalia. Nonplussed, Peter exclaimed: "Can any one forbid water for baptising these people who have received the Holy Spirit just as we have?" (10:47).

In a group discussion consider:

1. How do we overcome our cultural, educational and religious conditioning which is often prejudiced and exclusive?

2. How do we live as those who believe in a God who has no favourites?

God has no favourites!

Acts 10:1–16, 25–9, 34–5, 44–8.

¹ In Caesarea there was a man named Cornelius, a centurion of the Italian Cohort, as it was called. ² He was a devout man who feared God with all his household; he gave alms generously to the people and prayed constantly to God. ³ One afternoon about three o' clock he had a vision in which he clearly saw an angel of God coming in and saying to him, 'Cornelius'. ⁴ He stared at him in terror and said, 'What is it, Lord?' He answered. 'Your prayers and your alms have ascended as a memorial before God. ⁵ Now send men to Joppa for a certain Simon who is called Peter; ⁶ he is lodging with Simon, a tanner, whose house is by the seaside. ⁷ When the angel who spoke to him had left, he called two of his slaves and a devout soldier from the ranks of those who served him, ⁸ and after telling them everything, he sent them to Joppa.

⁹ After noon the next day, as they were on their journey and approaching the city, Peter went up on the roof to pray. ¹⁰ He became hungry and wanted something to eat; and while it was being prepared, he fell into a trance. ¹¹ He saw the heaven opened and something like a large sheet coming down, being lowered to the ground by its four corners. ¹² In it were all kinds of four-footed creatures and reptiles and birds of the air. ¹³ Then he heard a voice saying, 'Get up, Peter; kill and eat.' ¹⁴ But Peter said, 'By no means, Lord; for I have never eaten anything that is profane or unclean.' ¹⁵ The voice said to him again, a second time, 'What God has made clean, you must not call profane.' ¹⁶ This happened three times, and the thing was suddenly taken up to heaven . . . ²⁵ On Peter's arrival Cornelius met him, and falling at his feet, worshipped him. ²⁶ But Peter made him get up, saying, 'Stand up; I am only a mortal.' ²⁷ And as he talked with him, he went in and found that many had assembled; ²⁸ and he said to them, 'You yourselves know that it is unlawful for a Jew to associate with or to visit a Gentile; but God has shown me that I should not call anyone profane or unclean. ²⁹ So when I was sent for, I came without objection . . . ³⁴ Then Peter began to speak to them: 'I truly understand that God shows no partiality, ³⁵ but in every nation anyone who fears him and does what is right is acceptable to him . . . ⁴⁴ While Peter was still speaking, the Holy Spirit fell upon all who heard the word. ⁴⁵ The circumcised believers who had come with Peter were astounded that the gift of the Holy Spirit had been poured out even on the Gentiles, ⁴⁶ for they heard them speaking in tongues and extolling God. Then Peter said, ⁴⁷ 'Can anyone withhold the water for baptising these people who have received the Holy Spirit just as we have?' ⁴⁸ So he ordered them to be baptised in the name of Jesus Christ.

NRSV Bible

Session 6, Handout 3

B) Acts 16:14–15, 40 – Finding her voice

In the first generation of the Christian church, women were in key leadership roles. They sponsored and led churches that met in their homes. The earliest missionary stories in the New Testament reflect this situation. One such story features Lydia. There are four things that are important about Lydia.

1. She was the first European convert and first founder of the church at Philippi.

2. She was a wealthy businesswoman – "A dealer in purple cloth" (verse 14).

3. She lived in a considerable property (verse 40), big enough to host a house church in the city of Philippi.

4. She was the leader of this house congregation (verse 40), the reason why she was named in Acts.

◆ In the culture of the first-century Christian world Lydia, as a wealthy businessperson in her own right, and as the leader of a Christian church consisting of both women and men, was unusual. In fact it was radically different from the cultural norms in relation to the place of women in Greek and Roman societies. In a male-dominated society women generally stayed at home, did not even share in meals involving their husbands and his friends, and their opinions were usually considered unimportant.

◆ By the beginning of the second century, women were no longer allowed to be in leadership roles within the church. Bishops, priests and deacons were exclusively male.

Read the text and consider:

1. Why did this situation change?

2. How can the modern church reflect the earliest church practice as in the Lydia story?

Acts 16:11–15, 40 – Finding her voice

[11] We set sail from Troas and took a straight course to Samothrace, the following day to Neapolis, [12] and from there to Philippi, which is a leading city of the district of Macedonia and a Roman colony. We remained in this city for some days. [13] On the Sabbath day we went outside the gate by the river, where we supposed there was a place of prayer; and we sat down and spoke to the women who had gathered there. [14] A certain woman named Lydia, a worshipper of God, was listening to us; she was from the city of Thyatira and a dealer in purple cloth. The Lord opened her heart to listen eagerly to what was said by Paul. [15] When she and her household were baptized, she urged us, saying, 'If you have judged me to be faithful to the Lord, come and stay at my home.' And she prevailed upon us . . . [40] After leaving the prison they went to Lydia's home; and when they had seen and encouraged the brothers and sisters, they departed.

NRSV Bible

Session 6, Handout 4

Acts 17:16–31– It is always good to speak two languages

◆ We may be closer to the world of the early church than at any time since Paul stood before the Areopagus in Athens and engaged in an in-depth dialogue with the Athenians. We too live in the marketplace of ideas, a pluralistic and diverse world.

◆ In his dialogue, the texts he used are from Greek poets and not his Hebrew Scriptures. Transmitting the faith required him to be bilingual. Paul knew his audience: he had listened to the views of the marketplace and engaged with the people in the marketplace.

◆ Paul took the local context seriously in his dialogue. He knew the Athenians were attracted by new and competing ideas and that they engaged in the worship of many gods. Paul is prepared to speak their language.

In your group consider:

1. How do we bridge the growing gap between the church and people in the market place?

2. How might we share the Christian story in non-religious language as did Paul in Athens?

Acts 17:16–34 – It is always good to speak two languages

[16] While Paul was waiting for them in Athens, he was deeply distressed to see that the city was full of idols. [17] So he argued in the synagogue with the Jews and the devout persons, and also in the market-place' every day with those who happened to be there. [18] Also some Epicurean and Stoic philosophers debated with him. Some said, 'What does this babbler want to say?' Others said, 'He seems to be a proclaimer of foreign divinities.' (This was because he was telling the good news about Jesus and the resurrection.) [19] So they took him and brought him to the Areopagus and asked him; 'May we know what this new teaching is that you are presenting? [20] It sounds rather strange to us, so we would like to know what it means.' [21] Now all the Athenians and the foreigners living there would spend their time in nothing but telling or hearing something new. [22] Then Paul stood in front of the Areopagus and said, 'Athenians, I see how extremely religious you are in every way. [23] For as I went through the city and looked carefully at the objects of your worship, I found among them an altar with the inscription, "To an unknown god." What therefore you worship as un-known, this I proclaim to you. [24]The God who-made the world and everything in it, he who is Lord of heaven and earth, does not live in shrines made by human hands, [25] nor is he served by human hands, as though he needed anything, since he himself gives to all mortals life and breath and all things. [26] From one ancestor he made all nations to inhabit the whole earth, and he allotted the times of their existence and the boundaries of the places where they would live; [27] So that they would search for God and perhaps grope for him and find him – though indeed he is not far from each one of us. [28] For 'In him we live and move and have our being'; as even some of your own poets have said, "For we too are his offspring." [29] Since we are God's offspring, we ought not to think that the deity is like gold or silver, or stone, an image formed by the art and imagination of mortals. [30] While God has overlooked the times of human ignorance, now he commands all people everywhere to repent, [31] because he has fixed a day on which he will

have the world judged in righteousness by a man whom he has appointed, and of this he has given assurance to all by raising him from the dead.' [32] When they heard of the resurrection of the dead, some scoffed; but others said, 'We will hear you again about this.' [33] At that point Paul left them. [34] But some of them joined him and became believers, including Dionysius the Areopagite and a woman named Damaris, and others with them.

NRSV Bible

Session 7 Introduction

Walking together on common ground
Exploring what we share

In this session we will be exploring what it means to behave with 'strong tolerance' toward others. The primary resource for this consideration will be Paul's letter to the Romans. The context for this letter and the particular insights Paul brings to an understanding of tolerance are to be found in the course 'Living Faith At The Edge' under the session title 'A plea for tolerance' (page 74).

In our common parlance, to behave towards another with tolerance is to show patience toward others whose opinions or practices differ from our own. The difficulty of maintaining such a position is reflected in the Oxford dictionary's use of the terms 'to bear' and 'to endure', in defining what it means 'to tolerate' another. To act with tolerance, then, is to be prepared to set aside our own agendas and prejudices in an attempt to create the necessary space to listen to and understand the beliefs and practices of those who differ from us. This is no easy task but it is a necessary one if an open, equitable and tolerant society is to be nurtured and fully realised.

Session 7 Plan

Welcome and introduction (5 minutes)

Blue-sky thinking (10 minutes)

  What is understood by the word tolerance?

  Attitudes to tolerance.

Feedback (10 minutes)

Background to text (15 minutes)

  Historical setting

  Paul's letter to the Romans

Read text – Romans 14:1–15:7 (5 minutes)

Role-play (45 minutes)

  Roman House Church Conference

  Outline and preparation (15 minutes)

  Role-play (20 minutes)

  Debriefing (10 minutes)

Group work exercise 1 (15 minutes)

There were a number of cultural, ethnic and religious differences between these Jewish and Gentile Christians. In asking them to practice strenuous tolerance, Paul was also suggesting to them that for all their differences they shared a great deal in common. He pointed out that their common ground was more important than the issues that divided them.

From your reading of the text and your awareness of the background to the issues within the Roman house churches consider:

What was their common ground?

What common ground do we walk on together and how does it rise above the cultural and even religious differences?

Plenary feedback (15 minutes)

Overhead 1

Historical Setting

◆ It is 49 CE, seven or eight years before Paul wrote Romans.

◆ There were riots in Jewish synagogues between Jewish Christian agitators and zealous Jewish opponents.

◆ There was no central Jewish authority to mediate the dispute; therefore, the emperor Claudius expelled a large number of Jewish and Christian leaders from Rome and the Jews lost their right to assemble.

◆ The remaining Christians were almost exclusively Gentiles who formed separate congregations from the synagogues.

◆ They developed their own form and pattern and new Latin and Greek leaders emerged.

◆ Many would have had 'charismatic' views of the ministry and a liberal outlook on ethical questions.

◆ 54 CE Nero became emperor and the situation changed.

◆ Original Jewish-Christian leaders like Prisca and Aquila returned.

◆ They found a changed and threatening situation.

◆ Long smouldering anti-Semitic Roman tendencies emerged in leadership struggles.

◆ Two years before Paul wrote, conflicts between Jewish and Gentile Christians, conservatives and liberals, old and new Christians, increased and festered.

Overhead 2

◆ Paul's letter to the Roman Church

◆ Paul did not found the church of Rome.

◆ Paul intends to visit Rome on his way to Spain and he desires support and contacts to open his Spanish mission.

◆ He sets out in his letter to clarify the nature of the gospel to be preached and to overcome factions in the Roman house churches over the status of Jews and Greeks in the plan of salvation.

◆ He knows a large number of people in Rome by name, greeting them, along with at least five separate house churches, in chapter 16.

◆ As he knows the situation well, he is able to address it carefully.

◆ The letter was written primarily to the Gentile Christian majority, calling them to live together with Jewish Christians, recognising them as legitimate members of the community.

Session 7, Handout 1

Romans 14:1–15:7

[1] Welcome those who are weak in faith, but not for the purpose of quarrelling over opinions. [2] Some believe in eating anything, while the weak eat only vegetables. [3] Those who eat must not despise those who abstain, and those who abstain must not pass judgement on those who eat; for God has welcomed them. [4] Who are you to pass judgement on servants of another? It is before their own lord that they stand or fall. And they will be upheld, for the Lord is able to make them stand. [5] Some judge one day to be better than another, while others judge all days to be alike. Let all be fully convinced in their own minds. [6] Those who observe the day, observe it in honour of the Lord. Also those who eat, eat in honour of the Lord, since they give thanks to God; while those who abstain, abstain in honour of the Lord and give thanks to God.

[7] We do not live to ourselves and we do not die to ourselves. [8] If we live, we live to the Lord, and if we die, we die to the Lord; so then, whether we live or whether we die, we are the Lord's. [9] For to this end Christ died and lived again, so that he might be Lord of both the dead and the living.

[10] Why do you pass judgement on your brother or sister? Or you, why do you despise your brother or sister? For

we will all stand before the judgement seat of God. [11] For it is written, 'As I live, says the Lord, every knee shall bow to me and every tongue shall give praise to God.' [12] So then, each of us will be accountable to God.

[13] Let us therefore no longer pass judgement on one another, but resolve instead never to put a stumbling-block or hindrance in the way of another. [14] I know and am persuaded in the Lord Jesus that nothing is unclean in itself; but it is unclean for anyone who thinks it unclean. [15] If your brother or sister is being injured by what you eat, you are no longer walking in love. Do not let what you eat cause the ruin of one for whom Christ died. [16] So do not let your good be spoken of as evil. [17] For the kingdom of God is not food and drink but righteousness and peace and joy in the Holy Spirit. [18] The one who thus serves Christ is acceptable to God and has human approval. [19] Let us then pursue what makes for peace and for mutual edification. [20] Do not, for the sake of food, destroy the work of God. Every-thing is indeed clean, but it is wrong for you to make others fall by what you eat. [21] it is good not to eat meat or drink wine or do anything that makes your brother or sister stumble. [22] The faith that you have, have as your own conviction before God. Blessed are those who have no reason to condemn themselves because of what they approve. [23] But those who have doubts are condemned if they eat, because they do not act from faith; for whatever does not proceed from faith is sin. Chapter 15 We who are strong ought to put up with the failings of the weak, and not to please ourselves. [2] Each of us must please our neighbour for the good purpose of building up the neighbour. [3] For Christ did not please himself; but, as it is written: 'The insults of those who insult you have fallen on me.' [4] For whatever was written in former days was written for our instruction, so that by steadfastness and by the encouragement of the scriptures we might have hope. [5] May the God of steadfastness and encouragement grant you to live in harmony with one another, in accordance with Christ Jesus, [6] and so that together you may with one voice glorify the God and Father of our Lord Jesus Christ. [7] Welcome one another, therefore, just as Christ has welcomed you, for the glory of God.

NRSV Bible

Session 7, Handout 2

'Roman House Church Conference'

Characters:

◆ Minority Jewish Christian group

◆ Majority Gentile group

◆ Christian group

◆ Paul

Scenario:

The house churches in Rome have all received the letter from Paul. As a follow-up to the letter, representatives from the Jewish Christian and Gentile Christian groups travel to Ephesus to meet Paul. Their intention is to represent their positions to him. Both groups need to be prepared to argue with Paul.

Task:

In your group, take on the role you have been assigned, imagine your way into it, consider your position and what you will say when you meet Paul.

Questions for debriefing:

1. How did you feel in your role?

2. What were the real tensions you faced?

3. What insights did you gain on the nature and practice of tolerance?

Session 7, Handout 3

Minority Jewish Christian group

◆ In 49 CE, Emperor Claudius closed the Jewish synagogues and banished key Jewish leaders from Rome. This followed Jewish and Christian rioting in the city. Jewish Christian leaders, like Prisca and Aquila, were among those sent into exile. They are representative of your minority Jewish Christian group in the Roman house churches.

◆ In 54 CE when Nero allowed you to return, you discover the house churches are completely controlled by the majority Gentile Christians.

◆ There is no place for your Jewish culture and identity and you are looked upon as inferior.

◆ In Rome there is also anti-Semitic feeling.

◆ In Paul's letter you are referred to as 'the weak', which is what the Gentile majority call you. You are perceived as traditionalists who do not want to change but who wanted to preserve the traditional Jewish identity in some of your practices, eg the food laws, the practice of circumcision and the observance of Jewish festivals.

◆ The question facing you is do the Gentiles see a place for you in the church?

Session 7, Handout 4

Majority Gentile Christian group

◆ Following the exile of Jewish Christian leaders in 49 CE, as a result of the Jewish Christian riots, your group was left in control. This enabled you to establish some of your own house churches.

◆ Though your faith has its roots in the Jewish tradition, you see no need for any Jewish cultural or religious trappings in the life and worship of your house churches.

◆ When the Jewish Christian leaders returned in 54 CE tensions developed. You perceived yourselves as the strong and as superior to the Jewish Christians. You did not want any reintroduction of Jewish practices, like food laws, circumcision and observance of festivals. In your view if the Jewish Christians are to be part of the Christian church then all things Jewish have to disappear.

◆ You are in fact saying that to be Christian, Jewish Christians must become like you.

Session 7, Handout 5

Paul's view in Romans – Chapter 14:1–15:3

◆ You advocate 'mutual tolerance' between the factions in the Roman Church on the grounds of maintaining personal integrity and seeking harmony in the church.

◆ You admonish both traditionalists ('weak') and progressives ('strong') to remain true to their doctrinal convictions and their varying liturgical practices, while accepting one another in Christ.

◆ You selected the extreme positions of opposite ends of the liberal–conservative spectrum in Rome, absolute vegetarian and complete libertarian, to make the principle of tolerance inclusive of all positions in the range (14:1–3).

◆ You remind all of them that their opponents are acceptable to God and that they have no right, therefore, to discriminate against each other on the basis of differences in lifestyle (14:4).

◆ You also remind them that each Christian has the responsibility to retain integrity in the quest for truth (14:5).

◆ The relational basis of genuine tolerance is stressed by you. It is your belief that what unites people is not their liturgical or ethical preferences but their proper relationship to God, to whom alone praise is due (14:6).

◆ You suggest ways of protecting the integrity of one's adversaries. Each side has an obligation to see that the other lives up to its own standards, by creating the space for the other to exercise personal integrity (14:13–23).

◆ You point out that strong tolerance is not based on moral ambivalence or finding the lowest common denominator but on the action of God in Christ. Tolerance in the Christian community gives glory to God (15:7).

◆ By transcending the differences between Greeks and Jews you firmly hold that the gospel reaches out to include the entire human race. The Good News that finally transforms the world is that God has called conservatives as well as liberals, Greeks as well as Jews, to live in praise of God's mercy (15:9–13).

Session 7, Handout 6

Group work exercise 1

There were a number of cultural, ethnic and religious differences between these Jewish and Gentile Christians. In asking them to practice strenuous tolerance, Paul was also suggesting to them that for all their differences they shared a great deal in common. He pointed out that their common ground was more important than the issues that divided.

From your reading of the text and your awareness of the background to the issues within the Roman house churches, consider:

1. What was their common ground?

2. What common ground do we walk on together and how does it rise above the cultural and even religious differences?

Session 8 Introduction

Dreaming dreams, creating pathways
Formulating a twenty-first-century vision for church

Change is one of the very few certitudes of life. This is not a static universe. Change has been built into its very constitution. God might even be described as the great change agent.

These dynamic processes of change have implications for the church and the practice of spirituality. Some institutions are more conservative than others and the church tends towards conservatism. Having said that the church has always changed, slowly maybe but historical perspective shows change at work. Sometimes tradition is no older than a generation! It wasn't always the way it is and it will not always be the way it is.

Yet change can be painful and difficult:

Times of transition in cultures and societies mean permanent, social tension and conflict. They bring widespread experiences of dislocation. Established institutions and practice undergo changes and loss of coherence. Assumptions that have guided public and private patterns of life without much examination become problematic and suffer questions of legitimation.

(James W Fowler, *Faithful Change: The Personal and Public Challenges of Postmodern Life*, Abingdon, 1996, p 160.)

Trying to envision what kind of Northern Ireland we want to live in 25 years from now is a difficult task, even frightening. Already we are in a time of transition in which we are aware of ferment, social tension, conflict and experiences of dislocation. These experiences may be around for some time. Looking forward and dreaming dreams is a necessary challenge. Without vision there is no future possibility and there is no future possibility without change.

The church has always had to live in changing contexts. Since the Jesus story can only be lived in this world of changing contexts, the church not only has a contribution to make towards visioning a new society, it also needs to revision itself for times of transition and change. What kind of church, then, is needed for the twenty-first century?

The church needs a new vision of God. There are visions of God that no longer seem credible or important. Such images of God need to be allowed to die:

◆ the God who legitimised the collusion between thrones and alters and blessed the accompanying patterns of economic power and social class systems;

◆ the God of nationalistic doctrines of 'manifest destiny' and world imperialism;

◆ the God of the gospel of wealth;

◆ the male-gendered God (Ibid, p 192).

What shapes and patterns of God's active presence will we need for a new context? God's movement may be looked for in:

◆ the enhancing of freedom and the shaping of just communities.

◆ the breaking of systemic oppression and the reconstitution of institutions.

◆ the healing of the injured and the broken and the deep equalisation of life's chances.

◆ care for nature and for our reconciliation in mutuality with earth, sky, water, and our brother and sister humans and animals. (James W Fowler, p 194).

If the church is to engage in a public rethinking of God's presence and action, then it will need the normative and imaginative resources of the Bible. That will mean rediscovering God through a re-reading of the key biblical metaphors such as covenant, exodus, exile, reign of God, cross, resurrection, community, body, new heavens and new earth.

A church for the twenty-first century revisioning God will be a public church. Such a public church will no longer be closely allied with the public and political structures of power, nor will it hold a place of privilege and status in society. From the edge it will offer its witness in publicly visible and publicly intelligible ways. Not from the centre but from the edge it will articulate its vision of the common good in partnership with others, and if need be lobby and protest, but above all seek to live in public places the gospel story.

A church for the twenty-first century will be a life-sustaining community. To be in the world or the public place begins with and is sustained by supportive community. Such a community provides the faithful with space to celebrate together all that is good and true as the gift of divine grace. Within supportive community there is development and growth into more authentic personhood within the social experience of equality and freedom. There is a deep solidarity of forgiven sinners and people on the journey together. Within community there is shared forgiveness, reconciliation and healing.

Church for the twenty-first century will be an agent of healing for the world. The experience of God in a life-sustaining community is not contained within the walls or boundaries of the church. It holds before the world an authentic vision of community which has at its heart the vision of the whole human family reconciled and living together in justice and peace. The vision is an integrated one in which humanity and nature are reconciled.

This will lead the community of faith to oppose the idols of nationalism, greed, elitism, militarism, violence and consumerism. It will speak with the poor, oppressed, hungry and suffering. The biblical standards of right relations and compassion will be central. Since compassion is rare in a society of fear and distrust, in living compassionately the church will enable people to build trust and overcome fear.

Church for the twenty-first century will be a community of liberating spirituality. Growing numbers of people experience disillusionment with and alienation from the institutional church. This may be due to dying or dead images of God which are still offered. It may be because of a lack of authentic community or a meaningful engagement with contemporary questions and issues around society. The church as a model of control does not offer liberation and the possibility to grow up and become adult witnesses to faith.

The search for spirituality is the search for meaning, connectedness, community and wholeness, all of which is social. It is about connecting with a "co-creative God who co-creates with us, humans (and with all other creatures), in bringing about a world order, a worthy abode in which the new reign of God can unfold and flourish" (Diarmuid O Murchu in *Spiritual Questions for the 21st Century: Essays in Honour of Joan D Chittister*, Orbis Books, 2001, p 80).

It is the kind of spirituality in which Joan Chittister challenges us:

. . . to reappropriate the most challenging of gospel values, to outgrow the congested world of ecclesiastical holiness (with its many noble and heroic achievements of the past), and to embrace more fully the call to be agents for that love, justice, and liberation which belong essentially to building up the reign of God at the heart of creation.

(Ibid, p 80.)

As we dream dreams for a new society, what models of church are emerging?

Session 8 Plan

Welcome and introduction (5 minutes)

Group work exercise 1 (20 minutes)

'Dreaming dreams for Northern Ireland'

The year is 2020. In groups, consider the following question and record responses on flip chart sheets:

What kind of Northern Ireland would you like to see?

Feedback (10 minutes)

Discussion (10 minutes)

Is a common vision for Northern Ireland in the year 2020 emerging?

Group work exercise 2 (20 minutes)

'Dreaming dreams of church'

In the same groups, consider the following question and bring responses to the larger group:

What sort of church is going to be needed for that kind of society?

Plenary feedback (25 minutes)

Questions for consideration in the plenary:

What models of church are emerging?

How will our present churches need to change to reflect these models of church?

What role do we have?

Are we a people of hope?

Prayer service (30 minutes)

Prepare in advance a short prayer service that will leave space for participants' reflections on the course.

Session 8, Handout 1

Group work exercise 1

    The year is 2020. In groups, consider the following question and record responses on flip chart sheets:

    What kind of Northern Ireland would you like to see?

Group work exercise 2

    In the same groups, consider the following question and bring responses to the larger group:

    What sort of church is going to be needed for that kind of society?

Plenary discussion questions

    1. What models of church are emerging?

    2. How will our present churches need to change to reflect these models of church?

    3. What role do we have?

    4. Are we a people of hope?

Course Two Outline

Living faith at the edge
The Bible in the public square

Course description

Through exploration of biblical texts, this course provides an opportunity to explore the following.

◆ The challenge and insight to take responsibility for the enemy.

◆ What it means to be tolerant.

◆ The challenge and responsibility to build civic society and transform culture.

◆ The implications of embracing the equality agenda.

◆ Biblical insights into creating inclusive community for a new context.

Course outline

Session 1   So what about your enemy then?

Rereading the Sermon on the Mount

Session 2   A plea for tolerance!

Exploration of Romans 14:1–15:7

Session 3   Civic responsibility – the future!

Implications of Philippians 2 for building civic society

Session 4   Faith transforming culture

What can be learned from a study of the prophet Hosea?

Session 5   Embracing the equality agenda

Revisiting our covenant story in Exodus and Jeremiah

Session 6   Inclusive community for a new context

An exploration of 3rd Isaiah, Jonah And Ruth

Session 1 Introduction

So what about your enemy then? Re-reading the Sermon on the Mount

In conflict regions there is no shortage of perceived enemies. The enemy is a person or a group perceived as hostile by another individual, group or community. Enemies are those against us and are quickly demonised and dehumanised. We cope with enemies by treating them as inferior, less than human or not human at all. Whatever the situation of conflict, this is always a distorted feature of the other person or group. They are not the demons we make them but human beings like ourselves. Like us they have histories and experiences. Like us they have been shaped by those histories and experiences. Like us they have made wrong choices, taken wrong turnings, put their faith in negative ideologies or causes. At the same time they also resemble us in being loving sons, daughters, parents, spouses and friends. Such is the ambivalence of being human. What we demonise in the other may well be a mirror image. Not only do we demonise the other quickly in a conflict, but we perpetuate the conflict by continuing to demonise and dehumanise. The challenge from a Christian perspective is to rehumanise the enemy. That seems to be at the heart of the relation-centred ethic of Jesus.

When reading the Sermon on the Mount we are at the heart of the ethic of Jesus. That is what Matthew's Gospel intends to convey. Shaping the Gospel around the Jewish Torah, this Gospel portrays Jesus as a second Moses, the law giver. Law, though, is not to be confused with legalism and it is a distortion to set the Torah or Jewish law over against a gospel of grace. Matthew's Gospel after all is keen to stress that Jesus did not come to abolish the law but to fulfil it (Matthew 5:17). Torah in Jewish and Matthean thinking is life-giving wisdom of God, positive directions for holistic living in community. Love of neighbour is at the heart of the Sermon on the Mount and the most radical form of neighbour love is love of the enemy. It is "the perfect form of love of neighbour which accords with good and thus with justice" (Jurgen Moltmann, *Creating a Just Future*, SCM Press, 1989, p 42).

Such radical love is not retributive but creative since it removes the enemy's enmity and breaks the spirit of conflict and the cycle of violence. By doing so we are taking responsibility for the enemy and at the same time responsibility for the larger common good and well-being of community. It is also the recognition that both the enemy and ourselves can change. Love of the enemy is transformative of ourselves, the other and the conflict situation.

For Jesus such radical love was and is rooted in the nature and practice of God. The Matthean text ends with words that either bewilder or frighten us: "Be perfect therefore, as your heavenly Father is perfect" (5:48). The Luken version has the word 'compassionate' instead of 'perfect'. The latter often suggests to us a kind of moral perfection, which we know we can never reach. Luke's word is more relational and is closer to what is intended. Behind the Matthean 'perfect' is an Aramaic word, which was the language of Jesus, which is also profoundly relational. It means 'all-inclusive', 'all-embracing'. We are to be all-inclusive and all-embracing as God is all-inclusive and all-embracing. It may still strike us as a tall order, but it is a strategy for dealing with enemies and the enmity on the way to a non-violent and peaceful community. The Sermon's ethic is not about passive resistance but creative, proactive love that finds ways of breaking spirals and cycles of conflict and violence. The text is not just about love of the enemy but love of enemies and non-violence. The challenge of the text is real and concrete. "It is impossible to determine what love of enemies and non violence mean apart from the social, situation in which these demands are made and practiced" (Gerd Theissen, *Social Reality and the Early Christians: Theology, Ethics, and the World of the New Testament*, T and T Clarke, 1993, p 130).

The two overheads on the Political World of Jesus are important for understanding the first-century socio-political context in which such teaching was first heard. Jesus and the movement which followed him lived in a real, concrete, historical world. It was a world of Roman domination. Indeed the Jewish people had lived through centuries of political and military domination apart from almost a century of political independence following the Maccabean revolt from the Greeks in 167–142 BCE. The emerging imperial power of Roman conquered Palestine in 63 BCE, after which Emperor Pompey installed a native client king and introduced the tribute, an imperial tax. In 40 BCE the smaller Parthean empire ruled but in three years the Romans regained control, installing Herod the Great and a long and brutal reign which came to an end in 4 BCE. Apart from Herod's police state, the Romans had ultimate control and were equally if not more brutal. The Roman spin doctors propagated the myth of Pax Romano but the so-called peace was the peace of brutal military domination. When Jerusalem was conquered by Pompey, the city was besieged and the Holy of Holies within the temple violated, not only by the Roman occupying presence but by the sacrilege of Roman symbols. Tribute was exacted by force and the Romans were adept at the slaughter of people and destruction of towns. Any resistance in town, village or country was brutally put down. After one such rising in the region of Galilee, Cassius, a Roman military leader, enslaved 30,000 Galilean men. After a revolt in Sepphoris, a Herodian-built Hellenistic city, the Romans simply executed 2,000 Jewish males.

In 37 BCE Herod became king over the Jewish territories. From then until 4 BCE he ruled as an oppressive tyrant. His paranoia with personal safety and his political security led him to murder members of his own family whom he believed to be a threat to his power. He maintained a widespread system of unfairness and established a police state because of his obsession with security. His ego drove him to extravagant and massive building projects from water aqueducts to Hellenistic cities. His egotistical building schemes required enormous financial resources, which could only be met through taxation. Taxation was a particular burden on Jewish peasants who were the majority of the population. They suffered from triple taxation imposed on them by the Romans, the Herodian kings and the Temple system. The tax rate ran at 40% which left many peasants in slavery to debt, displaced from their land on which they became economic slaves to the élite landowners.

As well as bearing crippling taxation, the peasants of Galilee served as the breadbasket for the Hellenistic cities, which was a form of economic exploitation. Galilee suffered double oppression: "It was increasingly controlled by the political and economic forces of Hellenistic urban penetration. Symbolically and socio-economically it was controlled by Jerusalem in the south" (Ched Myers, *Binding the Strong Man: A Political Reading of Mark's Story of Jesus*, Orbis Books, 1988, p 54). Galilean people were exhausted economically and oppressed politically and militarily: " . . . Galilee was riven by deep structural tensions, by tensions between Jews and Gentiles, town and country, rich and poor, rulers and ruled" (Gerd Theissen and Annette Merz, *The Historical Jesus*, SCM Press, 1998, p 175).

When Jesus proclaimed the reign of God, it was in contrast to the reign of the Romans and the Herodians. There was no shortage of enemies in Palestine and in his native Galilee. When Herod died in 4 BCE discontent and revolt erupted in every district. The Romans attempted to deal with this by dividing Herod's kingdom but from 6–66 CE there was widespread discontent and turbulence. The massive Jewish revolt happened in 66–70 CE and was ruthlessly put down by the Romans. Matthew's Gospel was shaped by the Jewish situation after 70 CE. The catastrophic failure of the revolt against Rome is the backdrop to the conflicts and tensions experienced by the Matthean faith community. In the years after the Jewish war, love of enemies might have different meaning. There is still the challenge in a changed context for love of enemies, peacemaking and non-violence to be practiced. Whatever the context or situation, radical discipleship still means rehumanising the enemy, breaking the spiral of violence and going beyond the enmity to peace.

Session 1 Plan, Alternative 1

Welcome and introduction (10 minutes)

Blue-sky thinking (10 minutes)

When you hear or see the word 'enemy' written, what are your feelings, thoughts, associations?

Reading of text – Matthew 5:43–48 (5 minutes)

Political world of Jesus – Roman domination (5 minutes)

Political world of Jesus – Herod's tyranny (5 minutes)

Rereading of text (5 minutes)

Group work exercise 1 (30 minutes)

Read Matthew 5:43–48 and from the perspective of one of the following groups consider the questions which follow:

Roman army commanders

Herod and palace supporters

Jesus community

Peasants

Galilean Resistance Force

Who are your enemies?

How does Jesus' teaching challenge you?

In your context is Jesus' teaching realistic?

Feedback (20 minutes)

An enemy is a person or group perceived as hostile by another individual, group or community or who attempts to do damage or cause harm to another person, community or property.

In the context of Northern Ireland, consider:

What causes hostility?

Who are perceived as enemies? (10 minutes)

Plenary (15 minutes)

What does it mean to take responsibility for the enemy in the context of Northern Ireland?

Reading of poem 'Cross-Border Peace Talks' (5 minutes)

Session 1 Plan, Alternative 2

Welcome and introduction (10 minutes)

Blue-sky thinking (10 minutes)

When you hear or see the word 'enemy' written, what are your feelings, thoughts, associations?

Reading of text – Matthew 5:43–48 (5 minutes)

Political world of Jesus – Roman domination (5 minutes)

Political world of Jesus – Herod's tyranny (5 minutes)

Rereading of text (5 minutes)

Role-play (50 minutes)

Outline and preparation (15 minutes)

Role-play (20 minutes)

Debriefing (15 minutes)

Group work exercise 1 (10 minutes)

An enemy is a person or group perceived as hostile by another individual, group or community. In the context of Northern Ireland, identify:

What causes hostility?

Who are perceived as enemies?

Plenary discussion (15 minutes)

What does it mean to take responsibility for the enemy in our context?

Reading of poem 'Cross-Border Peace Talks' (10 minutes)

Session 1, Handout 1

Matthew 5:43–8

[43] You have heard that it was said, you shall love your neighbour and hate your enemy. [44] But I say to you, Love your enemies and pray for those who persecute you, [45] so that you may be children of your Father in heaven; for he makes his sun rise on the evil and on the good, and sends rain on the righteous and on the unrighteous. [46] For if you love those who love you, what reward do you have? Do not even the tax-collectors do the same? [47] And if you greet only your brothers and sisters, what more are you doing than others? Do not even the Gentiles do the same? [48] Be perfect, therefore, as your heavenly Father is perfect.

NRSV Bible

Overhead 1

The political world of Jesus

Roman domination

◆ Oppression and revolt

◆ Pompey conquered Palestine.

◆ Jerusalem besieged and Holy of Holies violated.

◆ Jewish territories forced to pay tribute.

◆ Roman brutality, slaughter and destruction of towns.

◆ Cassius enslaved 30,000 men in Galilee

◆ Heavy taxation

Overhead 2

The political world of Jesus

Herod's tyranny

◆ Herod became king over Jewish territories in 40 BCE.

◆ From 37–4 BCE Herod was an oppressive tyrant.

◆ Maintained a police state

◆ Undertook massive building projects

- Imposed a huge burden of taxation – exhausted people economically
- When Herod died in 4 BCE, discontent and revolt erupted in every district.
- Romans dealt with revolts by dividing Herod's kingdom.
- From 6–66 CE – widespread discontent and turbulence.
- Massive Jewish revolt in 66–70 CE
- Heavy taxation
  - Roman tax-collectors/collaborators
  - Kings
  - Temple
- Tax rate – 40%
  - Peasants in debt/slavery
  - Displaced from land
  - Became slaves on their own land
- Hellenistic economic exploitation

Session 1, Alternative 1, Handout 2

Peace negotiations

Background:

Two to three miles from Nazareth lies the city of Sepphoris. A recent rebellion against Roman occupation resulted in the crucifixion of 2,000 Jewish men by the Romans. Among those crucified was a GRF (Galilean Resistance Force) leader. Galilee is consequently a time bomb waiting to explode. The role-play will be about the possibility of dealing with this potential explosion of conflict.

Characters:

◆ Roman army commanders

◆ Herod

◆ Galilean Resistance Force

◆ Jesus community

◆ Peasants

◆ Observers

Scenario:

There will be a negotiation scenario opened up and one of the groups will take an initiative in that. Each group will be given information regarding their character to help them in their preparation for the role-play.

Task:

In your group, imagine yourself into your role. What will your response be? How will you deal with what is going on from your perspective? The role-play will begin when one group takes an initiative. You will know when that happens.

Questions for debriefing session:

1. How did you feel in your role?

2. What dynamics were going on?

3. Who is the enemy?

4. How did you deal with the enemy and the conflict?

5. On reflection would you have done anything differently?

Session 1, Alternative 1, Handout 3

Roman army commanders:

◆ Oppressive occupying force.

◆ Little understanding of Jewish religion and culture.

◆ Roman peace maintained by militarism.

◆ Only concerned to build their empire.

◆ Palestine is on the trade routes. Roman economic power is dependent on keeping control and ensuring safe passage for traders.

Herod:

◆ You are a Roman puppet king dependent on the goodwill of the Romans to stay in power.

◆ You cannot afford to have the Galileans resisting, agitating and disturbing the Roman status quo ('Peace').

Jesus community:

◆ You are committed to non-violence, taking responsibility for one's enemy and finding an alternative way based on the radical ethic of Jesus, expressed in Matthew 5:43–8, as a way of resolving community conflict.

Peasants:

◆ Majority of population in Galilee were peasants who were poorly paid and suffered economic exploitation and oppression.

◆ They blamed the Romans and Herod for their abuse and regarded the heavy taxation both imposed as robbery and illegitimate.

◆ They also resented the erosion of their way of life under Roman rule.

◆ They supported the GRF and viewed them as heroic victims of Roman injustice; they offered them protection from the Romans.

◆ They believed God would soon act within history to vindicate them and establish justice and peace.

Observers:

◆ Your role is to observe all that is going on during the role-play and be prepared to comment on these observations at the end.

◆ Pay particular attention to the dynamics going on within and between groups.

◆ Are there questions you would like to ask any of the players?

◆ In your opinion who is the enemy and how was the conflict dealt with?

Session 1, Alternative 1, Handout 4

Galilean Resistance Force (GRF)

◆ You are resistance fighters.

◆ You believe God has mandated you to liberate the country from Roman occupation.

◆ You believe the only way forward is through the use of violence.

◆ You operate in small cell groups from hideaways in the hillsides around Galilee, coming out to strike the enemy and quickly disappearing.

◆ Your slogan is 'For God and Galilee'.

Instructions for role-play:

1. Issue a list of demands to the Romans.

2. Issue an ultimatum to Herod to take action against the Romans to liberate the Jewish people.

3. Following the Roman response, take a Roman commander hostage to hide out in the hills.

Session 1, Alternative 2, Handout 5

Peace negotiations

Group work exercise 1

Read Matthew 5:43–8 and from the perspective of one of the following groups (background information provided) and consider the questions which follow:

◆ Roman army commanders

◆ Herod and palace supporters

◆ Jesus community

◆ Peasants

◆ Galilean Resistance Force

Questions for discussion within your group

1. Who are your enemies?

2. How does Jesus' teaching challenge you?

3. In your context, is Jesus' teaching realistic?

Task: Ask a representative from your group to give feedback on the above questions to the whole group.

Session 1, Alternative 2, Handout 6

Roman army commanders:

◆ You are an oppressive occupying force.

◆ You have little understanding of Jewish religion and culture.

◆ You maintain peace by militarism.

◆ You are only concerned to build your empire.

◆ Palestine is on the trade routes. You recognise that Roman economic power is dependent on keeping control and ensuring safe passage for traders.

◆ Your role is to maintain the 'Pax Romana' by whatever means is necessary.

Herod and his palace supporters:

◆ Herod is a Roman puppet king dependent on the goodwill of the Romans to stay in power.

◆ Herod cannot afford to have the Galileans resisting and agitating and disturbing the Roman status quo ('Peace').

◆ Herod is hated by Jews because of the imposed taxation.

◆ Herod is also despised because ethnically he is only half Jewish.

◆ Herod's insecurity and paranoia has led him to create a police state.

Jesus community:

◆ You are committed to non-violence, taking responsibility for one's enemy and finding an alternative way based on the radical ethic of Jesus, expressed in Matthew 5:43–8, as a way of resolving community conflict.

◆ You are largely from the peasant community (see heading 'Peasants' below).

Peasants:

◆ The majority of the population in Galilee are peasants who are

poorly paid and suffer economic exploitation and oppression.

◆ You blame the Romans and Herod for your abuse and regard the heavy taxation both impose as robbery and illegitimate.

◆ You also resent the erosion of your way of life under Roman rule.

◆ You are supportive of the GRF and view them as heroic victims of Roman injustice; you offer them protection from the Romans.

◆ You believe God will soon act within history to vindicate you and establish justice and peace.

Galilean Resistance Force (GRF)

◆ You are resistance fighters.

◆ You believe God has mandated you to liberate the country from Roman occupation.

◆ You believe the only way forward is through the use of violence.

◆ You operate in small cell groups from hideaways in the hillsides around Galilee, coming out to strike the enemy and quickly disappearing.

◆ Your slogan is 'For God and Galilee'.

Session 1, Handout 7

'Cross-Border Peace Talks'

There is a place

beyond the borders

where love grows,

and where peace is not the frozen silence

drifting across no man's land from two heavily-defended entrenchments,

but the stumbling, stammering attempts of long-closed throats

to find words to span the distance;

neither is it a simple formula

that reduces everything to labels,

but an intricate and complex web of feeling and relationship which spans a wider range than you'd ever thought possible.

The place is not to be found on the map

of government discussions

or political posturing.

It does not exist within the borders

of Catholic or Protestant,

Irish or British,

male or female,

old or young.

It lies beyond,

and is drawn with different points of reference.

To get to that place,

you have to go

(or be pushed out)

beyond the borders,

to where it is lonely, fearful, threatening,

unknown.

Only after you have wandered for a long time

in the dark,

do you begin to bump into others,

also branded,

exiled,

border-crossers,

and find you walk on common ground

It is not an easy place to be,

this place beyond the borders.

It is where you learn that there is more pain in love

than in hate,

more courage in forbearance than in vengeance,

more remembering needed in forgetting,

and always new borders to cross.

But it is a good place to be.

(Kathy Galloway (ed), *Pushing The Boat Out*, Wild Goose Publications, 1995, pp 65–6.)

Session 2 Introduction

A plea for tolerance
Exploration of Romans 14:1–15:7

There are many examples throughout our world of the dangers inherent in living within a context where tolerance is viewed with suspicion or altogether absent. Whether the reason for the intolerance be contested identity, land, culture or religion, the worst excesses of it are apparent in the violent conflicts raging in areas of contested space and diverse ethnic groupings: Israel and Palestine, Sri Lanka and Kashmir, to mention but a few. As with the conflict in Northern Ireland, an inability to act with tolerance toward the 'perceived' enemy hinders the move toward reconciliation and the creation of inclusive and harmonious relations.

Paul in the letter to the Romans is concerned to promote the relational basis of genuine tolerance between Jewish and Gentile Christians. It is Paul's intention to visit Rome on his way to Spain and he hopes to gain support from the Romans for this mission to the Gentiles in Spain. He recognises that if the Roman Christians are to be truly effective in their support they need to overcome hostilities between factions in the Roman house churches and be clear as to the nature of the gospel to be preached. Paul recognised that it is easier for us to accept those who are like us; the difficulty arises when we are faced with those who are different. The challenge to deal with difference in a faith context is at the heart of Paul's letter to the Romans. He obviously knows a large number of people in Rome and he greets them by name along with at least five separate house churches in chapter 16. Knowing the situation well, he is in a position to address it intelligently and carefully.

The Roman house churches had their origins in small Greek-speaking synagogues in Rome. As the Jewish community had no central governing board, and there was no supervisory body in Rome itself to oversee and control the zeal of Christian propagandists, the excesses and zeal of newly converted Christians led to increased factions, and disputes, between Christian and traditional Jewish members of the synagogues. When riots broke out involving the Jewish Christian agitators and their Jewish opponents in 49 CE, the emperor, viewing it as a Jewish problem, expelled a large number of Jewish and Christian leaders from Rome. He also took away the Jews' right to assemble. The remaining Christians, almost exclusively Gentile in origin, were forced to form congregations separate from the synagogues. When Nero became emperor five years later he held a more tolerant attitude toward the Jews and allowed Jewish exiles to return to Rome. On their return, Jewish Christians found the situation much changed.

The majority church is Gentile, and the liberal, free-thinking culture promoted within the pluralistic Roman Empire has pervaded the Christian communities. Consequently, Gentile Christians have rejected more traditional styles of worship and thinking, held within Jewish religious practice, in favour of an open, free and liberal approach. Long-smouldering anti-Semitic tendencies, which viewed the laws and traditions of the Jewish people as uncivilised, exclusive and somewhat strange, have influenced the Gentile Christian outlook to such an extent that the climate for returning Jewish Christians is both threatening and oppressive. In the two years prior to Paul's writing his letter to the Romans, Jewish and Gentile Christian relationships disintegrate even further. Wolfgang Wiefel is of the opinion that Paul wrote his letter to the Romans, "to assist the Gentile Christian majority, who are the primary addressees of the letter, to live together with the Jewish Christians in one congregation, thereby putting an end to their quarrels about status" (Wiefel, quoted in Robert Jewett, *Christian Tolerance: Paul's Message to the Modern Church*, The Westminster Press, 1982, p 29).

Living post-Shoah, our history and memories are scarred by the terrible atrocities and decimation of a people that results when anti-Semitism is pushed to its limits. We have learnt that the person who is not accepted is soon driven out and in extreme cases exterminated. Paul, in his own context, recognised the importance of solidarity and 'strenuous tolerance' in the face of sectarian divisiveness and conflict.

Paul warns the Gentile Christians that God has not rejected the Jews and that the roots of their faith are in Judaism; they are to keep in mind their indebtedness to the Jewish faith as "it is not you that support the root but the root that supports you" (Romans 11:18b). Lest the Jewish Christians use the argument of primacy to claim superiority, Paul also warns that no one can 'boost' for all have sinned and are in need of the free gift of God's grace (Romans 5:13) available to us through faith in Jesus Christ.

Paul employs the term 'weak' and 'strong' to define the hostile groups. It is likely that these terms have been adopted by the 'strong', who viewed their challenging of traditional values and holding fast to a more 'liberal' outlook as an example of spirited courage. It is also likely that this group boasted members from diverse racial and socio-economic backgrounds whose opinions and beliefs were not always in concord. Those labelled as 'weak' are thus named because they are more 'conservative' in their attitude to laws and traditions. Temperamentally the so-called 'weak' are equally forceful in maintaining the rightness of their own convictions and condemning the misguided lifestyle of the self-confessed liberals.

Paul's opposition to the divisions in the Roman house churches is informative. Rather than debating the rightness or wrongness of the 'weak' or the 'strong' position, or issues of food, worship or circumcision, Paul seeks to find common ground. By advocating a spirit of strenuous tolerance, for the entire range of views held, Paul is effectively endorsing a culture of mutual acceptance.

If God in God's wisdom accepts all, then the onus is on us to "welcome one another" (Romans 15:8). As a guiding principle, Paul reminds them that each person has a responsibility to retain integrity in the living out of their doctrinal convictions or practices. What is more, commitment to living in truth, in communities of integrity, is demonstrated by an equal concern to create space for the other to exercise their conscience and live by it. Paul recognised that it is only in living with tolerance, and forgiving each other the offences caused by living according to different standards, that the relational basis of community living is truly honoured and respected.

In spite of opposition in the early Christian church, Paul struggles to stay faithful to this approach (to be a Greek to the Greeks and a Jew to the Jews – Corinthians 9:21) in his own work. He is convinced of the integrity of living truthfully according to one's own standards and insights. How does this principle operate in practice? Paul advocates that those who choose to keep Jewish feast days in honour of the Lord should be encouraged to do so; equally, those who choose to work on these days, honouring God in their activities, should be supported in this choice. Similarly in relation to food, what is important is not whether one eats meat or abstains from eating it but one's relationship with God and with others in the community.

The letter which was written to and for a divided Christian community, where there was much intolerance, reaches its key insight and challenge in chapter 15:7: "Welcome one another, therefore, just as Christ has welcomed you, for the glory of God." Paul is urging the Roman Christians to put an end to their hostilities and recognise the legitimacy of the other's position. A similar message is given to the Ephesian churches, which experienced something of a reconciliation between Jews and Gentiles of different cultures and ethnicities. It is through the cross of Christ that God has reconciled both Jews and Gentiles into one body, putting an end to the earlier hostilities (Ephesians 2:16). The same letter reminds us that accepting the principle of reconciled diversity in Christ, and living according to its precepts, are two very different things. The struggle to live "with humility and gentleness, with patience, bearing with one another in love, making every effort to maintain the unity of the Spirit in the bond of peace" (Ephesians 4:2–3) is ongoing, requiring constant application.

The challenge to listen to those who are different and accept those differences while taking them seriously is a painful process. Keeping sight of the importance of the individual and the relationship when faced with divergent and sometimes contradictory politicised, religious and cultural perspectives is hard work. Yet in an increasingly multi-cultural and multi-faith society the practice of tolerance, whereby relationships transcend doctrines, dogmas and principles, is increasingly necessary. Living in a spirit of freedom, while taking responsibility for the other, places the building of relational community at the top of the church's agenda. Tolerance assumes concrete form in community with other people. Strenuous tolerance for Paul is rooted in the very nature of God who welcomed us while we were God's enemies and reconciled us to God's self by the life and death of Jesus Christ (Romans 5:8, 10). Strenuous tolerance for Paul is grounded in the love of God. We can, therefore, be generous in "welcoming others" because God has been generous in welcoming us. In acting with strenuous tolerance toward others we are effectively giving glory to God.

Session 2 Plan

Buzz and feedback on what is tolerance? (10 minutes)

Background to text:

Historical setting (5 minutes)

Paul's letter to the Romans (5 minutes)

Questions for clarification (5 minutes)

Read text (5 minutes)

Role-play

'Roman House Church Conference' (30 minutes)

Characters:

Minority Jewish Christian Group

Majority Gentile Christian Group

Paul

Task:

The house churches in Rome have all received the letter from Paul. In your group take on the role you have been assigned, imagine your way into it, and consider your response to the following questions:

1. From your perspective what kind of church would you like to see in first-century Rome?

2. What tensions exist in the Roman churches and why?

3. How can these tensions be resolved?

4. In resolving the tensions, what steps need to be taken?

Feedback (30 minutes)

Discussion (10 minutes)

What insights did you gain on the nature and practice of tolerance?

Group work exercise (10 minutes)

What does Paul's plea for tolerance mean in practical terms for the church and society in Northern Ireland?

Plenary (10 minutes)

Overhead 1

Historical Setting:

◆ It is 49 CE, seven or eight years before Paul wrote Romans.

◆ There were riots in Jewish synagogues between Jewish Christian agitators and zealous Jewish opponents.

◆ There was no central Jewish authority to mediate the dispute, therefore the Emperor Claudius expelled a large number of Jewish and Christian leaders from Rome and the Jews lost their right to assemble.

◆ The remaining Christians were almost exclusively Gentiles who formed separate congregations from the synagogues.

◆ They developed their own form and pattern and new Latin and Greek leaders emerged.

◆ Many would have had 'charismatic' views of the ministry and a liberal outlook on ethical questions.

◆ In 54 CE Nero became emperor and the situation changed.

◆ Original Jewish-Christian leaders like Prisca and Aquila returned.

◆ They found a changed and threatening situation.

◆ Long smouldering anti-Semitic Roman tendencies emerged in leadership struggles.

◆ Two years before Paul wrote, conflicts between Jewish and Gentile Christians, conservatives and liberals, old and new Christians, increased and festered.

Overhead 2

Paul's letter to the Roman Church:

◆ Paul did not found the church of Rome.

◆ Paul intends to visit Rome on his way to Spain and he desires support and contacts to open his Spanish mission.

◆ He sets out in his letter to clarify the nature of the gospel to be preached and to overcome factions in the Roman house churches over the status of Jews and Greeks in the plan of salvation.

◆ He knows a large number of people in Rome by name, greeting them, along with at least five separate house churches, in chapter 16.

◆ As he knows the situation well, he is able to address it carefully.

◆ The letter was written primarily to the Gentile Christian majority, calling them to live together with Jewish Christians, recognising them as legitimate members of the community.

Session 2, Handout 1

Romans 14:1–15:7

[1] Welcome those who are weak in faith, but not for the purpose of quarrelling over opinions. [2] Some believe in eating anything, while the weak eat only vegetables. [3] Those who eat must not despise those who abstain, and those who abstain must not pass judgement on those who eat; for God has welcomed them. [4] Who are you to pass judgement on servants of another? It is before their own lord that they stand or fall. And they will be upheld, for the Lord is able to make them stand. [5] Some judge one day to be better than another, while others judge all days to be alike. Let all be fully convinced in their own minds. [6] Those who observe the day, observe it in honour of the Lord. Also those who eat, eat in honour of the Lord, since they give thanks to God; while those who abstain, abstain in honour of the Lord and give thanks to God.

[7] We do not live to ourselves and we do not die to ourselves. [8] If we live, we live to the Lord, and if we die, we die to the Lord; so then, whether we live or whether we die, we are the Lord's. [9] For to this end Christ died and lived again, so that he might be Lord of both the dead and the living.

[10] Why do you pass judgement on your brother or sister? Or you, why do you despise your brother or sister? For we will all stand before the judgement seat of God. [11] For it is written, 'As I live, says the Lord, every knee shall bow to me and every tongue shall give praise to God.' [12] So then, each of us will be accountable to God. [13] Let us therefore no longer pass judgement on one another, but resolve instead never to put a stumbling-block or hindrance in the way of another. [14] I know and am persuaded in the Lord Jesus that nothing is unclean in itself; but it is unclean for anyone who thinks it unclean. [15] If your brother or sister is being injured by what you eat, you are no longer walking in love. Do not let what you eat cause the ruin of one for whom Christ died. [16] So do not let your good be spoken of as evil. [17] For the kingdom of God is not food and drink but righteousness and peace and joy in the Holy Spirit. [18] The one who thus serves Christ is acceptable to God and has human approval. [19] Let us then pursue what makes for peace and for mutual edification. [20] Do not, for the sake of food, destroy the work of God. Every-thing is indeed clean, but it is wrong for you to make others fall by what you eat. [21] it is good not to eat meat or drink wine or do anything that makes your brother or sister stumble. [22] The faith that you have, have as your own conviction before God. Blessed are those who have no reason to condemn themselves because of what they approve. [23] But those who have doubts are condemned if they eat, because they do not act from faith; for whatever does not proceed from faith is sin.

Chapter 15 We who are strong ought to put up with the failings of the weak, and not to please ourselves. [2] Each of us must please our neighbour for the good purpose of building up the neighbour. [3] For Christ did not please himself; but, as it is written: 'The insults of those who insult you have fallen on me.' [4] For whatever was written in former days was written for our instruction, so that by steadfastness and by the encouragement of the Scriptures we might have hope. [5] May the God of steadfastness and encouragement grant you to live in harmony with one another, in accordance with Christ Jesus, [6] and so that together you may with one voice glorify the God and Father of our Lord Jesus Christ. [7] Welcome one another, therefore, just as Christ has welcomed you, for the glory of God.

NRSV Bible

Session 2, Handout 2

'Roman House Church Conference'

Characters

◆ Minority Jewish Christian Group

◆ Majority Gentile Christian Group

◆ Paul

◆ Observers from Ephesus

Scenario:

The house churches in Rome have all received the letter from Paul. As a follow up to the letter representatives from the Jewish Christian and Gentile Christian groups travel to Ephesus to meet Paul. Their intention is to represent their positions to him. Both groups need to be prepared to argue with Paul.

Task:

In your group take on the role you have been assigned, imagine your way into it, consider your position and what you will say when you meet Paul.

Questions for debriefing session:

1. How did you feel in your role?

2. What were the real tensions you faced?

3. What insights did you gain on the nature and practice of tolerance?

Session 2, Handout 3

Minority Jewish Christian Group

◆ In 49 CE emperor Claudius closed the Jewish synagogues and banished key Jewish leaders from Rome. This followed Jewish and Christian rioting in the city. Jewish Christian leaders, like Prisca and Aquila, were among those sent into exile. They are representative of the minority Jewish Christian group in the Roman house churches.

◆ In 54 CE when Nero allowed you to return, you discover the house churches are completely controlled by the majority Gentile Christians.

◆ There is no place for your Jewish culture and identity and you are looked upon as inferior.

◆ In Rome there is also anti-Semitic feeling.

◆ In Paul's letter you are referred to as 'the weak', which is what the Gentile majority call you. You are perceived as traditionalists who do not want to change but who wanted to preserve the traditional Jewish identity in some of your practices, eg the food laws, the practice of circumcision and the observance of Jewish festivals.

◆ The question facing you is do the Gentiles see a place for you in the church?

Session 2, Handout 4

Majority Gentile Christian Group

◆ Following the exile of Jewish Christian leaders in 49 CE, as a result of the Jewish Christian riots, your group was left in control. This enabled you to establish some of your own house churches.

◆ Though your faith has its roots in the Jewish tradition, you see no need for any Jewish cultural or religious trappings in the life and worship of your house churches.

◆ When the Jewish Christian leaders returned in 54 CE tensions developed. You perceived yourselves as the strong and as superior to the Jewish Christians. You did not want any reintroduction of Jewish practices, like food laws, circumcision and observance of festivals. In your view, if the Jewish Christians are to be part of the Christian church then all things Jewish have to disappear.

◆ You are in fact saying that to be Christian, Jewish Christians must become like you.

Session 2, Handout 5

Paul's view in Romans 14:1–15:13

◆ You advocate 'mutual tolerance' between the factions in the Roman church on the grounds of maintaining personal integrity and seeking harmony in the church.

◆ You admonish both traditionalists ('weak') and progressives ('strong') to remain true to their doctrinal convictions and their varying liturgical practices, while accepting one another in Christ.

◆ You selected the extreme positions of opposite ends of the liberal–conservative spectrum in Rome, absolute vegetarian and complete libertarian, to make the principle of tolerance inclusive of all positions in the range (14:1–3).

◆ You remind all of them that their opponents are acceptable to God and that they have no right, therefore, to discriminate against each other on the basis of differences in lifestyle (14:4).

◆ You also remind them that each Christian has the responsibility to retain integrity in the quest for truth (14:5).

◆ The relational basis of genuine tolerance is stressed by you. It is your belief that what unites people is not their liturgical or ethical preferences but their proper relationship to God, to whom alone praise is due (14:6).

◆ You suggest ways of protecting the integrity of one's adversaries. Each side has an obligation to see that the other lives up to its own standards, by creating the space for the other to exercise personal integrity (14:13–23).

◆ You point out that strong tolerance is not based on moral ambivalence or finding the lowest common denominator but on the action of God in Christ. Tolerance in the Christian community gives glory to God (15:7).

◆ By transcending the differences between Greeks and Jews you firmly hold that the gospel reaches out to include the entire human race. The Good News that finally transforms the world is that God has called conservatives as well as liberals, Greeks as well as Jews, to live in praise of God's mercy (5:9–13).

Session 2, Handout 6

Observers from the Churches in Ephesus

In the Ephesian house churches Gentile and Jewish Christians had found some expression of unity. In a letter written to you, much later than the one written to the Romans, and perhaps written even a generation later than Paul, you were encouraged to think of:

◆ yourselves as the Body of Christ, or a new human being. This image gives expression to the reality of diversity in unity.

◆ how you have been helped to see yourselves as a new creation, as a community of people for whom Christ has broken down the dividing wall of hostility.

◆ in this later letter which you received, you are even encouraged to see yourselves beyond your identity as a local community and to perceive your identity in a world setting.

◆ how you are to be a model of God's purpose for all humanity, which is to unite all things in Christ.

Your role is to:

1. observe the discussion between the Roman house church members and Paul;

2. note the disagreements and the difficulties, which each group is facing;

3. at the end of the discussion be prepared to make your observations known to the group, ask them questions and suggest, from your own experience as Ephesians, how the Roman Christians might resolve their difficulties.

Session 3 Introduction

Civic responsibility – the future!
Implications of Philippians 2 for building civic society

The notion of 'civic' or 'civil' society has its roots in the ancient Greek and Roman worlds; the modern idea has its roots in the eighteenth-century Enlightenment period. Political theorists at that time developed the idea of a civil society, separate from, but parallel to, the state. The growing demand for liberty, demonstrated in the American and French Revolutions and the rise of individualism, private property and market competition, formed the context for a groundswell of support for the promotion of a civic society.

The term fell into disuse in the nineteenth century as attention focused instead on the Industrial Revolution and the resulting social and political consequences. It gained in popularity again after World War Two through the writings of the Marxist Antonio Gramsci who critiqued capitalist dictatorships. In the 1970s and 1980s the common cry for a civic society was vocalised by those opposing the various political guises dictatorships assume. In our post-Cold War world there is a greater openness and commitment to the development of civic society as a means of social renewal.

What is civic society? Civic society encompasses organisations, institutions and interest groups that exist outside the state and the market. It includes non-governmental organisations, labour unions, professional associations, chambers of commerce, religious organisations, student groups, sports groups, cultural and ethnic groupings, to name but a few. Where civic society is weak there can be a lack of engagement and trust in the society; where it is operating effectively it can ensure that people's interests are taken seriously and encourage greater involvement in political and social life.

Paul in his letter to the Philippian house churches explores what it means to take seriously civic responsibilities while living "as citizens worthy of the gospel". What do we know of the context into which Paul was writing?

Philippi was a loyal colony of the Roman Empire; where public life was meant to mirror life in the empire and where Philippian citizens were expected, in their civic life, to demonstrate their allegiance to Rome. As in other Roman colonies, the practice of patronage operated in Philippi, whereby wealthy Roman citizens within and outside of the city offered individuals economic support and social prestige if they returned these favours by honouring their patron and showing loyalty. The system of patronage embedded inequalities into the social system, serving to distribute power from the top down, beginning of course from the emperor. This caused rivalry and factionalism within the city. In the public arena and in the civil courts individuals were treated according to prestige and social standing.

The Christian community in Philippi was viewed with suspicion and considered unworthy citizens of Rome by other Philippian citizens. This was because of their withdrawal from participation in the city's cult practices and their rejection of patronage. Living as they did in the centre of Philippian society, they were, however, influenced by the power struggles and partisan behaviour of public life. Consequently disputes over power and control, similar to those in the surrounding society, also arose within the Christian community. These disputes threatened the unity and ethos of the church.

Paul, aware of the situation, wrote his letter to the Philippian house churches to address this power struggle within the church. It seems likely that the original church at Philippi was of Gentile origin and began in Lydia's house. Women continued in leadership positions within the Philippian house churches and we learn that two in particular, Euodia and Syntyche, were involved in a very serious power struggle which was creating factions within the churches, leading to division. As the house churches were situated in the life of the city, their power struggle was spilling over into the wider community life and was publicly discrediting the gospel. Paul also feared that the private dispute could become so serious that it might be perceived as undermining public order by the Philippian authorities and be referred to the law and civil courts.

In his letter, then, Paul sought to encourage the Philippian Christians to live as "citizens worthy of the gospel of Christ". He reminds them that they are to be of "the same mind". His appeals for harmony and concord, mutual regard and affection within the ekklesia are deliberately opposed to the values of rivalry that permeate the surrounding culture. He seeks to remind them that their life on earth is to be governed by the heavenly commonwealth and that their lives should therefore reflect its laws and values, rather than those of the Roman Empire.

Living as they do in the centre of the public place, Paul recognises that the house churches are in a prime position to influence for good the surrounding community. His hope is that their efforts to publicly model a more participatory form of community might impact power relations within the life of the city. It is in this context, then, that they are to live "as citizens worthy of the gospel".

Paul calls on the Philippian Christians to renounce their rights and status as Roman citizens, an act that is also socially and politically subversive. Through their actions, Paul reminds them, they will be affirming their new Lord, Jesus Christ, who similarly chose to have no rights or status within the empire and was in fact convicted and executed as a traitor, rebel and slave.

This call is chiefly found in the Christological hymn that recounts Christ's choice to give up equality with God in order to become a slave. The Greek translation of the hymn reads: "[Jesus] who being in the form of God did not consider as something to be exploited equality with God but made himself nothing taking the form of a slave."

Christ did not cease to be in the form of God when he took the form of a slave, anymore than he ceased to be the Son of God when he became man. Paul makes the point that it was in his self-emptying and humiliation that he reveals what God is like and that it is through his taking the form of a slave that we see the form of God. This is not a God of almighty power reflected in the image of the Roman emperor. There is no absolutist, dominating, or coercive use of power here.

Paul argues that Jesus did not grasp at primacy, that is his equal status with God, and as a result Christ has been given a primacy of servanthood, which all creation will acknowledge.

The attitude appropriate to those who are 'in Christ', then, is shown by the historical person Jesus. Instead of grasping at dominance, the Philippian Christians are being challenged to empty themselves of dominating power and privileged status. This is a model of power that serves rather than dominates. Paul is suggesting it is a model of power for the public place.

Paul draws on first-century Philippian political vocabulary to compare the power displayed by the Roman Empire with the model of power he recommends for the Christian community. The empire's power is marked by 'unworthy' behaviour, namely, discord, strife, partisan activity, competitive party spirit, intense hatred and the need for primacy. The model Paul recommends, by contrast, is one that is worthy of followers of Christ. The values at the heart of this model of power are concord, harmony in public life, politics of friendship, freedom, political health and unity.

Paul in recommending that the community remain vulnerable to suffering is speaking out of his own experience. He is in fact writing this particular letter from prison where his sentence carries the death penalty. Looking back over his own life, Paul recounts for the Philippians what putting on "the mind of Christ" has meant for him: namely, giving up the privileges of belonging to the Jewish religious élite, renouncing the privileges of Roman citizenship, and in the course of his missionary work sharing in the sufferings of Christ.

At the heart of Paul's message to the Philippians is the notion that Christians should be prepared to be radically vulnerable for the sake of Christ as the cross is the foundation of the Christian community. The nature of the community and the social ethos Paul advocates is a direct challenge to the abuse of power and state control operating in the Roman Empire.

In Northern Ireland the movement toward the creation of a civic society is demonstrated in the commitment, contained in the Belfast Agreement, to a Civic Forum. Civic Forum members are drawn from non-party political structures in the community and have a mandate to work alongside the governing Assembly in an advisory capacity, representing the views and concerns of the general public to the government. Among other things the Civic Forum depends for its effectiveness on individuals and community groupings taking their civic responsibility seriously. In this changing context what does it mean to be "citizens worthy of the gospel"? What ethical and moral resources are available to shape the use of power in the public place? How can the core values of justice, equity and peace best be promoted and become the basis for establishing right relations throughout the society?

Session 3 Plan, Alternative 1

Blue-sky thinking (10 minutes)

What do you understand by the term 'civic society' and what are the different strands that constitute it?

Feedback (5 minutes)

Overhead on letter to the Philippians (15 minutes)

Role-play (65 minutes)

Outline and preparation (15 minutes)

Role-play (20 minutes)

Debriefing (15 minutes)

Reading text – Philippians 2:1–11 (5 minutes)

Overhead on Paul's response (10 minutes)

Plenary (20 minutes)

What does it mean in Northern Ireland today to live as citizens worthy of the gospel?

Reading of text Philippians 2:1–11 (5 minutes)

Session 3 Plan, Alternative 2

The Civic Forum consists of representatives drawn from the organisations and institutions which make up civic society. What is civic society? (5 minutes)

Feedback (5 minutes)

Overhead on Civic Society (5 minutes)

Group work exercise 1 (10 minutes)

Map out how civic society works in your local context and how the different elements relate.

What are the strengths?

What are the weaknesses?

What are the obstacles to improving civic society and how might these be overcome?

Feedback (10 minutes)

Overhead on letter to the Philippians (5 minutes)

Read text (Philippians 2:1–11)

Overhead on Paul's response (5 minutes)

Group work exercise 2 (20 minutes)

'Citizenship in Philippi'

Task:

Read the profiles of citizens who make up the community at Philippi. Consider the relationships within and between each of the groups and the underlying tensions operating in the society. Then address the following questions:

1. What are the obstacles to healthy civic society in Philippi?

2. What does it mean for each of these groups to be good citizens in Philippi?

3. In particular, what model of citizenship is Paul and his spokesperson, Syzygus, trying to encourage?

Prepare to feedback responses to the group.

Feedback (15 minutes)

Plenary (20 minutes)

Read text (Philippians 2:1–11) (5 minutes)

What does it mean in Northern Ireland today to live as citizens worthy of the gospel?

Alternative 2, Overhead 1

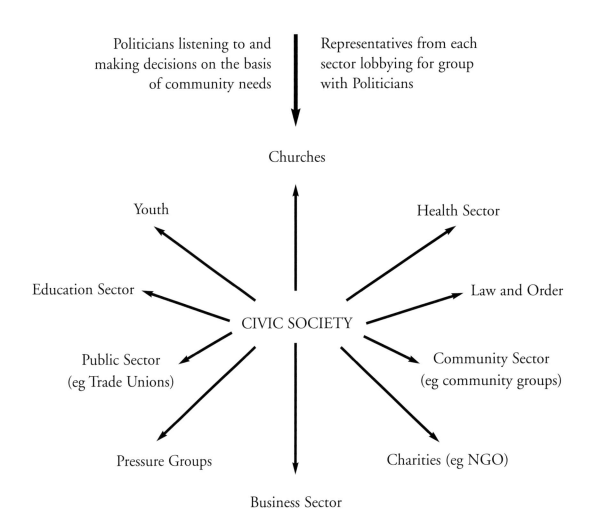

Politicians listening to and making decisions on the basis of community needs | Representatives from each sector lobbying for group with Politicians

Churches

Youth

Health Sector

Education Sector

Law and Order

CIVIC SOCIETY

Public Sector (eg Trade Unions)

Community Sector (eg community groups)

Pressure Groups

Charities (eg NGO)

Business Sector

Session 3, Alternative 2, Handout 1

Group work exercise 1

   1. Map out how civic society works in your local context and how the different elements relate.

   2. What are the strengths?

   3. What are the weaknesses?

   4. What are the obstacles to improving civic society and how might these be overcome?

Overhead 2

Paul's letter to the Philippians

Written to Philippian house churches around 59 CE to address a power struggle between house church leaders.

Much of Paul's language is drawn from first-century Philippian political vocabulary.

Unworthy – Discord	Worthy – Concord
Strife – Partisan Behaviour	Harmony in Public Life
Envy – Intense Hatred	Politics of Friendship
Faction– Party Spirit	Freedom
Vainglory – Primacy	Political Health
	Unity

The power struggle in Philippi could not merely be confined to the house churches. The house churches were situated in the life of the city .The struggle for supremacy between two church leaders, Euodia and Syntyche, was spilling over into the wider community life. The church was simply mirroring the party spirit and partisan behaviour of much of political life.

Such behaviour Paul does not consider to be good citizenship. Paul writes to encourage the Philippian Christians to live as citizens "worthy of the gospel of Christ" (Philippians 1:27). This means three things:

1. It applies to the whole of life in the public domain.

2. It is about living corporately in the public place.

3. It is the exercising of Christian civic responsibility in public life.

Session 3, Alternative 1 & 2, Handout 2

'Citizenship in Philippi'

Characters:

◆ Public leaders of city.

◆ Euodia and Syntyche – leaders of Philippian house churches and their supporters.

◆ Syzygus – Paul's loyal companion (Philippians 4:3).

◆ Gentile citizens of Philippi.

Scenario:

The public leaders in Philippi want to know what contribution Christians can make to civic life in the city. They have, therefore, invited representatives from the house churches to a public forum in Philippi to state their case.

Task:

In your group imagine yourself into your role. What will your response be? How will you deal with what is going on from your perspective.

◆ The public leaders represent people of power and wealth

◆ The two church leaders, who are in a power struggle, should prepare to state separately what each think the role of her house church is.

◆ Syzygus is aware of Paul's vision of citizenship and recognises that the church is sending wrong signals to the wider community. He sees his role as defending the church by not admitting too much about the real difficulties to the public leaders.

◆ Gentile citizens play the role of observers and commentators. When all the others have spoken, they will be asked to give their impression of what is being said.

Session 3, Alternative 2, Handout 3

Profiles

Public Leaders:

◆ People of power and wealth in Philippi who probably bought their way into public office through the system of patronage.

◆ They are the public leaders of a city in which politics is being shaped by party strife, partisan behaviour, ie favouritism, and struggles for supremacy.

◆ They are aware of the Philippian house churches and of the factionalism and power struggles between the leaders of the churches. They feel church members are not good citizens of Philippi and also are aware that the Christians believe themselves to be citizens of heaven.

◆ They wish to know if these Christians have any contribution to make to the life of the city.

Euodia and Syntyche:

◆ Church leaders in Philippian house churches, which points to the significant role of women in early church leadership. The first-century church in Philippi was actually founded by another woman, Lydia.

◆ Euodia and Syntyche are involved in a very serious power struggle – they are competing for primacy within the Philippian churches. This is creating factions within the churches, some very partisan behaviour on the part of each of these two leaders, and is even generating an intense hatred between divided church members.

Session 3, Alternative 1 & 2, Handout 4

Syzygus:

◆ Syzygus is described as a loyal companion of Paul. He has obviously worked with Paul and shared many difficulties and hardships.

◆ He knows the mind of Paul and is familiar with Paul's thinking and teaching. In this case he is familiar with the hymn Paul quotes in Philippians 2:3–16. This hymn was probably sung in the worship of the Philippian house churches.

◆ Syzygus is deeply troubled by the power struggle between the church leaders and is a key person in mediation and interpretation of Paul's approach to transforming this conflict and enabling the Philippian Christians to be good public citizens.

Gentile Citizens:

◆ The citizens of Philippi are proud Roman citizens. Philippi is a very loyal colony of the Roman Empire. Public life is meant to mirror life in the empire itself.

◆ The Gentile citizens are suspicious of the Christians in their city because they have heard that these Christians believe themselves to be citizens of heaven.

◆ Christians are viewed with suspicion as people without a sense of civic responsibility. Such people undermine the public well-being of society, especially by their internal struggles for primacy and their factional fighting.

Session 3, Alternative 1 & 2, Handout 5

Questions for debriefing session

1. How did you feel in your respective roles?

2. What were the strengths and weaknesses of the Christians' presentation?

3. Did Syzygus play a significant role?

4. Did any model of Christian citizenship emerge from the role-play?

Session 3, Alternative 1 & 2, Handout 6

Philippians 2:1–11

[1] If then there is any encouragement in Christ, any consolation from love, any sharing in the Spirit, and compassion and sympathy, [2] make my joy complete; be of the same mind, having the same love, being in full accord and of one mind. [3] Do nothing from selfish ambition or conceit, but in humility regard others as better than yourselves. [4] Let each of you look not to your own interests, but to the interests of others. [5] Let the same mind be in you that was in Christ Jesus, [6] who though he was in the form of God, did not regard equality with God as something to be exploited, [7] but emptied himself, taking the form of a slave, being born in human likeness. And being found in human form, [8] he humbled himself and became obedient to the point of death even death on a cross. [9] Therefore God has highly exalted him and gave him the name that is above every name, [10] so that at the name of Jesus every knee should bend, in heaven and on earth and under the earth, [11] and every tongue confess that Jesus Christ is Lord, to the glory of God the Father.

NRSV Bible

Session 3, Alternative 2, Handout 7

Group work exercise 2

'Citizenship in Philippi'

Task:

Read the profiles of citizens who make up the community at Philippi. Consider the relationship within and between each of the groups and the underlying tensions operating in the society. Then address the following questions.

1. What are the obstacles to healthy civic society in Philippi?

2. What does it mean for each of these groups to be good citizens in Philippi?

3. In particular what model of citizenship is Paul and his spokesperson, Syzycus, trying to encourage?

Prepare to feedback responses to the group.

Overhead 3

Paul's Response to the Church at Philippi

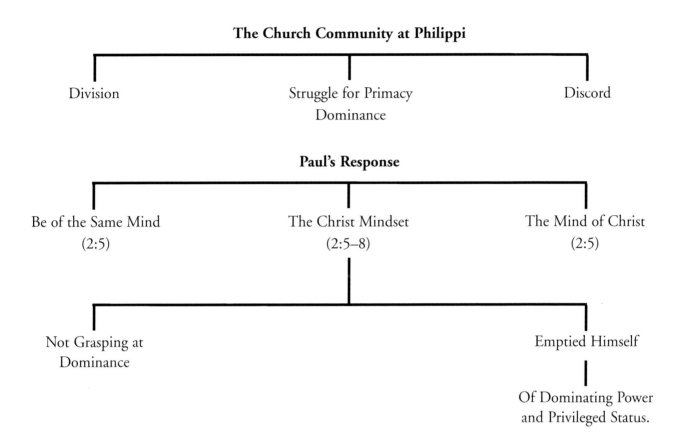

The Church Community at Philippi

Division　　　　Struggle for Primacy　　　　Discord
　　　　　　　　　Dominance

Paul's Response

Be of the Same Mind　　　The Christ Mindset　　　The Mind of Christ
(2:5)　　　　　　　　　(2:5–8)　　　　　　　　(2:5)

Not Grasping at　　　　　　　　　　　　　　Emptied Himself
Dominance

　　　　　　　　　　　　　　　　　　　Of Dominating Power
　　　　　　　　　　　　　　　　　　　and Privileged Status.

A model of power that serves rather than dominates

A model of power for the public place

Session 4 Introduction

Faith transforming culture
What can be learnt from a study of the prophet Hosea?

Cultural identity is often a major concern, especially for minorities or a community whose sense of identity seems under threat. There are political, social, economic and religious components to culture.

Robert Schreiter offers three important dimensions:

(a) Culture is ideational – it provides systems or frameworks of meaning which serve both to interpret the world and to provide guidance for living in the world. Culture . . . embodies beliefs, values, attitudes and rules for behaviour.

(b) Culture is performance – rituals that bind a culture's members together to provide them with a participatory way of embodying and enacting their histories and values.

(c) Culture is material – the artefacts and symbolisations that become a source of identity: language, food, clothing, music, and the organisation of space.

(Robert J Schreiter, *The New Catholicity: Theology Between the Global and the Local*, Orbis Books, 1997, p 29.)

One of the major questions, not necessarily new for the twenty-first century, is around the relationship between faith and culture. Faith cannot exist outside a culture. Faith is not lived in a culture-free zone. To be meaningful, faith is culturally embodied, whether it be Irish, African or Asian culture. Yet faith can become so identified with culture that it is no longer distant or critical and God becomes another cultural icon.

In the eighth century BCE the Hebrew prophet Hosea lived in a challenging cultural context and did so in a remarkably creative way.

Hosea was a prophet of the Northern Kingdom of Israel and lived through a time of intense political turmoil and insecurity. In a 23-year span from 745–722 BCE there were six monarchs. Four of them were assassinated, such was the political instability. This in turn produced widespread disillusionment among the people and a lack of confidence in the political institutions. The minority ruling élite, rather than take responsibility for the situation and attempt to change things for the better, became consumed by their own self-interest.

Not surprisingly the Kingdom of Israel was weak and was soon easily overrun by the emerging Assyrian superpower. Israel was not simply overrun but wiped from the map and eliminated from history. Hosea was a prophet during the final critical years of the Northern Kingdom.

As a prophet he was critical of the prevailing culture and especially critical of the widespread social injustices perpetrated by the self-serving ruling classes.

The book opens with prophetic, symbolic actions. The relationship between Hosea and Gomer is presented as a symbol of the relationship between God and Israel. His marriage experience became a paradigm of the God–people relationship. Hosea's wife became a temple prostitute in the religion of Baal. Israel's infidelity in abandoning Yahwism for Baalism was dramatically portrayed. Yahweh had been abandoned for cultural assimilation with the culture and religion of Baalism.

Baalism was the cultural and religious expression of Canaanite society. Ever since the Hebrew slaves found themselves in Canaan – and many of them may well have been disillusioned Canaanites – there was always deep tension between Yahwism and Baalism. In the Hebrew scriptures, Israelite and Canaanite are not racial, ethnic and cultural groups so much as systems of social, economic and political organisations diametrically opposed. Canaanite was a hierarchically organised and socially stratified system. This was the model of community it promoted and developed. It was a domination system supported and legitimised by the religion of Baal. At the heart of Baalism were fertility rites, which included the religious practice of both men and women consorting with male and female temple prostitutes. The purpose of this religion practice was mystical union with gods and goddesses in order to obtain fertility in farmlands, livestock and families. Baal controlled fertility and fertility was important for economic existence and livelihood. In reality the ruling élites, including the priests of Baal, controlled the religious, political and economic systems and reduced the majority of the Canaanite population to domination and subservience. Yahweh's covenantal religion was about an egalitarian society in which justice and equality were to be norms. Again and again Israel preferred the domination system and bought into the prevailing and pervasive culture of Baalism.

Yahwism offered an alternative social, economic and political organisation characterised by decentralised structures and institutions. The covenant idea was at the heart of Yahweh's community vision. It was a radical social vision of community and society based on justice, which was essentially distributive. The covenantal model of community reflected the time when Israel was a confederation of tribes. This confederation was characterised by decentralisation and provided for a more participatory society in which political power and economics were more justly spread and practiced. It was Solomon who dismantled the covenantal community and created and structured a society modelled on that of the Canaanites. This included building a temple modelled on the Canaanite one. Not only did this create a political and economic élite oppressive of the majority of the people, it also used God to legitimise the exploitation and oppression. Yet the earlier memory lingered on in the rural Israelite communities in the eighth century. Hosea, like many of the other prophets, was a radical conservative, calling people back to their roots and challenging them to return to the ideals of justice and egalitarian communal practice – in other words, to become a covenantal people again.

He did this in a remarkable and creative way. He developed his radical and conservative theology in dialogue with Canaanite culture. He was totally opposed to the Canaanite system and his personal experience gave him every right to detest Canaanite culture and religious practice. Yet he borrowed the best of its images, symbols and vocabulary to critique and reinterpret the covenant. He did this by incorporating Canaanite fertility language into Israel's worship and theology. Using the husband and wife language of Canaanite religious fertility rites, he recast covenant vocabulary. He borrowed and used terminology and imagery indigenous to Canaanite culture and religion. The most explicit use of the fertility language is in chapter 2:16–23. It is in verses 19–20 that he daringly reinterprets the Mosaic covenant in Canaanite terms.

It was a daring communicative strategy. Those who heard him would have recognised his vocabulary, perhaps been startled by it, but would have been pushed to rethink their anti-covenantal lifestyle and practice as well as encounter the old tradition in a new way. This was communitarian at its best, using contemporary and pervasive cultural metaphors, symbols and vocabulary to appeal to a neglected but transformative and more just tradition and vision of society.

At the same time Canaanite culture was challenged in a way that purified its best insights as well as giving new insights to Israel's covenantal tradition. It was the all-pervasive Canaanite culture that entitled the prophet to speak of God's love in terms of marital union and mystical depth. Hosea, by making critical use of Canaanite culture, gave Israel a new vision of God and community.

The book of Hosea is a model of faith challenging and transforming culture. Faith has the capacity to express itself through cultural images that connect with people's experiences within society. This is a process of challenge and critique that becomes transformative.

The perennial challenge is always to find new images and metaphors which can make the vision of God more accessible to people. This also enables people to language and imagine a new and transformed society.

In Northern Ireland the churches and the Christian faith have often been too closely allied with cultural identities. It might even be said that churches and faith live in cultural captivity. This would also include political captivity. There is not sufficient critical distance, and faith expressions and practices lack a critical edge. There is at times little evidence of a contrast culture community.

While faith always expresses itself through culture, it also needs to critique culture, including its own cultural expressions of faith. Faith will always affirm what is good in culture and always keep sufficient critical distance to be able to transform culture. Hosea is a model of the creative tension and the critical edge that is always required.

Session 4 Plan

In small groups, develop a profile of the primary cultural identities in Northern Ireland. (10 minutes)

Read Hosea 2:2–23 (5 minutes)

Overheads:

The challenging cultural context of Hosea (10 minutes)

Canaanite religious and social practice (10 minutes)

Group work exercise 1 (15 minutes)

How would you describe the contemporary context and role of religion and religious practice in Northern Ireland?

Feedback (10 minutes)

Overheads

Yahwist religion and social revolution (10 minutes)

Radical challenge to the pervading culture (10 minutes)

Group work exercise 2 (20 minutes)

The people Hosea met had so bought into the culture that they could not be distinguished as believers in Yahweh.

In what ways have the churches over-identified with cultural identities in Northern Ireland that they merely mirror society rather than the values of the reign of God?

How can the faith community transform culture in Northern Ireland?

Feedback and reflection points (20 minutes)

Session 4, Handout 1

Group work exercise 1

In small groups, develop a profile of the primary cultural identities in Northern Ireland.

Group work exercise 2

How would you describe the contemporary context and role of religion and religious practice in Northern Ireland?

Session 4, Handout 2

Hosea 2:2–23

[2] Plead with your mother, plead – for she is my wife, and I am her husband – that she put away her whoring from her face, and her adultery from between her breasts, [3] or I will strip her naked and expose her as the day she was born, and make her like a wilderness, and turn her into a parched land, and kill her with thirst. [4] Upon her children also will I have no pity, because they are children of whoredom. [5] For their mother has played the whore; she who conceived them has acted shamefully. For she said, I will go after my lovers; they give me my bread and my water, my wool and my flax, my oil and my drink. [6] Therefore I will hedge her way with thorns; and I will build a wall against her, so that she cannot find her paths. [7] She will pursue her lovers, but not overtake them; and she shall seek them, but shall not find them. Then she shall say, 'I will go and return to my first husband, for it was better with me then than now.' [8] She did not know that it was I who gave her the grain, the wine, and the oil, and who lavished upon her silver and gold that they used for Baal. [9] Therefore I will take back my grain in its time, and my wine in its season; and I will take away my wool and my flax, which were to cover her nakedness. [10] Now I will uncover her shame in the sight of her lovers, and no one shall rescue her out of my hand. [11] I will put an end to all her mirth, her festivals, her new moons, her Sabbaths and all her appointed festivals. [12] I will lay waste her vines and her fig trees, of which she said, 'These are my pay, which my lovers have given me.' I will make them a forest, and the wild animals shall devour them. [13] I will punish her for the festival days of the Baals, when she offered incense to them and decked herself with her ring and jewellery, and went after her lovers, and forgot me, says the Lord.

[14] Therefore, I will now persuade her, and bring her into the wilderness, and speak tenderly to her. [15] From there I will give her her vineyards, and make the Valley of Achor a door of hope. There she shall respond as in the days of her youth, as at the time when she came out of the land of Egypt. [16] On that day, says the Lord, you will call me, 'My husband', and no longer will you call me, 'My Baal'. [17] For I will remove the names of the Baals from her mouth, and they shall be mentioned by name no more. [18] I will make for you a covenant on that day with the wild animals, the birds of the air, and the creeping things of the ground; and I will abolish the bow, the sword, and war from the land; and I will make you lie down in safety. [19] And I will take you for my wife forever; I will take you for my wife in righteousness and in justice, in steadfast love, and in mercy. [20] I will take you for my wife in faithfulness; and you shall know the Lord. [21] On that day I will answer, says the Lord, I will answer the heavens and they shall answer the earth; [22] and the earth shall answer the grain, the wine, and the oil, and they shall answer Jezreel; [23] and I will sow him for myself in the land. And I will take pity on Lo-ruhamah, and I will say to Lo-ammi, 'You are my people'; and he shall say 'You are my God'.

NRSV Bible

Overhead 1

The challenging cultural context of Hosea 2:2–23

◆ Culture includes the   – political;

    – social;

    – economic;

    – religious.

◆ Hosea was a prophet in the Northern Kingdom of Israel.

◆ Assyria threatened Israel.

◆ It was an era of political turmoil.

◆ 745–722 BCE – six kings reigned during 23 years.

◆ Four kings were assassinated.

◆ Widespread disillusionment and self-interest, especially among the ruling élite.

◆ Hosea was a prophet during these final years of the Northern Kingdom.

◆ He was critical of social injustices, especially those perpetrated by the ruling classes.

◆ His marriage experience became a paradigm of Israel's relationship to God.

◆ Hosea's wife became a temple prostitute in the religion of Baal.

Overhead 2

Canaanite religious and social practice

◆ Israelite and Canaanite are not racial, ethnic and cultural groups.

◆ They are opposed systems of social, economic and political organisation.

◆ Canaanite was a hierarchically organised, socially stratified system.

◆ It promoted a community and society based on hierarchy and social stratification.

◆ This was supported and legitimised by the religion of Baal.

◆ At the heart of Baalism were Canaanite fertility rites.

◆ Men and women consorted with male and female temple prostitutes.

◆ Purpose was mystical union with gods and goddesses.

◆ To obtain fertility in farmlands, livestock and families.

◆ Canaanite religious and social practice was an all-pervading presence in the Northern Kingdom.

Overhead 3

Yahwist religion and social revolution

◆ An alternative social, economic and political organisation.

◆ Characterised by decentralised structures and institutions.

◆ Fostered an economic and political levelling process.

◆ Represented egalitarian ideals and vision of society.

◆ Rooted in the worship of the one God and by a covenant relationship.

◆ Covenant was a radical social vision of community and society based on justice.

◆ This model reflected the older tribal confederation practice.

◆ In the eighth century this was still the ideal for many rural Israelites.

◆ The prophets were radical conservatives challenging a return to the ideals of justice and egalitarian communal practice.

Overhead 4

Radical challenge to the prevailing culture

◆ Hosea develops his theology in dialogue with Canaanite culture.

◆ The prophet opposes the Canaanite system, yet adapts its language to critique and reinterpret the covenant.

◆ Fertility language is incorporated into Israel's worship and theology.

◆ Covenant language now uses 'husband and wife' imagery.

◆ Hosea uses terminology and imagery indigenous to Canaanite culture and religion.

◆ The most explicit use of fertility language is in 2:16–23.

◆ The Mosaic covenant is reinterpreted in Canaanite terms in 2:19–20.

◆ Canaanite culture was so challenged that its best insights were purified and given new life within Israel's covenantal tradition.

◆ Canaanite culture enabled prophet and people to speak of God's love in terms of marital union and mystical depth.

Session 4, Handout 3

Group work exercise 3

The people Hosea met had so bought into the culture that they could not be distinguished as believers in Yahweh.

1. In what ways have the churches over-identified with cultural identities in Northern Ireland that they merely mirror society rather than the values of the reign of God?

2. How can the faith community transform culture in Northern Ireland?

Overhead 5

Faith transforming culture

Reflection points

◆ Faith expresses itself through cultural images that connect with people's experiences within society.

◆ The process is also transforming the culture itself by challenging and critiquing it.

◆ The challenge is always to find new images and metaphors which can make the vision of God more accessible to people. This also enables people to language and imagine a transformed society.

Session 5 Introduction

Embracing the equality agenda
Revisiting our covenant story in Exodus and Jeremiah

The Belfast Agreement of 1998 highlighted the importance of an equality agenda as a key strand in building a more just and peaceful society. Conflict societies are often based on inequalities which are social, political, economic and cultural. Underlying this is usually a domination system, be it a ruling class or a one-party state. Domination systems are unjust and when they are dismantled it is important to replace them with a society and structures based on equality, otherwise one domination system is replaced by another; new inequalities are put in place.

Embracing the equality agenda is not easy, especially for those who once dominated and monopolised power. Equality presents itself as a threat and may be resisted. Yet equality in the longer term is for everyone's well-being. It is an essential ingredient of *shalom*, peace.

Equality is at the heart of the Hebrew vision of community. It is a key element in the Hebrew concept of covenant. The Hebrews did not invent covenant. It was familiar political language with near eastern peoples and was a socio-political contract between ruler and ruled. It was the radical reworking of a familiar concept that made Israel's community vision distinctive. Covenant provided a model of community subversive of the domination system and opened up new social possibilities. Its roots were in the historical experience of Egyptian oppression and the Exodus event.

It would be hard to overstate the central importance of the Exodus experience for Israel's understanding of itself and of its faith. In many ways the narrative of Exodus 1–15 may be considered the birth story of Israel as a people. The book of Exodus opens with Israel suffering oppressively as slaves in Egypt, but in the climactic moment of the story (Exodus 14–15) they are delivered by God's hand through the sea to new life. The struggles of wilderness begin (Exodus 16–18), but they are on the way to Mount Sinai where they will become God's covenant people.

(Birch, Brueggemann, Fretheim and Peterson, *A Theological Introduction to the Old Testament*, Abingdon, 1999, p 99.)

Exodus and wilderness are experiences of community formation and at Sinai the covenant is sealed between God and people, providing the subversive and radical vision of an egalitarian society. The community vision often eluded Israel as systems and structures were created which were anti-covenant and destructive of community. Yet the prophets kept calling Israel back to its foundational vision. Covenant was repeatedly reinterpreted for different historical and political contexts. Always the equality agenda was at the heart of prophetic challenges.

The oppressive economics and politics of Egypt provided the seeds of an alternative community vision. When the Hebrew slaves recognised the destructive power of empire and voiced their pain, then faith came alive and an alternative became possible. The cry of pain was Israel's first step towards alternative community formation.

God heard their cry and acted in solidarity and liberation. Exodus was a socio-political experience of liberation from oppression, injustice and inequality. The song of Moses in Exodus 15:1–18 celebrates a new social situation. It is beyond the wilderness that they publicly articulate a new social situation and reject the oppressive empire of Pharaoh for the liberating empire of Yahweh. Covenant is sealed and there is public commitment to be a covenant people embodying an alternative social and political reality.

Exodus was the foundational event providing the origins of community identity. The book of Exodus is not history writing but a theological proclamation written generations later, and for subsequent generations offering an encounter with the liberating God in any contemporary experience of oppression and domination. The final form of the Exodus text was reached during the Babylonian exile. The foundational story and vision is reclaimed by Hebrew exiles in a strange land. In the Babylonian exile and crisis the story takes on new meaning and urgency. In another historical experience a new Exodus is possible and a new beginning in community formation is offered.

The Exodus memory and its radical and subversive vision of socio-political reality remained and was reappropriated in different historical circumstances. The eighth-century prophet Amos radicalised the theological proclamation even more. He challenged Israel's exclusive interpretation of Exodus. Amos proclaimed Exodus in the plural and pointed beyond the narrow confines of Israel to the God of Exodus at work in the histories of the Philistines and Arameans. Exodus happens wherever people are in situations of economic, social, political and cultural oppression. The God of Exodus is at work to liberate peoples from inequalities to alternative possibilities (Amos 9:7).

The God of the Exodus has particular qualities. Exodus also provided Israel with a vision of God on which their vision of society was based. The community theologians wrote of God in descriptive terms of what Yahweh characteristically does. Israel's credo was expressed through verbs and adjectives. The key text for Israel's credo is Exodus 34:6–7: "We may begin with this text, both because it occurs in such a poignant context, on which the entire future of Israel seems to pivot, and because the statement itself appears to be a rich convergence of Israel's preferred adjectives for Yahweh" (Walter Brueggemann, *Theology of the Old Testament: Testimony, Dispute, Advocacy*, Fortress, 1997, p 215).

This is a credo of adjectives arising out of the incident of the ill-conceived golden calf made by Aaron and from the request by Moses to see Yahweh's glory (Exodus 33:18). All that Yahweh will show to Moses is "my back" (Exodus 33:23). It is not said whether Moses saw Yahweh's front or back but the credo of adjectives is a self-disclosure by Yahweh "which provides the grounds for the continued life of Israel, after the unparalleled affront to Yahweh in the golden calf" (ibid, p 216).

We are surprised and perhaps disturbed by verse 7b, with its emphasis on 'inequity' that is visited on as many as four generations. From a more human perspective it does alert us to the reality that historical choices and actions arising out of abuses of power can be generational in their effect. Structures and systems of inequality and their destructiveness can take generations to unravel. We may express such historical processes with less direct and casual reference to God than did the Hebrews. Yet the negative historical experience is all too real and Northern Ireland may be such an historical model of experience.

From Israel's theological perspective there is the God dimension. Exodus 34:7b "alerts Israel to the reality that Yahweh's full character is not subsumed under Yahweh's commitment to Israel in solidarity.

There is something in Yahweh's sovereign rule – Yahweh's own self-seriousness – that is not compromised or conceded, even in the practice of solidarity" (Ibid, pp 217–18).

In a very different historical experience, Jeremiah re-read the Sinai covenant and called upon the people of his generation to rebuild their society on the old covenant vision of egalitarian community. At a time when the new superpower of Babylon was threatening the kingdom of Judah's existence, Jeremiah envisaged the possibility of a new covenant which was about radical inner and moral transformation. This also was about deep social transformation. This promise of a new community of equality was closely connected to the vision of God. Jeremiah was saying that 'there will be no new community on earth until there is a fresh articulation of who God is' (Walter Brueggemann, *A Social Reading of the Old Testament: Prophetic Approaches to Israel's Communal Life*, Fortress, 1994, p 47).

Jeremiah's covenant is not new in the sense that it replaces the old covenant. It is the old covenant applied to a new situation. The prophet's emphasis on newness may even be heard as caustic. Israel has so abandoned the covenant vision of community and has long since forgotten it, that to talk of covenant will be heard as something 'brand new'.

The vision of new covenant or new community is Torah-centred. This is not moralism or a moralistic basis for community but is about "weighty matters of justice, mercy and righteousness" (Ibid, p 48).

All will know God in an equality of knowledge. 'Knowing God' is socially related and is attending to human needs. For Jeremiah to know God is to do justice and justice has to do with equality and fairness of treatment as well as opportunity.

Forgiveness is also at the centre of covenant community but not as an individualistic or pietistic idea. It is about drawing a line under the past in that there will be no "grudging, careful management of old hurts but rather a genuine yielding of the past for a hope" (Ibid, p 49).

Forgiveness is also about real redistribution of power, "a redress of power in which the weak and the strong, the least and the greatest derive their life from each other" (Ibid, p 50).

In keeping with the old covenant vision, which he is reinterpreting for his historical moment, Jeremiah is calling for a radical inner and social transformation which has radical implication for communal, social and political relationships. To become God's covenanted people is to practice equality at the heart of political relationships and power structures.

Session 5 Plan

Word associations on equality (5 minutes)

Read Exodus 34:1–10 (5 minutes)

Group work exercise 1 (20 minutes)

Summarise the meaning of the Exodus event for the Hebrew people.

Compile a profile of God from the Exodus story.

Feedback (10 minutes)

Overheads (50 minutes)

Exodus (10 minutes)

Qualities of Yahweh (Exodus 34) (10 minutes)

Word association on covenant (10 minutes)

Biblical covenant (10 minutes)

Introduction to Jeremiah (10 minutes)

Jeremiah in a different situation from Sinai envisioned a new covenant. Read Jeremiah 31:31–34.

Jeremiah was living in a different time when the kingdom of Judah was about to collapse under the threat of Babylonian invasion. He envisaged the possibility of a new covenant. His new covenant was about radical inner and moral transformation, which was also the deep social transformation of society.

Group work exercise 2 (15 minutes)

We are also a covenanted people. In the light of Exodus and Jeremiah, what does it mean to live as covenant community in a changing political context which requires new structures and relationships.

Feedback and discussion (15 minutes)

Session 5, Handout 1

Exodus 34:1–10

The Lord said to Moses, 'Cut two tablets of stone like the former ones, and I will write on the tablets the words that were on the former tablets, which you broke. [2] Be ready in the morning, and come up in the morning to Mount Sinai and present yourself there to me, on the top of the mountain. [3] No one shall come up with you, and do not let anyone be seen throughout all the mountain; and do not let flocks or herds graze on the front of that mountain.' [4] So Moses cut two tablets of stone like the former ones; and he rose early in the morning and he went up on Mount Sinai, as the Lord had commanded him, and took in his hand the two tablets of stone. [5] The Lord descended in the cloud and stood with him there, and proclaimed the name, 'The Lord.' [6] The Lord passed before him, and proclaimed, 'The Lord, The Lord, a God merciful and gracious, slow to anger, and abounding in steadfast love and faithfulness, [7] keeping steadfast love for the thousandth generation, forgiving iniquity and transgression and sin, yet by no means clearing the guilty, but visiting the iniquity of the parents upon the children and the children's children, to the third and the fourth generation.' [8] And Moses quickly bowed his head towards the earth, and worshipped. [9] He said, 'If now I have found favour in your sight, O Lord, I pray, let the Lord go with us. Although this is a stiff-necked people, pardon our iniquity and our sin, and take us for your inheritance.' [10] He said 'I hereby make a covenant. Before all your people I will perform marvels, such as have not been performed in all the earth or in any nation; and all the people among whom you live shall see the work of the Lord; for it is an awesome thing that I will do with you.

NRSV Bible

Session 5, Handout 2

Group work exercise 1

1. Summarise the meaning of the Exodus event for the Hebrew people.

2. Compile a profile of Yahweh from the Exodus story.

Overhead 1

Exodus

◆ A concrete historical memory which shapes Jewish experience. The event is remembered as formative for contemporary identity.

◆ Israel's faith develops in protest against the destructive and oppressive power of the Egyptian empire.

◆ The Israelite cry of pain begins the formation of a counter community in which there is an alternative way of perceiving social relationships. Though not addressed to Yahweh, nevertheless Yahweh heard their cry.

◆ When they realised that they could no longer live under the Egyptian system, the Israelites were open to Yahweh's social alternative.

◆ The public processing of pain gives the Israelites the ability, courage and will to hope, imagine, design and implement an alternative social vision.

◆ The Song of Moses celebrates a changed social situation, asserting a new sense of freedom (Exodus 15:1–18).

◆ At Sinai the Israelites publicly articulated another way of being community. They rejected the kingship of Pharaoh and affirmed the kingship of Yahweh (Exodus 19:4–6).

◆ Later prophets, like Amos, reappropriate the Exodus memory, challenging the exclusive interpretation of it. They remind us that the same God has wrought exoduses for the Philistines and Arameans. Yahweh enacts exoduses wherever people are in oppressive situations (Amos 9:7).

Overhead 2

Qualities of Yahweh referred to in Exodus 34

◆ Merciful ('rhm') shares same root with word womb – pointing to the compassionate, motherly nature of Yahweh's love.

◆ Gracious ('hnn') – Yahweh acts freely and generously.

◆ Steadfast love ('hsd') – Yahweh shows tenacious fidelity and loyalty in a relationship.

◆ 'Abounds in Faithfulness' ('emeth') refers to Yahweh's complete trustworthiness and reliability.

◆ Yahweh abides for Israel in complete fidelity, even toward those who enact ' iniquity, transgression and sin' (verse 7a)

◆ However, Yahweh takes affront at iniquity. So seriously does Yahweh treat it we are told in verse 7b that it affects the relationship for as many as four generations. There is something in Yahweh's own self- seriousness that is not compromised or conceded, even in the practice of solidarity.

Overhead 3

The biblical covenant

- ◆ God initiating a divine–human partnership
- ◆ Pledged relationships
- ◆ Community solidarity
- ◆ Inclusive relationships – all the nations of the earth – Abrahamic covenant
- ◆ Ecological relationships – Noahic covenant
- ◆ Rooted in social, economic and political justice
- ◆ Alternative political vision in contrast to Canaanite city states surrounding the Hebrews
- ◆ An egalitarian vision of society
- ◆ Alternative or contrast community life
- ◆ New arrangement of public relationships and public power

Session 5, Handout 3

Jeremiah – Jeremiah in a different situation from Sinai envisioned a new covenant.

Jeremiah 31:31–4

[31] The days are surely coming, says the LORD, when I will make a new covenant with the house of Israel and the house of Judah. [32] It will not be like the covenant that I made with their ancestors when I took them by the hand to bring them out of the land of Egypt – a covenant that they broke, though I was their husband,' says the LORD. [33] But this is the covenant that I will make with the house of Israel after those days, says the LORD: I will put my law within them, and I will write it on their hearts; and I will be their God, and they shall be my people. [34] No longer shall they teach one another, or say to each other, 'Know the LORD', for they shall all know me, from the least of them to the greatest, says the LORD; for I will forgive their iniquity and remember their sin no more.

NRSV Bible

Jeremiah was living in a different time when the kingdom of Judah was about to collapse under the threat of Babylonian invasion. He envisaged the possibility of a new covenant. His new covenant was about radical inner and moral transformation, which was also the deep social transformation of society.

Session 5, Handout 4

Group work exercise 2

We are also a covenanted people. In the light of Exodus and Jeremiah, consider what it means for us to live as a covenant community in a changing political context that requires new structures and relationships?

Ask a representative in your group to report your reflections.

Session 6 Introduction

Inclusive community for a new context
An exploration of 3rd Isaiah, Jonah and Ruth

Rebuilding a community following conflict is a process fraught with tensions and difficulties. Sensitivities are usually raw following a traumatic historical experience. The new context requires inclusivity. A new community needs to be inclusive and if any group is excluded there are the seeds for future disintegration. Exclusion creates alienation, which leads to resistance and maybe even new forms of violence.

The rebuilding process also needs to deal with competing visions of community. Not all see the future in the same way. There are diverse needs, cultures and traditions with different perspectives. This is a particular challenge to inclusivity. How can competing visions of the future be held together? How can competing aspirations be accommodated? It is easier to pursue the dominant vision but that will lead to another domination system, cultural or political. How can a plurality of identities, traditions and visions each find space to flourish, not in isolation but in interdependence?

The reconstruction process in Northern Ireland can no longer speak of two communities or two traditions. The Catholic and Protestant traditions contain pluralism within themselves. There is no one Protestant or Catholic identity or culture. Though geographically small, Northern Ireland has within its boundaries at least 40 different ethnic groups and a number of spoken languages. In a post-Troubles society the challenge to build a truly inclusive community is huge and will require commitment to a lengthy process.

Scripture again provides a model of historical experience. In 538 BCE Cyrus the Persian came to power and his empire replaced the Babylonian one. For the Hebrews exiled in Babylon this opened up the possibility of a return to their homeland. The Edict of Cyrus in 538 BCE (Ezra 1:1–4) allowed for such a return with state support and what today might be called Persian grant aid.

Even with state financial aid, the return was slow. It happened in phases over approximately 150 years. Those who did return in the early phases found that Jerusalem needed rebuilding, not only with a temple and city walls but a complete community infrastructure. Not least, relationships required rebuilding since Jerusalem was already inhabited by a range of groups, including historical enemies. There were also land issues as returnees expected to reclaim the land which had belonged to their families almost two generations earlier. Those threatened with displacement were not amused!

Nehemiah 4:1–8 reflects the tensions on rebuilding, mainly between Jews and Samaritans. In 398 BCE Ezra reorganised and reconstituted the Jewish community. The community was constituted on the basis of Torah but Torah interpreted in a rigid way. Legislation was passed which ensured ethnic purity. This forbade inter-marriage and even called for the dissolution of marriages contracted with Gentiles. What Ezra and Nehemiah rebuilt and constituted in Jerusalem was an exclusive community whose purity of identity was narrowed and people of mixed identities were pushed to the margins. The only pure and authentic Jews were those who had suffered in exile. This vision of ethnic and racial purity created not only an exclusive community but one with a fortress mentality.

There were alternative visions but it is important to try and understand the Ezra mindset:

The Jewish community of the early postexilic period was very fragile. Not only were its members still haunted by the remembered devastation of homeland and of exile, but in addition internal divisions had begun to threaten the viability of the new vassal state even before it had become established.

(Paul D Hanson, *The People Called: The Growth of Community in the Bible*, Harper and Row, 1986, p 260.)

In such a situation of fragility and insecurity it is understandable that identity and purity became a key issue. Rigid exclusivity is a recognisable response to a threatening situation. Yet what it creates is an identity myth, an imagined construct that has no basis in history or reality. Ezra and Nehemiah were not the first or last to invent the myth of ethnic purity, including religious purity.

The situation in Jerusalem consisted of multiple conflicts but of particular significance was the conflict between rival priestly groups:

In particular, Ezekiel 44 indicates that the Zadokite priests were determined to establish themselves as undisputed heads over the cult, in continuity with the pre-eminence they had come to enjoy in Babylon. The effect of their efforts was to complete the process begun during the reign of Josiah, namely demoting the Levites to a rank explicitly subservient to the Zadokites.

(Ibid, p 260.)

This priestly conflict, which has to do with power relations and different theological visions of God and community, has a significant role in the tensions around the reconstruction process.

The demoted and excluded Levites did have an alternative vision of society. They were convinced:

1. that they stood for the classic principles of Yahwism;

2. that the Zadokites had profaned these principles through a combination of accommodation to worldly powers and dedication to personal ambition (Ibid, p 261).

At the same time the Zadokites had a:

carefully defined theological basis of their program. It had been refined in detail by Ezekiel and the authors of the Priestly Writing. Its aim was nothing less than the restoration of a communal sanctity that would re-establish a suitable habitation for Yahweh's 'Glory' (KABOD), that is, for the indwelling of the divine Presence that alone could preserve SALOM in the land.

(Ibid, p 261.)

These priestly groups represent two competing visions of community and the future, yet each has authentic insights. Inclusive community has to deal with a plurality of truths, often in opposition yet authentic.

The hopes and dreams of the Levites are probably expressed in 3rd Isaiah, chapters 56–66. The most graphic description of a new envisioned society is in Isaiah 65:17–25. Third Isaiah builds on themes from 2nd Isaiah (chapters 40–55) from the time in exile. Third Isaiah is set in the post-exilic context.

Other writings emerged from this same post-exilic period and though in short-story form, are forms of protest against the rigid and exclusive purity of identity, which seems to dominate the rebuilding process.

Ruth is a story of human love and affection yet poses uncomfortable and challenging questions: "Can a non-Israelite become part of Yahweh's people? How do women survive in a patrilineal culture? What is the lineage of David?" (Birch, Brueggemann, Fretheim and Peterson, *A Theological Introduction to the Old Testament*, Abingdon, 1999, p 442). There is no myth of purity or identity. Even great King David has hated and despised Moabite blood in his veins!

The short book of Jonah, best described as a narrative parable, was almost certainly written in the Persian period. It "challenged the ancient Yahwistic reader to contemplate the ways in which God might relate to non-Jews" (Ibid, p 438). Again, Israel's ancient enemies feature. The Phoenician mariners make vows to God and the Ninevites (Assyrians) repent and believe God. This is too much for the theological purity and integrity of Jonah. Here is a God whose love and embrace goes beyond the theologically defined boundaries. God embraces the non-Israelite and Israelite alike. The sting in the tail is that God not only loves the Ninevites but their animals as well!

Building inclusive community is essential for *shalom* but is difficult, given the often competing visions. How can exclusive and inclusive visions be held together? Israel never quite resolved the tensions, yet the canon of Scripture includes contrasting visions of community. The post-exilic visions of community may reflect the contemporary Northern Ireland experience and encourage the struggle to build an inclusive community for a new context.

Session 6 Plan

Buzz session: (20 minutes)

Identify the different groups that make up the Northern Ireland community.

Feedback

Who are the excluded?

Feedback

Overheads (20 minutes)

Return from exile.

Visions of community:

Dominant vision of community

Alternative vision of community

Questions for clarification (10 minutes)

Group work exercise 1 (30 minutes)

Read Isaiah 56:3–8 and Ezra 9:1–4, 10:1–5 and consider the following questions:

1. What are the strengths and weaknesses of the contrasting visions of community?
2. What hopes and fears lie behind each of these visions of community?
3. Can the different perspectives be reconciled and become inclusive of contrasting visions?
4. How can a community live with different community visions?

Feedback (20 minutes)

Plenary (20 minutes)

How does the post-exile story challenge us as we try to rebuild community in Northern Ireland?

What insights does it offer?

Overhead 1

Return from exile

◆ 587 BCE – Babylon destroys kingdom of Judah and the cream of the population of Judah is exiled in Babylon.

◆ 538 BCE – Edict of Cyrus permits the exiles to return to their homeland. The return was slow, almost reluctant and happened in phases over approximately 150 years.

◆ Jerusalem needed reconstructing – new Temple, city walls, infrastructure, community.

◆ Jerusalem was occupied by a range of groups:

   – Jews who remained at home

   – Jews in the diaspora

   – Samaritans who had been put in control of the territory

   – Moabites

   – Edomites

   – People who had owned land two generations ago and on return discovered it occupied.

◆ Nehemiah 4:1–8 reflects the tension of rebuilding, mainly between the Jews and the Samaritans. The Jews refused the Samaritans' offer of help to rebuild the temple because their religion was not pure. The Samaritans opposed the reconstruction of the walls of Jerusalem.

◆ 398 BCE – Ezra reorganises the Jewish community:

   – He re–established purity of faith and affirmed a rigid definition of Jewishness defined by circumcision and Sabbath observance.

   – He forbade intermarriage and dissolved marriages contracted with Gentiles.

   – He imposed the Torah as the central authority in the life of the community.

   – The community was reconstructed as an exclusive community, where purity of identity was narrowed and people of mixed identities were pushed out.

Overhead 2

Dominant vision of community

◆ The dominant shapers of the community are Ezra and Nehemiah.

◆ The early chapters of Ezra recount the rebuilding of the temple as a response to the Persian edicts. In Ezra 7, Ezra is authorised to travel to Jerusalem and to institute a religious and civil order.

◆ A key phrase in Ezra is "the congregation of the exiles" (Ezra 10:8). The books of Ezra and Nehemiah make clear that the leadership of the new community is in the hands of those who have returned from Babylon.

◆ The true Israel is the group that lived in Babylonian exile.

◆ A key issue for Ezra is intermarriage. Ezra is against mixing the holy seed with the peoples of the land (Ezra 9:2). The issue for Ezra is purity of identity.

◆ The destroyed Jerusalem was a shunned place, a city without honour (Nehemiah 1:3). Nehemiah's concern is with rebuilding the walls. Rebuilding walls is not so much defence against enemies but is rather a matter of honour for God and God's people. Rebuilt walls means esteem for Israel and shame for their neighbours (Nehemiah 6:1–16).

◆ In Nehemiah 13, foreigners are expelled from the city before the beginning of the Sabbath and are kept outside until Sabbath is over (Nehemiah 13:19–22).

◆ Ezra with his focus on intermarriage and Nehemiah with his commitment to the rebuilding of walls are both concerned with boundaries, ie purity of Jewish identity.

◆ The issues of identity (ethnicity) and status (honour/shame) are being addressed in the areas of family, community and city structure.

◆ Ezra/Nehemiah feel that all of this is important to enable the community to clearly stand in the great religious traditions of their past which for them also means avoiding religious and cultural compromise.

Overhead 3

Alternative visions of community

◆ This group represents a minority Levite priesthood who have been excluded by the controlling Zadokite priesthood in Jerusalem. The Levites have been marginalised for a long time and are looked upon as inferior. Their hopes and dreams for an inclusive community are expressed in Isaiah chapters 56–66.

◆ Their vision is in opposition to Ezra and Nehemiah's rigid interpretation of the purity laws.

◆ The new envisioned society is most graphically described in Isaiah 65:17–25 which concerns a new heaven and a new earth, a rejoicing Jerusalem, new economics and new piety. The dream of God and Israel is for the establishment of a new social order which will embody peace, justice, freedom, equity and well-being.

◆ The story of Ruth, a woman in a man's world and a foreigner, also represents an alternative vision of community. Ruth is a Moabite and Moabites were long-standing despised and hated enemies of the Hebrew people. As far as the returning exiles are concerned, the Moabites should never have had any place in a Jerusalem society. The story of Ruth illustrates how when the marginal are brought into the centre, the community is enriched. The memory of Ruth, a Moabite and ancestor of David, shows how inclusion is already part of the Jewish identity.

◆ The story of Jonah also contains a valuable lesson on the inclusiveness of Yahweh's vision of community. Jonah, sent to preach judgement to the Assyrians, refuses and from the sea is swallowed up in death (exile). When he is restored to his mission he is dismayed when the Assyrians, including the king, repent. In Jonah's rebuke by God (Jonah 4:9–11) is the reassertion of the radical freedom of God who will extend salvation to whomever it pleases God to redeem.

◆ The stories of Ruth and Jonah were written in this period as protest literature against narrow exclusive visions of identity and community. Both stories include representatives of Israel's despised enemies from earlier periods of history.

Session 6, Handout 1

Group work exercise 1

Read Isaiah 56:3–8 and Ezra 9:1–4, 10:1–5 and consider the following questions:

1. What are the strengths and weaknesses of the contrasting visions of community?

2. What hopes and fears lie behind each of these visions of community?

3. Can the different perspectives be reconciled and become inclusive of contrasting visions?

4. How can a community live with different community visions?

Choose a member of your group to feedback to the larger group.

Session 6, Handout 2

Isaiah 56:3–8

³ Do not let the foreigner joined to the Lord say, 'The Lord will surely separate me from his people'; and do not let the eunuch say, 'I am just a dry tree.' ⁴ For thus says the Lord: To the eunuchs who keep my Sabbaths, who choose the things that please me and hold fast my covenant, ⁵ I will give, in my house and within my walls, a monument and a name better than sons and daughters; I will give them an everlasting name that shall not be cut off. ⁶ And the foreigners who join themselves to the Lord, to minister to him, to love the name of the Lord, and to be his servants, all who keep the Sabbath, and do not profane it, and hold fast my covenant – ⁷ these I will bring to my holy mountain, and make them joyful in my house of prayer; their burnt-offerings and their sacrifices will be accepted on my altar; for my house shall be called a house of prayer for all peoples. ⁸ Thus says the Lord God, who gathers the outcasts of Israel, I will gather others to them besides those already gathered.

NRSV Bible

Session 6, Handout 3

Ezra 9:1–4, 10:1–5

¹ After these things had been done, the officials approached me and said, 'The people of Israel, the priests, and the Levites have not separated themselves from the peoples of the lands with their abominations, from the Canaanites, the Hittites, the Perizzites, the Jebusites, the Ammonites, the Moabites, the Egyptians, and the Amorites. ² For they have taken some of their daughters as wives for themselves and for their sons. Thus the holy seed has mixed itself with the peoples of the lands, and in this faithlessness the officials and leaders have led the way.' ³ When I heard this, tore my garment and my mantle, and pulled hair from my head and beard, and sat appalled. ⁴ Then all who trembled at the words of the God of Israel, because of the faithlessness of the returned exiles, gathered around me while I sat appalled until the evening sacrifice . . . Chapter 10 While Ezra prayed and made confession, weeping and throwing himself down before the house of God, a very great assembly of men, women, and children gathered to him out of Israel; the people also wept bitterly. ² Shecaniah son of Jehiel, of the descendants of Elam, addressed Ezra, saying, 'We have broken faith with our God and have married foreign women from the peoples of the Land, but even now there is hope for Israel in spite of this. ³ So now let us make a covenant with our God to send away all these wives and their children, according to the counsel of my lord and of those who tremble at the commandment of our God; and let it be done according to the law. ⁴ Take action, for it is your duty, and we are with you; be strong, and do it.' ⁵ Then Ezra stood up and made the leading priests, the Levites, and all Israel swear that they would do as had been said. So they swore.

NRSV Bible

Course Three Outline

Being authentic community for the twenty-first century

Exploring the biblical tension between institutional religion and community

Course Description

What do we mean by authentic community? Is institutional religion a help or a hindrance to the building of community? In the Bible story the temple features large at the heart of community. The temple was more than just a building; it embodied the spiritual, social, economic and political life of the people. There is often a tension between what the temple stood for and what authentic community might be. This course will explore the dynamics of that tension. The theme will relate to our contemporary struggle to build authentic community in church and society in Northern Ireland.

Course Outline:

Section 1   Solomon's temple: house of cards or household of God?

                 Exploring foundations for authentic community

Section 2   Delusions of grandeur!

                 Demolishing the myth of 'God on our side' in 1st Isaiah and Jeremiah

Section 3   Behind the walls! Beyond the walls!

                 Inclusive or exclusive community: exploring the tensions in Ezra, Nehemiah and 3rd Isaiah

Section 4   And the walls came tumbling down

                 Jesus in conflict with the religion, economics and politics of the temple

Section 5   Fashion me a people

                 Paul on forming alternative community

Section 6   A community without a temple!

                 Can religious institutions survive in the new Northern Ireland?

Session 1 Introduction

Solomon's temple – house of cards or household of God? Exploring foundations for authentic community

The biblical story of Solomon is found in 1 Kings 1–11. The popular image of Solomon is of great political and economic achievements and a reputation for personal wisdom. The biblical tradition, though aware of this profile, is much more critical. When reading these texts we need to recognise royal propaganda and what today we call the 'spin doctors'. There is satire also in the text. The biblical writers may be setting up Solomon to knock him down. A literal reading of his story diverts us from critical questions concerning both Solomon and our contemporary world, church and society. The biblical story is brutally honest and critical. Whatever his reputation for wisdom – and he may well have established a wisdom school in Israel – he was a political and moral fool who deeply compromised the radical covenantal faith of Israel. This covenantal faith had to do with a vision of just and egalitarian socio-economic and political structures in society. Solomon abolished these, ie he broke the covenant and this led eventually to the destruction of the kingdom itself.

1. The development of the monarchy

Israel's early existence was as a confederation of tribes. There was no centralised social, economic or political system. At the heart of community life and structures was the Exodus–Sinai covenant tradition. The confederation of tribes, though, was surrounded by Canaanite city states which were heavily stratified social, economic and political systems. They were characterised by hierarchical power relations and were systems of domination. The covenant tradition was always threatened by Canaanite culture and ideology.

The opening chapters of 1 Samuel show Israel in crisis. There were pressures both within and without, internal and external, which were pushing Israel towards a monarchy. There was much tension around the concept of kingship.

(a) Internal pressures

Israel's religious practice was under pressure because the priestly system at the heart of it had become corrupt. This would have weakened the covenant vision for society. The tribal confederacy was cracking and weaknesses were appearing in the decentralised organisation. The push was more and more towards the centre and the need for centralised power. Population increase created greater demand for resources. It was becoming increasingly difficult to meet agricultural supply and demand and diversity of cultural groups seemed to demand greater central control if a strong sense of identity was to hold. Some were becoming wealthy and, in contrast to the covenant ideal, were not inclined to share wealth. Accumulated wealth needed to be defended and protected.

What is portrayed in the early chapters of Samuel and in Judges is a society in crisis, with growing conflict between tribal groups. Judges chapters 17–21 reflect this conflict. In chapter 21:25 there is depicted a situation where there is no authority or unity in Israelite society. Everyone is doing their own thing. Social chaos is evident.

(b) External pressures

The tribal confederacy was never an insulated island. The power politics of the Near East always impinged on life and security. This is a time of Philistine expansionism, with the ruling Canaanites being replaced in the geopolitical power play. There is particular tension between the Philistines and two southern tribes, Judah and Dan.

The military strategy of the Philistines was to dominate the Israelite hill country. In 1 Samuel 4–6 there is the story of a major defeat for Israel. Key symbols of identity are destroyed, eg the Ark of the Covenant is captured and the key city of Shiloh and its sanctuary are destroyed. Shiloh is occupied by the Philistines who establish military garrisons.

All of this pressure increased the call for institutions of government and military leadership. Many were disillusioned by the confederacy system. It had been powerless to stop Philistine expansionism. The demand grew for a centralised monarchy. Israel wanted a king "so that we also may be like other nations, and that our king may govern us and go out before us and fight our battles" (1 Samuel 8:19–20).

The tension developed around the idea of an earthly king replacing Yahweh as king. "Kingship raises the issue of accommodation to the world over against the call of God to alternative community in the world. This will remain a central issue in the whole history of Israel's kings" (Bruce C Birch, *Let Justice Roll Down: The Old Testament, Ethics and Christian Life*, Westminster/John Knox Press, 1991, p 207).

2 Meet King Solomon

In the end Israel opted for a king like the other nations. This was not merely the appointment of a new figurehead. It changed the whole structure on which Israelite society was built. Saul was the first king, but was really no more than a chieftain and one who was a tragic failure. It was David who constructed the institution of monarchy in Israel. What he built was modelled on the Canaanite city states. Whatever heroic qualities David had (he became key to Messianic memory), his model of monarchy was the beginning of the anti-covenant trend. "It is the beginning of a royal ideology which is in deep tension with the resistance to kingship and professional militarism which was part of the ideology of God's kingship in Israel" (ibid, p 213).

If David constructed the institution of monarch, Solomon built an empire with all the trappings of power and elitism. This is the story or the critical evaluation, which is made in 1 Kings 1–11. It was empire building, which like all empires had within it the seeds of its own destruction. It was characterised by injustice and oppression.

(a) Solomon's oppressive politics

When Solomon came to power he ruthlessly purged the old Davidic regime to establish complete control. He demonstrated brutal power by executing key political and military figures from David's reign. The high priest at Shiloh was banished, which removed the connection with the older covenant traditions. Zadok was appointed as permanent high priest, even though he had very loose claims to Israelite lineage. Right at the beginning of his reign, Solomon used brutal power to control the political and religious institutions.

Solomon was dismantling the covenantal society and practice and replacing them with the Canaanite model. He built a temple and a palace modelled not only on Canaanite architecture, but also on the Canaanite system. The palace was the much greater of the two buildings which made its own statement about Solomon's ideology. His prayer at the dedication of the temple, often used as a sermon text at the opening of new church buildings, was nothing more than pious spin-doctoring. It was the use of prayer as royal ideology propaganda.

Solomon developed a police state. Garrison towns were strategically built, intended to give subjects the impression that they were well defended from external enemies. It was more a way of controlling subjects by fear. There was no criticism of the system allowed in Solomon's kingdom!

His empire-building needed funding which resulted in a system of heavy taxation including a forced labour policy. Not surprisingly, the subjects in the hill country were becoming restless.

(b) Solomon's administrative policies

In pursuit of power and empire Solomon dismantled the Exodus–Sinai covenantal society. Modelling his society on the Canaanite city states, he replaced covenant economic equality by an economics of privilege. A small élite at the top of the social pyramid became the possessors of wealth. He also displaced covenantal justice with élitist political power. The tribal confederacy had been decentralised, providing tribes with decision-making power and participation in their own systems. Solomon placed power in the hands of the élite again at the top of the pyramid. He created a system of domination.

By building the temple, Solomon was not expressing great piety and religious devotion, his prayer of dedication notwithstanding. Before Solomon, the covenant God was envisioned and experienced as radically free, not under the control of any system or institution. Solomon locked God into the temple. God was now under control and the religious practice of the king's subjects was also under control. Solomon nationalised God in that God became his state sponsor. God was the national deity, on the side of Solomon's empire. Solomon used God, therefore, to legitimise the economics of privilege and the politics of power élites. The God in the temple blessed Solomon's oppressive economics and politics.

3 Consequences of Solomon's reign

The Solomon story written in 1 Kings 1–11 was written much later and is a critical, prophetic judgement on his reign. When later prophets of Israel evaluated Solomon's contribution to the life of the Hebrew community, their verdict was critical, even devastating. Solomon had completely undermined the covenant of Moses. He did this by undermining the covenantal concerns for equality and justice. The prophetic judgement was that Solomon was an idolater who ultimately destroyed the kingdom. His idols were wealth and power and a God created in the image of empire which was really a way of using religion to sanction oppression, domination, exploitation and all forms of injustice.

Not surprisingly, his subjects grew restless. Rebellions broke out towards the end of his reign. They were of course seen as rebellions and not resistance movements. Significantly the prophets condemned not the 'rebels' but Solomon and his royal ideology for the crisis and the violence that destroyed the kingdom and the covenantal society.

When Solomon died Jeroboam led a revolution. He made representation to Solomon's successor, Rehoboam, who rejected any idea of reform. Nothing was changed by those who held power and worse was to follow. In 922 BCE the kingdom was partitioned, with Jeroboam established as king of the northern tribes.

After Solomon matters went downhill fast. The destructive momentum set off in Solomon's reign had repercussions which rolled on for centuries. The consequences were far-reaching. In 721 BCE the Northern Kingdom was powerless in the face of the advancing Assyrian empire. The defeat was so total that the Northern Kingdom disappeared from the map and from history. Its end was final and complete. The Southern Kingdom survived for a little longer. Then in 587 BCE the Southern Kingdom of Judah was destroyed by the new Babylonian empire. Only the poor were left to exist in the ruins of Jerusalem, with the educated and wealthy exiled to the rivers of Babylon. Solomon's anti-covenant economics, politics and religion were ultimately destructive. The crisis of 587 BCE was to burn its way deeply into the Jewish psyche. The roots of that catastrophic suffering were traced back to Solomon's reign. So what did Solomon build : the household of God or a house of cards? Was he a wise king or a political fool?

Session 1 Plan

Welcome (10 minutes)

Blue-sky thinking (10 minutes)

What is your experience of church and in your view what is church for?

Overhead (10 minutes)

The development of monarchy

Blue-sky thinking (5 minutes)

Who was Solomon?

Overheads (10 minutes)

Meet King Solomon

Consequences of Solomon's reign

Group work exercise 1 (three groups) (25 minutes)

Group 1 will explore the economics of privilege.

Task: From the following texts, build up an economic profile of Solomon's reign: 1 Kings 4:22–23, 26–7; 1 Kings 10:26–9

Group 2 will explore the politics of power.

Task: From the following texts, build up a political profile of Solomon's reign: 1 Kings 4:1–7, 20–1, I Kings 5:13–18

Group 3 will explore the nationalisation of God.

Task: What do these texts tell us about how Solomon used religion?: 1 Kings 8:12–21, 1 Kings 11:1–13

Feedback (15 minutes)

Group work exercise 2: (15 minutes)

Are the churches places for the economically privileged?

Have the churches been over identified with the politics of power?

In what ways do the churches use God for political ends?

Feedback and discussion (15 minutes)

Closing reflection (5 minutes)

What does the Lord require of us? Reading from Micah 6:6–8

Overhead 1

Development of the monarchy

The opening chapters of 1 Samuel show Israel in crisis. There are internal and external pressures towards a monarchy.

Internal Pressures

◆ The priestly system has become corrupt

◆ Israel's tribal confederacy is being pushed in the direction of centralisation

◆ Increased population

◆ Diverse cultural groups

◆ Agricultural limitations

◆ Accumulation of wealth needing to be defended

◆ Judges chapters 17–21 reflect violent conflicts between tribal groups. There is no authority or unity (Judges 21:25).

External Pressures

◆ Philistine expansionism – the Philistines are replacing the ruling Canaanites.

◆ Conflict between the Philistines and the two southern tribes of Judah and Dan.

◆ Philistine military campaigns to dominate Israelite hill country. First Samuel chapters 4–6 recount a major defeat for Israel: the Ark of the Covenant is captured; city of Shiloh and the sanctuary are destroyed; occupation by Philistine garrisons.

◆ Internal and external pressure for new institutions of centralised government and military leadership. Israel looked toward the model of its neighbours (1 Samuel: 8:19–20).

◆ There is tension around the idea of being ruled by an earthly king, replacing Yahweh alone as king.

Overhead 2

Meet King Solomon

◆ Israel opted for a model of monarchy like other nations.

◆ Saul was no more than a chieftain.

◆ David constructed an institutional monarchy modelled on the Canaanite city states.

◆ Solomon built an empire (1 Kings:1–11).

Solomon's oppressive politics

Solomon ruthlessly purged the old Davidic regime to establish complete control.

Solomon dismantled covenantal practices and replaced them with Canaanite institutions:

1. He built a temple and palace modelled on the Canaanite system.

2. He developed a police state.

3. He instituted heavy taxation, including a forced-labour policy.

Solomon's administrative policies

1. He replaced covenant economic equality by an economics of privilege.

2. He displaced covenantal justice with élitist political power.

3. He displaced the radically free God of the covenant with a nationalised God. God became the state sponsor. God legitimised the economics of privilege and the politics of power élites.

Overhead 3

Consequences of Solomon's reign

◆ Solomon undermined the covenantal concerns for equity and justice.

◆ The prophetic judgement was that Solomon was an idolater who destroyed the kingdom.

◆ Rebellions broke out towards the end of his reign.

◆ On Solomon's death Jeroboam leads a revolution. Rehoboam, who succeeded Solomon, rejected the idea of reform.

◆ In 922 BCE the kingdom was divided. Jeroboam was established as king of the northern tribes.

◆ In 721 BCE the Northern Kingdom was destroyed by the Assyrians.

◆ In 587 BCE the Southern Kingdom was destroyed by the Babylonians.

Session 1, Handout 1

Group work exercise 1

Group 1 – will explore the economics of privilege.

Task: From the following texts, build up an economic profile of Solomon's reign.

1 Kings 4:7, 22–3, 26–7

[7] Solomon had twelve officials over all Israel, who provided food for the king and his household; each one had to make provision for one month in the year . . . [22] Solomon's provision for one day was thirty cors of choice flour, and sixty cors of meal, [23] ten fat oxen, and twenty pasture-fed cattle, one hundred sheep, besides deer, gazelles, roebucks, and fatted fowl . . . [26] Solomon also had forty thousand stalls of horses for his chariots, and twelve thousand horsemen. [27] These officials supplied provisions for king Solomon and for all who came to king Solomon's table, each one in his month; they let nothing be lacking.

NRSV Bible

1 Kings 10:26–9

[26] Solomon gathered together chariots and horses; he had fourteen hundred chariots and twelve hundred horses, which he stationed in the chariot cities and with the king in Jerusalem. [27] The king made silver as common in Jerusalem as stones, and he made cedars as numerous as the sycamores of the Shephelah. [28] Solomon's import of horses was from Egypt and Kue, and the king's traders received them from Kue at a price. [29] A chariot could be imported from Egypt for six hundred shekels of silver, and a horse for one hundred and fifty; so through the king's traders they were exported to all the kings of the Hittites and the kings of Aram.

NRSV Bible

Session 1, Handout 2

Group work exercise 1

Group 2 – will explore the politics of power.

Task: From the following texts build up a political profile of Solomon's reign.

1 Kings 4:1–7, 20–21

[1] King Solomon was king over all Israel, [2] and these were his high officials: Azariah son of Zadok was the priest; [3] Elihoreph and Ahijah sons old Shisha were secretaries; Jehoshaphat son of Ahilud was recorder; [4] Benaiah son of Jehoiada was in command of the army; Zadok and Abiathar were priests; [5] Azariah son of Nathan was priest and king's friend; [6] Ahishar was in charge of the palace; and Adoniram son of Abda was in charge of the forced labour. [7] Solomon had twelve officials over all Israel, who provided food from the king and his household; each one had to make provision for one month in the year . . . [20] Judah and Israel were as numerous as the sand by the sea; they ate and drank and were happy. [21] Solomon was sovereign over all the kingdoms from the Euphrates to the land of the Philistines, even to the border of Egypt; they brought tribute and served Solomon all the days of his life.

NRSV Bible

1 Kings 5:13–18

[13] King Solomon conscripted forced labour out of all Israel; the levy numbered thirty thousand men. [14] He sent them to the Lebanon, ten thousand a month in shifts; they would be a month in the Lebanon and two months at home; Adoniram was in charge of the forced labour. [15] Solomon also had seventy thousand labourers and eighty thousand stonecutters in the hill country, [16] besides Solomon's three thousand three hundred supervisors who were over the work, having charge of the people who did the work. [17] At the king's command, they quarried out great, costly stones in order to lay the foundation of the house with dressed stones. [18] So Solomon's builders and Hiram's builders and the Gebalites did the stonecutting and prepared the timber and the stone to build the house.

NRSV Bible

Session 1, Handout 3

Group work exercise 1

Group 3 – will explore the nationalisation of God.

Task: What do these texts tell us about how Solomon used religion?

1 Kings 8:12–21

[12] Then Solomon said, 'The Lord has said that he would dwell in thick darkness. [13] I have built you an exalted house, a place for you to dwell for ever.' [14] Then the king turned round and blessed all the assembly of Israel, while all the assembly of Israel stood. [15] He said, 'Blessed be the Lord, the God of Israel, who with his hand has fulfilled what he promised with his mouth to my father David, saying [16] 'Since the day that I have brought my people Israel out of Egypt, I have not chosen a city from any of the tribes of Israel in which to build a house, that my name might be there; but I chose David to be over my people Israel.' [17] My father David had it in mind to build a house for the name of the Lord, the God of Israel. [18] But the Lord said to my father David, 'You did well to consider building a house for my name; [19] nevertheless, you shall not build the house, but your son who shall be born to you shall build the house for my name.' [20] Now the Lord has upheld the promise that he made; for I have risen in the place of my father David; I sit on the throne of Israel, as the Lord promised, and have built the house for the name of the Lord, the God of Israel. [21] There I have provided a place for the ark, in which is the covenant of the Lord that he made with our ancestors when he brought them out of the land of Egypt.

NRSV Bible

1 Kings 11:1–13

[1] King Solomon loved many foreign women along with the daughter of Pharaoh: Moabite, Ammonite, Edomite, Sidonian, and Hittite women, [2] from the nations concerning which the Lord had said to the Israelites, 'You shall not enter into marriage with them, neither shall they with you; for they will surely incline your heart to follow their gods;' Solomon clung to these in love. [3] Among his wives were seven hundred princesses and three hundred concubines; And his wives turned away his heart. [4] For when Solomon was old, his wives turned away his heart after other gods; and his heart was not true to the Lord his God, as was the heart of his father David. [5] For Solomon followed Astarte the goddess the Sidonians, and Milcom the abomination of the Ammonites. [6] So Solomon did what was evil in the sight of the Lord, and did not completely follow the Lord, as his father David had done. [7] Then Solomon built a high place for Chemosh the abomination of Moab and for Molech the abomination of the Ammonites, on the mountain east of Jerusalem. [8] He did the same for his foreign wives, who offered incense and sacrifice to their gods. [9] Then the Lord was angry with Solomon, because his heart had turned away from the Lord, the God of Israel, who had appeared to him twice, [10] and had commanded him concerning this matter, that he should not follow other gods; but he did not observe what the Lord commanded. [11] Therefore the Lord said to Solomon, 'Since this has been your mind and you have not kept my covenant and my statutes that I have commanded you, I will surely tear the kingdom from you and give it

to your servant. [12] Yet for the sake of your father David I will not do it in your lifetime; I will tear it out of the hand of your son. [13] I will not, however, tear away the entire kingdom; I will give one tribe to your son, for the sake of my servant David and for the sake of Jerusalem, which I have chosen.

NRSV Bible

Session 1, Handout 4

Group work exercise 2

1. Are the churches places for the economically privileged?
2. Have the churches been over-identified with the politics of power?
3. In what ways do the churches use God for political ends?

Session 1, Handout 5

Reflection

Micah 6:6–8

[6] 'With what shall I come before the Lord,

and bow myself before God on high?

Shall I come before him with burnt offerings,

with calves a year old?

[7] Will the Lord be pleased with thousands of rams,

with tens of thousands of rivers of oil?

Shall I give my firstborn for my transgression,

the fruit of my body for the sin of my soul?'

[8] He has told you O mortal what is good;

And what does the Lord require of you

But to do justice, and to love kindness,

And to walk humbly with your God?

NRSV Bible

Session 2 Introduction

Delusions of grandeur!
Demolishing the myth of 'God on our side' in 1st Isaiah and Jeremiah

In the Hebrew Scriptures there is constant tension between royal theology and covenant theology. The people are being challenged to choose between the two. Each theology has its spokespersons. The classical prophets of Israel repeatedly call for a commitment to covenant theology. Other prophets, usually portrayed as 'false prophets', support the royal theology. Royal theology tends to be the establishment position and more often the status quo. There is often a clash between these two conflicting theologies.

Royal theology may be described as the civil religion of the monarchy. Covenant theology is critical theology and is radical in the sense of that word, getting back to roots. It is a radical conservative call to return to the Exodus–Sinai covenant made with Moses. The clash between the theologies is not a matter of religious practice in the sense of piety or devotion. It is a clash between two different models of society; two different ways of organising structures, economic systems and political power relations. Covenant was a radical socio-economic and political vision of society, which was egalitarian and based on distributive justice. Royal theology was about the economic and political élitism of the monarchy; a system of domination experienced by the majority as unjust, oppressive and exploitative. Religious claims were made by both theologies.

Solomon's reign was a classical example of royal theology. What David started Solomon took to the nth level. Solomon created royal theology, which was really a theology of privilege and power. Solomon's use of God was to claim God on his side. Solomon was not the first or the last to make such claims. After all, he modelled his temple and palace on the architecture and system of the Canaanite city states. The 'God on our side' theology has lived on, not only in much of the story of Israel's monarchy, but in the empires of history and in national identities and ideologies. Royal theology or civil religion has never gone away! It also has a tendency to believe in its indestructibility (see handout on 'Meet Jeremiah'). It is a serious delusion and the classical prophets were often critical and attempted to undermine and demolish the perspective.

In this session there is an exploration of texts from two of Israel's prophets, Isaiah and Jeremiah. Over a century separates them, yet in different historical contexts they encountered the royal theology.

Isaiah of Jerusalem (chapters 1–39 – the rest of the book belongs to two later historical experiences, eg exile and return) belongs to the mid-eighth century. He was a prophet in Israel for over half a century. Ironically he seems to be associated with life at the palace, drawing much of his language and imagery from Jerusalem's royal traditions. It is in the temple, in the dramatic activity and symbolism of the temple worship, that his life-transforming experience of God's holiness occurs. Isaiah 6:1–13, the account of his sense of prophetic vocation, is in itself a coronation hymn.

His prophetic ministry is placed in the context of concrete historical events and crises. The experience of God and religious faith is always in the public place. The handout on 'Isaiah in context' makes this clear. It is in the context of very public events and from within the royal court that Isaiah of Jerusalem critiques the delusions of his time.

Jeremiah belongs to another time of crisis. He begins his prophetic ministry hopefully. The Assyrian empire was in decline and a new king of the Southern Kingdom of Judah, Josiah, had begun a reform movement. The story goes that during temple renovation an old scroll was found which expressed the covenantal faith and practice of Moses from the Exodus–Sinai experience. Josiah realised how far kings and people had departed from the covenant and so he set about liturgical, social, economic and political reform. What Josiah's builders discovered during the renovation project was believed to be the basis of our present book of Deuteronomy, hence Josiah's Deuteronomic reform.

The Deuteronomic vision of society was rooted in the Exodus–Sinai covenant. Jeremiah was a radical conservative steeped in this Mosaic tradition and in Josiah's reform, taking place in a new historical moment, Jeremiah has hope. It was cautious hope, because he did not seem to think that the reform movement was radical enough. When Josiah was killed in 609 BCE at the battle of Carchemish, Jeremiah may well have lost hope in an in-depth reform really happening.

Politically the Egyptians were threatening and interfering. Much worse, a new and dominant political power was emerging, the Babylonians. Another empire was on the march.

Caught in a political and military tug-of-war between the Egyptians and the Babylonians, and with the reform movement turning out to be a superficial project, Jeremiah saw nothing else for it but to 'make friends' with the Babylonians. He saw the writing on the wall and opposed the 'independence at all costs' dogmas of the ruling classes. The royal theology was alive and well, not least in the line put out by the royal propagandists. This was a message of peace, that all was well, that Jerusalem was inviolable, the Davidic kingdom permanent and the temple indestructible. God was on their side, independence therefore was an absolute position.

Jeremiah opposed this ideology in his sermons within the temple itself (Jeremiah 7 and 26). The royal theologians were in no mood to hear him. "The priests and the prophets laid hold of him, crying, 'You must be put to death!'" (26:8). By this stage Jeremiah's horizon of hope had abandoned the reform movement and looked forward to a rebirth of community beyond exile.

The clash between the true and false prophet is expressed in the confrontation between Jeremiah and Hananiah (Jeremiah 27–28). This was not so much a confrontation between truth and falsehood – it was no intellectual or scholastic struggle – but rather "a question of point of view of differing class-based perspectives on the same situation". It was not even that they made differing evaluations of the situation. What was being expressed were two "different programmes of action for confronting the situation" (Anthony R Ceresho, *Introduction to the Old Testament: A Liberation Perspective*, Orbis, 1992, p 208). Royal theology versus covenant theology was not about formulations of doctrine. It was about conflicting courses of action involving social and political justice issues and the future shape of the community and its relationships and infrastructure. Theology always translates into socio-economic, political and public relationships, even international relations. 'God on our side' may be the ultimate idolatry and delusion.

Session 2 Plan

Welcome (5 minutes)

Personal reflection (10 minutes)

Each person will receive a page with the following three quotations and task on it.

'In God we trust' (American dollar)

'For God and Ulster'

'For God and Ireland'

When you read these slogans, draw a symbol to represent the image of God they evoke.

Group discussion (10 minutes)

Share your image with a small group and discuss what your image suggests about the people who created the slogans.

Overhead (5 minutes)

Isaiah in context

Group work exercise (15 minutes)

Read Isaiah 1:16–31 and consider:

1. What were Isaiah's criticisms?

2. The prophet uses two key words: 'righteousness' and 'justice.' Reading the text in its context, what do you think Isaiah means by each of these terms?

Feedback (10 minutes)

Overheads (20 minutes)

Jeremiah in Context

Meet Jeremiah

Questions for clarification

Role-play (25 minutes)

Royal theology versus Covenant theology

Reflection (10 minutes)

1. How did you feel in your role?

2. What were the key issues that were emerging?

Plenary question (10 minutes)

How do we relate the criticisms of Isaiah and Jeremiah to our modem forms of God on our side?

Session 2, Handout 1

Delusions of grandeur

Personal reflection

Read the following quotations and draw a symbol, or find an image, to represent the image of God they evoke.

1. 'In God We Trust' (On the American dollar)

2. 'For God and Ulster'

3. 'For God and Ireland'

Symbol/image: (drawing or description)

Group work

In small groups, share your symbol/image and discuss what your symbol/image suggests about the people who created the slogans.

Overhead 1

Isaiah in context

◆ Isaiah's life as a prophet began in the year that king Uzziah died – 742 BCE (Isaiah 6).

◆ He continued his prophetic work through the reigns of three kings: Jotham, Ahaz and Hezekiah. His work ended with the siege of Jerusalem by Sennacherib in 701 BCE.

◆ Isaiah's language and imagery is drawn from the royal traditions of Jerusalem. He is closely associated with palace and temple and the royal theology. Royal theology is about the centrality and permanence of Jerusalem. It is about Jerusalem as the dwelling place of God on earth and an unending Davidic dynasty.

◆ Isaiah's close association with temple and palace is expressed in his coronation hymn (Isaiah 6:1–13). His experience of prophetic vocation was located in the temple.

◆ Isaiah chapters 1–12 have been described as the prophet's memoirs. The historical setting is the Syro–Ephraimite crisis of 735 BCE. The growing power of Assyria is advancing to take over seaports and trading routes. Small city states and regions form an alliance under the leadership of the northern Israelite king Pekah and the Syrian king of Damascus, Rezin. The southern king Ahaz refused to join the alliance.

◆ Rezin and Pekah feared the Assyrians would force Ahaz into an Assyrian coalition. They, therefore, threatened an attack on Jerusalem.

◆ Isaiah and Ahaz encounter each other when the latter is inspecting Israel's defences.

◆ Isaiah is against an alliance with the Syro-Ephraimites and any submission to Assyria. The prophet calls Ahaz to:

> trust in the covenantal God;
>
> remain neutral in relation to international power politics.

Session 2, Handout 2

Group work exercise 1

Read text from Isaiah 1:16–31

[16] Wash yourselves; make yourselves clean; remove the evil of your doings from before my eyes; cease to do evil,
[17] learn to do good; seek justice, rescue the oppressed, defend the orphan, plead for the widow.

[18] Come now, let us argue it out, says the Lord: though your sins are like scarlet, they shall be like snow; though they are red like crimson, they shall become like wool. [19] If you are willing and obedient, you shall eat the good

of the land; [20] but if you refuse and rebel, you shall be devoured by the sword; for the mouth of the Lord has spoken.

[21] How the faithful city has become a whore! She that was full of justice, righteousness lodged in her – but now murders! [22] Your silver has become dross, your wine is mixed with water. [23] Your princes are rebels and companions of thieves. Everyone loves a bribe and runs after gifts. They do not defend the orphan, and the widow's cause does not come before them.

[24] Therefore says the Sovereign, the Lord of hosts, the Mighty One of Israel: Ah, I will pour out my wrath on my enemies, and avenge myself on my foes! [25] I will turn my hand against you; I will smelt away your dross as with lye and remove all your alloy. [26] And I will restore your judges as at the first, and your counsellors as at the beginning. Afterwards you shall be called the city of righteousness, the faithful city. [27] Zion shall be redeemed by justice, and those in her who repent, by righteousness. [28] But rebels and sinners shall be destroyed together, and those who forsake the Lord shall be consumed. [29] For you shall be ashamed of the oaks in which you delight; and you shall blush for the gardens that you have chosen. [30] For you shall be like an oak whose leaf withers, and like a garden without water. [31] The strong shall become like tinder, and their work like a spark; they and their work shall burn together, with no one to quench them.

NRSV Bible

Consider:

1. What were Isaiah's criticisms?

2. The prophet uses two key words: 'righteousness' and 'justice'. Reading the text in its context, what do you think Isaiah means by each of these terms?

Overhead 2

Jeremiah in context

◆ Jeremiah was called to be a prophet when Josiah was king of Judah in 627–626 BCE.

◆ The Assyrian empire was in decline.

◆ Josiah had introduced the Deuteronomic reform movement. The reform was cut short by the king's death in battle in 609 BCE.

◆ Josiah's successor and son, Jehoahaz, was removed after three months by the Egyptians. Jehoahaz's brother, Jehoiakim, succeeded him and was loyal to Egypt for four years.

◆ Babylon was emerging as the key player in power politics.

◆ Jehoiakim revolted against the Babylonians and was assassinated. Jehoiakim's son and successor, Jehoiachin, was taken into captivity, along with court officials, to Babylon in 597 BCE.

◆ The Babylonians put Zedekiah on the throne as a 'puppet' king. He led a revolt, anticipating

Egyptian help that never arrived.

◆ In 587 BCE King Zedekiah and his sons were executed, the royal palace and temple were burned down and the city walls reduced to rubble.

◆ These troublesome times form the foreground to Jeremiah's life and work.

Overhead 3

Meet Jeremiah

◆ Jeremiah supported Josiah's reform movement.

◆ He remained a significant voice when the reform collapsed.

◆ He indicted Jehoiakin for failing to continue his father's social reforms, eg renewal of worship in the temple and creating a socially just society.

◆ Jeremiah condemned the king's building programme. He advocated submission to Babylon, instead of resistance and independence at all costs.

◆ Jeremiah saw submission as a way to mitigate the injustice and suffering of the majority.

◆ This would provide opportunity to continue the social reforms begun by Josiah.

◆ Jeremiah opposed the royal theology, ie the theology of the palace and the temple. Royal theology upheld:

  – the inviolability of Jerusalem;

  – the permanence of the Davidic kingdom;

  – the indestructibility of the temple;

  – the irrevocable promise of God's permanent temple presence;

  – the absolute belief of 'God on our side'.

◆ Jeremiah's opposition to royal theology is in his temple sermon (chapters 7 & 26).

Session 2, Handout 3

Royal theology versus Covenant theology

Preparatory reading, Jeremiah: 28:1–16.

[1] In the same year, at the beginning of the reign of King Zedekiah of Judah, in the fifth month of the fourth year, the prophet Hananiah son of Azzur, from Gibeon, spoke to me in the house of the Lord, in the presence of the priests and all the people. saying: [2] 'Thus says the Lord of Hosts, the God of Israel: I have broken the yoke of the king of Babylon. [3] Within two years I will bring back to this place all the vessels of the Lord's house, which King Nebuchadnezzar of Babylon took away from this place and carried to Babylon. [4] I will also bring back to this place King Jeconiah son of Jehoiakim of Judah, and all the exiles from Judah who went to Babylon, says the Lord, for I will break the yoke of the king of Babylon.'

[5] Then the prophet Jeremiah spoke to the prophet Hananiah in the presence of the priests and all the people who were standing in the house of the Lord; [6] and the prophet Jeremiah said 'Amen! May the Lord do so; may the Lord fulfil the words that you have prophesied, and bring back to this place from Babylon the vessels of the house of the Lord, and all the exiles. [7] But listen now to this word that I speak in your hearing and in the hearing of all the people. [8] The prophets who preceded you and me from ancient times prophesied war, famine, and pestilence against many countries and great kingdoms. [9] As for the prophet who prophesies peace, when the word of that prophet comes true, then it will be known that the Lord has truly sent the prophet.'

[10] Then the prophet Hananiah took the yoke from the neck of the prophet Jeremiah, and broke it. [11] And Hananiah spoke in the presence of all the people, saying, 'Thus says the Lord: This is how I will break the yoke of King Nebuchadnezzar of Babylon from the neck of all the nations within two years.' At this, the prophet Jeremiah went his way.

[12] Some time after the prophet Hananiah had broken the yoke from the neck of the prophet Jeremiah, the word of the Lord came to Jeremiah: [13] 'Go, tell Hananiah, Thus says the Lord: You have broken wooden bars only to forge iron bars in place of them! [14] For thus says the Lord of Hosts, the God of Israel: I have put an iron yoke on the neck of all these nations so that they may serve King Nebuchadnezzar of Babylon, and they shall indeed serve him; I have even given him the wild animals.' [15] And the prophet Jeremiah said to the prophet Hananiah, 'Listen, Hananiah, the Lord has not sent you, and you made this people trust in a lie. [16] Therefore, says the Lord: 'I am going to send you off the face of the earth. Within this year you will be dead, because you have spoken rebellion against the Lord.'

NRSV Bible

Session 2, Handout 4

Role-play

Royal theology versus Covenant theology

Characters:

◆ Jeremiah group

◆ Hananiah group

◆ Group of rural peasants and Jerusalem citizens.

Scenario:

A meeting takes place in the outer court of the temple in Jerusalem. In attendance are a group of rural peasants and citizens of Jerusalem alongside supporters of both the prophet Jeremiah and the prophet Hananiah. At the meeting both prophets will be given an opportunity to address the people gathered to put their views and concerns regarding the present situation in Israel. The people gathered will then have an opportunity to consider what they have heard, ask questions of the prophets and decide which of the two contradictory messages is to be believed.

Preparatory reading for role-play

◆ Jeremiah 7:1–10 (key verses 5–7)

◆ Jeremiah 27:1–8, 28:1–4,:15–16.

Questions for reflection after role-play

Staying in role, consider the following:

1. How did you feel in your role?

2. What were the key issues that were emerging?

Out of role consider:

1. How do we relate the criticisms of Isaiah and Jeremiah to our modem forms of 'God on our side'?

Session 2, Handout 5

Background information

◆ The confrontation between Hananiah and Jeremiah is found in Jeremiah chapters 27 and 28. Both are prophets. Hananiah belongs to the temple court and is an advocate of the royal theology. Jeremiah is coming from the rural communities. The clash between them is not a question of what is true against what is false. It is about two different class-based perspectives on the same situation.

◆ Hananiah is reading the situation through the eyes of the economic and political élite and therefore, the status quo. Jeremiah is reading the situation through the eyes of the rural, marginalised, disempowered and oppressed people.

◆ Jeremiah warns that if Judah does not submit to Babylon there will be nothing but destruction and suffering. Hananiah contradicts Jeremiah and claims that within two years the temple will be restored and those who were taken away in 597 BCE will return.

◆ Hananiah bases this on his royal theology (ie the theology of palace and temple). Royal theology upheld:

  – the inviolability of Jerusalem;

  – the permanence of the Davidic kingdom;

  – the indestructibility of the temple;

  – the irrevocable promise of God's permanent temple presence;

  – the absolute belief of 'God on our side'.

◆ Jeremiah based his view on the covenant theology, which opposed the injustices of heavy taxation and forced labour that supported the military adventures and luxurious lifestyle of the king and the royal court ruling classes.

◆ Jeremiah believes that the royal temple theology is false because it is divorced from the covenant demands of social and political justice and right living.

Session 3 Introduction

Behind the walls! Beyond the walls!
Inclusive or exclusive community: exploring the tensions in Ezra, Nehemiah and 3rd Isaiah

The great watershed event in the history of the Hebrew people was the Babylonian exile in 587 BCE. It was a catastrophic experience that shattered the illusory certainties, the false hopes and the royal theology that Jeremiah confronted, at the time unsuccessfully in the Jerusalem temple. The temple, believed to be indestructible, was razed to the ground in 587 BCE. It was not just a building that was torn down. The social, economic, political, cultural and religious systems were destroyed. Exile was a major socio-political and theological crisis.

Only the poor and the 'nobodies' were left among the ruins of Jerusalem. The pain and desolation they experienced can be heard and indeed felt in the book of Lamentations. What else could they do but lament? The professionals, educated and better off were taken by the Babylonians into captivity. The pathos of their experience can be heard in Psalm 137: "By the rivers of Babylon we sat down and wept . . . how can we sing the Lord's song in a strange land?" They could not envisage ever singing again!

Strangely though, they did learn to sing again in Babylon. In fact the exiles became very creative. Not only did they sing songs like Psalm 95, but engaged with a remarkable literary project. They wrote and revised their story all the way back to their foundational event at the Exodus. Some of them undertook a massive editorial exercise. Most of the Hebrew Scriptures as we now have them were edited and shaped during the exile. The book we call Isaiah was finally shaped after the exile, bringing together writings that span over 200 years. The book is the work of three different prophets each declaring a message at different historical moments and in different contexts.

Shaped into its final form by the editors, perhaps an Isaianic school, the book in its totality offers a model of historical experience. How does a community move beyond crisis, conflict and an experience of exile/captivity? The book of Isaiah suggests that there needs to be an honest critique made of the social and religious structures. There are honest judgements to be made that go beyond denial and scapegoating. The pain then needs to be named. It is in the public naming of pain that healing begins. Only when pain is named is there the release of imagination to enable the visioning of a new future. The experiential process of the book of Isaiah provides a model for societies struggling to emerge from histories of crisis and pain.

A particular focus in this session is on the third part of the scroll. What we encounter in chapters 56–66 is less the work of an individual than in all probability a school of visionaries. The Edict of Cyrus in 538 BCE allowed the exiles to return to their homeland. There was no immediate rush to join the trek to Jerusalem. After all, many were second generation in Babylon. Jeremiah had told their parents to make

THE ISAIAH SCROLL

8th Century	6th Century	6–5th Century
Isaiah of Jerusalem Assyrian crisis	'Isaiah' of Babylon Babylonian exile	'Isaiah' of The Return Rebuilding community
Chapters 1–39	Chapters 40–55	Chapters 56–66

Critique of society	Public naming of pain	Released imagination for a new future

the best of it – "seek the welfare of the land" (Jeremiah 29:7). They had, and by the rivers of Babylon they were singing again, had built houses, made money and some were even in the Persian civil service. The new Persian empire promised much. Cyrus was tolerant and benevolent. Life might even get better by the River Chebar! There were only ruins in Jerusalem and a population of undesirables, many of them ancient enemies.

Despite the Edict of Cyrus, the return was not immediate. Those who did return did so in four phases over a period of 150 years! The Persians did everything to encourage them, including substantial financial support for the rebuilding of the city and its walls. Nehemiah, a fairly high-ranking Persian civil servant, was named governor by the Persians and sent to provide new social, economic and administrative infrastructure. He was Jewish and probably arrived in Jerusalem around 435 BCE. He had not been born when Cyrus issued his Edict of liberation!

Ezra arrived later still with the largest group of returnees, around 5,000. Ezra officially established the Jewish Law in a solemn public ceremony. The Law may have been the Holiness Code of Leviticus chapters 17–26, given its final shape in the exile period.

The challenge of the return from exile was to rebuild community in and around Jerusalem. It was a time of religio-political conflict. The returning exiles and the Samaritans were long-standing antagonists. In terms of religion they were first cousins, which often does intensify conflict. The Samaritans offered help in rebuilding the temple but were aggressively rebuffed. They then opposed the rebuilding project and began interfering and meddling in the temple politics.

There were other ancient enemies, including Edomites and Moabites who were on a permanent exclusion order (Deuteronomy 23:3–4). Some had intermarried and Nehemiah and Ezra opposed such "mixing of the holy seed" (Ezra 9:2). They eventually legislated against mixed marriages, with Jewish men consenting to divorce their Gentile spouses, thereby putting women and children in socially and economically marginalised and vulnerable situations. Purity of identity – ethnic, racial, cultural and religious – was paramount.

There was internal religious conflict, which had to do with power and control. The key issue was who controlled Jerusalem and this led to a power play between two priestly groups. The roots of this power conflict went back to the time of Solomon. The antagonism between the Zadokites and Levite priests was centuries old. Solomon, in his brutal purge of David's regime, banished the Levites and permanently installed the Zadokites, even though they had no pure Hebrew lineage. Ironically, Nehemiah and Ezra legislating for purity of the 'holy seed' were backing the Zadokites! There are always blind spots in power play!

It is the excluded Levites who are thought to be behind the third part of the book of Isaiah. They were a group of disadvantaged and marginalised priests, who were again being excluded from the religious institutions of the reconstructed Jerusalem. They were visionary dissenters opposed to the exclusive legislation and community structures of Ezra and Nehemiah. For them identity and belonging in the community being reconstructed were too narrow. Isaiah chapters 56–66 represent not only their protest but also their vision for a new Jerusalem. The key texts envision an inclusive community.

The Zadokites were the traditionalist party and were in power in the rebuilt temple as they had been since Solomon's time and probably had remained dominant even in exile.

Ezekiel was a Zadokite priest who had been among the first phase of exiles in 597 BCE when the Babylonians had first invaded Jerusalem. He had been a member of the temple personnel in Jerusalem before the terrible destruction. Ezekiel was profoundly affected by the events of 597 and 587 BCE. Even the death of his wife was insignificant in comparison with the loss and destruction of Jerusalem (24:15–18, 21, 24). Yet out of this deep sense of trauma and disorientation he produced some very powerful and imaginative poetry and images, some even bizarre. For Ezekiel the exile was an intellectual, psychological, emotional, theological and institutional catastrophe. He was one of the privileged classes and he did survive, providing for the first generation of exiles a future hope based on ancient roots. Everything had been shaken to the foundations but this priestly prophet still had foundations deep beneath the rubble of the historical crisis.

As a priest he not surprisingly dreamt of a restored temple. His future temple visions are in chapters 40–48. In chapter 44 the vision sounds an exclusive note. Charges of idolatry were made against the Levites and they were excluded from the officiating priesthood. Such an exclusive attitude jars with the spirituality of Ezekiel, which emerges from his struggle. It is believed that in the editorial process which happened during the later part of exile and even into the early period of return, the Zadokites had reworked chapter 44 and narrowed Ezekiel's original vision. This would reflect the depth of the tension between Zadokites and Levites and it expresses the tension between two different visions of community. In the reconstruction of Jerusalem, which was not merely about bricks and mortar but about humanity and human relations, is the new community to be inclusive or exclusive? Are there always tensions around building community? How do we deal with competing visions and can the conflict between opposing visions be resolved?

Session 3 Plan

Welcome (5 minutes)

Group work exercise 1 on the recent political past (10 minutes)

Share what some of your thoughts and feelings have been on the working of the Northern Ireland Executive and Assembly.

1. What tensions have you observed in the attempt to build a new society?

Overhead (10 minutes)

Return from exile

Questions for clarification (5 minutes)

Overhead (10 minutes)

Religio-political conflict

Questions for clarification (5 minutes)

Group work exercise 2 (20 minutes)

A vision for a new community

Working with one of two texts – Ezekiel 44:9–23 and Isaiah 56:1– 8 the group will create a profile for either the Zadokite or Levite vision for a new community

Feedback (10 minutes)

Plenary questions (15 minutes)

1. What are the key issues of conflict between these respective visions?

2. Is it possible to resolve this conflict?

Group work exercise 3 on the following questions (15 minutes)

1. Can the tensions you observed around building a new society be resolved and reconciled?

2. What needs to happen for this to take place?

3. What role has the faith community in building this new society?

Feedback (10 minutes)

Session 3, Handout 1

Group work exercise 1

Group reflection on the recent political past.

1. Share what some of your thoughts and feelings have been on the working of the Northern Ireland Executive and Assembly.

2. What tensions have you observed in the attempt to build a new society?

Overhead 1

Return from exile

◆ In 587 BCE Judah was destroyed by the Babylonians and the cream of its people exiled in Babylon.

◆ The exile was a social, political, cultural and theological crisis.

◆ In 538 BCE the Edict of Cyrus, the new Persian leader, allows the exiles to return to their homeland.

◆ The return from exile is in four phases.

1. 538 BCE – a small group undertakes a feasibility study and prepares the groundwork for future returns.

2. 520 BCE – Zerubbabel is the chief officer and Joshua is the high priest. Under their leadership the former exiles begin to rebuild the temple (Ezra 2:2–70, Nehemiah 7:7–72).

◆ The prophets who encouraged the rebuilding of the Jerusalem temple were Haggai and Zechariah. By 515 BCE the restored temple was dedicated and regular worship was carried out.

3. In 435 BCE Nehemiah, with Persian financial support, is named as the governor of Jerusalem. He undertakes the rebuilding and fortification of the city walls. He repopulates the city with rural residents and he reforms the temple worship (Nehemiah 2:4–9).

◆ Nehemiah provided a new economic and administrative infrastructure.

4. In the late fifth century BCE Ezra led 5,000 exiles home to Judah. In a ceremony in the town square he officially proclaims and establishes the Jewish law (Nehemiah 8:1–3). The law may have been the Holiness Code of Leviticus chapters 17–26 (Nehemiah 8:1–3).

Overhead 2

Religio-political conflict

◆ Conflict in Jerusalem between returned exiles and resident Samaritans.

◆ The Samaritans oppose the rebuilding of the temple. They interfere and meddle in the temple politics (Ezra 4).

Internal religious conflict

◆ The key issue is who controls Jerusalem. This power issue involves two groups – Zadokite priests and Levites

Internal religious conflict and dissenting visionaries

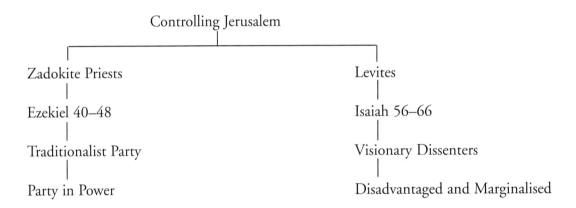

```
                        Controlling Jerusalem

      Zadokite Priests                        Levites
             |                                   |
      Ezekiel 40–48                       Isaiah 56–66
             |                                   |
    Traditionalist Party                Visionary Dissenters
             |                                   |
      Party in Power              Disadvantaged and Marginalised
```

Session 3, Handout 2

Group work exercise 2

A Vision for a new community

Working with one of two texts – Ezekiel 44:9–23 and Isaiah 56 – the group will create a profile for either the Zadokite or Levite vision for a new community.

Representative feedback to large group.

1. What are the key issues of conflict between these respective visions?

2. Is it possible to resolve this conflict?

Session 3, Handout 3

Ezekiel 44:9–23

[9] Thus says the Lord God: 'No foreigner, uncircumcised in heart and flesh, of all the foreigners who are among the people of Israel, shall enter my sanctuary. [10] But the Levites who went far from me, going astray from me after their idols when Israel went astray, shall bear their punishment. [11] They shall be ministers in my sanctuary, having oversight at the gates of the temple, and serving in the temple; they shall slaughter the burnt-offering and the sacrifice for the people, and they shall attend on them and serve them. [12] Because they ministered to them before their idols and made the house of Israel stumble into iniquity, therefore I have sworn concerning them, says the Lord God, that they shall bear their punishment. [13] They shall not come near to me, to serve me as priest, nor come near any of my sacred offerings, the things that are most sacred; but they shall bear their shame, and the consequences of the abominations that they have committed. [14] Yet I will appoint them to keep charge of the temple, to do all its chores, all that is to be done in it. [15] But the levitical priests, the descendants of Zadok, who kept the charge of my sanctuary when the people of Israel went astray from me, shall come near to me to minister to me; and they shall attend me to offer me the fat and the blood, says the Lord God. [16] It is they who shall enter my sanctuary, it is they who shall approach my table, to minister to me, and they shall keep my charge. [17] When they enter the gates of the inner court, they shall wear linen vestments; they shall have nothing of wool on them, while they minister at the gates of the inner court, and within. [18] They shall have linen turbans on their heads, and linen undergarments on their loins; they shall not bind themselves with anything that causes sweat. [19] When they go out into the outer court to the people, they shall remove the vestments in which they have been ministering, and lay them in the holy chambers; and they shall put on other garments, so that they may not communicate holiness to the people with their vestments. [20] They shall not shave their heads or let their locks grow long; they shall only trim the hair of their heads. [21] No priest shall drink wine when he enters the inner court. [22] They shall not marry a widow, or a divorced woman, but only a virgin of the stock of the house of Israel, or a widow who is the widow of a priest. [23] They shall teach my people the difference between the holy and the common, and show them how to distinguish between the unclean and the clean.'

NRSV Bible

Session 3, Handout 4

Isaiah 56:1–8

[1] Thus says the Lord: 'maintain justice, and do what is right, for soon my salvation will come, and my deliverance be revealed. [2] Happy is the mortal who does this, the one who holds it fast, who keeps the Sabbath, not profaning it, and refrains from doing any evil. [3] Do not let the foreigner joined to the Lord say, "The Lord will surely separate me from his people"; and do not let the eunuch say, "I am just a dry tree." [4] For thus says the Lord: To the eunuchs who keep my Sabbaths, who choose the things that please me and hold fast my covenant, [5] I will give, in my house and within my walls, a monument and a name better than sons and daughters; I will give them an everlasting name that shall not be cut off. [6] And the foreigners who join themselves to the Lord, to minister to him, to love the name of the Lord, and to be his servants, all who keep the Sabbath, and do not profane it, and hold fast my covenant – [7] these I will bring to my holy mountain, and make them joyful in my house of prayer; their burnt offerings and their sacrifices will be accepted on my altar; for my house shall be called a house of prayer for all peoples. [8] Thus says the Lord God, who gathers the outcasts of Israel, I will gather others to them besides those already gathered.'

NRSV Bible

Session 3, Handout 5

A vision for a new community: background information

◆ The Zadokite priests are the priestly family of Solomon's temple and remained until the temple was destroyed before the exile. They are the people who, when the temple is rebuilt, take control.

◆ The tribe of Levi, which is a priestly tribe, is given no land because Yahweh is its portion. The Levites have a more prominent role in the history of Chronicles than they do in Samuel and Kings. Their tasks were overseeing admission to the temple and performing in the temple choir.

◆ On return from exile there is strife between these two priestly groups (Zadokites and Levites). Ezekiel 44 shows that the Zadokite priests were determined to establish themselves as the undisputed leaders over the temple and cult.

◆ The Zadokites were determined to complete what had begun in Josiah's reign, which was to demote and make the Levites subservient to the Zadokites.

◆ The Zadokites had compromised their faith through accommodation with the political powers of Persia. The Zadokites were backed by the Persian crown and acted with Persian authority. They were intent on creating religious purity which by its very nature was exclusive.

◆ The Zadokites were supported by the prophets Haggai and Zechariah. Within a divided community the Zadokites asserted authority, repressed dissent and mobilised resources for the rebuilding of the temple.

◆ Ezekiel was a Zadokite priest. His vision of the restored temple (Ezekiel chapters 40–48) was narrowed by the Zadokites to fabricate charges of idolatry against the Levites and bar them from the officiating priesthood.

◆ Chapter 44 is probably a Zadokite reworking of part of Ezekiel's original vision.

◆ The Levites were a marginalised, repressed group who protest against the narrow, exclusive vision of the Zadokites. The Levite vision is of universal peace and an inclusive temple.

◆ The special social concerns within the Deuteronomic reform were in favour of the less fortunate, which included the widow, the orphan, the resident alien and the Levite.

◆ The Levites inclusive vision is expressed in 3rd Isaiah chapters 56–66, which is placed in the era of return from exile (Isaiah 56:6–8, 65:17–25).

Session 3, Handout 6

Group work exercise 3

1. Can the tensions you observed around building a new society be resolved and reconciled?

2. What needs to happen for this to take place?

3. What role has the faith community in building this new society?

Session 4 Introduction

And the walls came tumbling down
Jesus in conflict with the religion, economics and politics of the temple

In the Gospel story of Mark, Jesus is never far away from conflict. Jesus opposed the political, economic and religious order of his own world. That is not how we often read the Jesus story. Somewhere along the line we have successfully domesticated him. We have been able to do this by building spiritual bypasses. Jesus has no context, no concrete, historical world. He has become universal and timeless, without roots, even Jewish roots. Our starting point is often, even unconsciously, the creedal formulations. We even treat these without context.

When the word became flesh it was not merely human flesh, but Jewish flesh. Even more specifically, Jesus was Galilean Jewish. Theologically, God was very particularist when it came to the incarnation!

Jesus lived in a real world, a very particular and real world. The conflict scenarios are not therefore surprising. To understand Jesus is to understand the Galilean world of his time. To understand that world is to understand the socio-political and historical realities of first-century Palestine and Galilee in particular. Ched Myers dramatically paints the world of Mark's Gospel in a short sentence: "The Gospel reflects the daily realities of disease, poverty and disenfranchisement that characterised the social existence of first-century Palestine's other 95%" (Ched Myers, *Binding the Strong Man: A Political Reading of Mark's Story of Jesus*, Orbis, 1995 ed, p 39).

In the Gospel of Mark much of the conflict is with the institution of the temple in Jerusalem. The temple is but one institution, experienced as heavily oppressive by the common people who were the "95%". The world behind the Gospels is a world of imperial domination and resistance to empire, or at least critical distance. There is a political, economic and religious landscape lying behind the words of the Gospels. Not merely the background but the foreground of the Gospels is the power of the Roman Empire, the splendour of Herodian Jerusalem and the dehabilitating poverty of rural Galilee and urban Judea. It was also a world of popular resistance movements and messianic pretenders.

The Palestine of Jesus was occupied territory. After almost a century of independence, Pompey invaded and Palestine became another subject of the expanding Roman Empire. That was in 63 BCE. Between 40 and 37 BCE the Parthians ruled but Rome soon reconquered Palestine and installed a client king called Herod the Great. From 37 BCE to 4 CE Herod ruled with brutality. When Herod died in 4 CE there were popular uprisings. The Romans introduced a policy of divide and rule and then in 44 CE imposed direct rule. The so-called Pax Romano was maintained by military oppression as well as economic oppression. The populace suffered from triple taxation: firstly, there were the Roman tribute and toll taxes; secondly, Herod also enforced taxation to fund his lavish building projects; and thirdly there was the temple tax and various tithes which enabled the high priests to live in extravagant luxury in

Jerusalem. The small farmer taking his produce to the city markets was met with toll taxes and tariffs before he could even set up his stall. The "other 95%" referred to by Ched Myers were the poor because the wealth and the land were owned by the 5% élite.

Galilee, where Jesus spent most of his time, was a province where tension was especially acute. The Herodians had built a number of Greek cities. There was a serious cultural clash between the Hellenistic cities and the Jewish towns and villages. Furthermore, Galilee was the breadbasket for the Greek cities which added to the economic oppression. Galilee and its people suffered a triple oppression: occupied by the imperial might of Rome, it was also increasingly controlled by the political and economic forces of the Greek cities, and then there was the socio-economic pressure from the religious centre of Jerusalem. Galileans lived with the military ideology of empire, the brutality of client kings, the cultural and economic conflict with Hellenism and the religio-economic oppression of Jerusalem. In the village of Nazareth, only four miles away from one of the Hellenistic cities, a young Jesus was raised. Shaped by this context, familiar with the sufferings of his Galilean people, "Jesus came to Galilee, proclaiming the good news of God, and saying, The time is fulfilled, and the Kingdom of God has come near, repent and believe in the good news" (Mark 1:14).

We cannot, therefore, understand Jesus and the significance of Jesus unless we understand something of this very real world in which he lived and in which he was executed by the imperial power. Jesus did not oppose this world from a distance. He was often direct in his challenge to the violently oppressive powers. There is nothing 'gentle, meek and mild' in his opposition to the temple and the economic and religious oppression it imposed on the common people.

Two stories illustrate this, but only if re-read in the context of his world.

The entry into Jerusalem was a very dramatic challenge to dominating power. The Herodian dynasty was hated by the ordinary Jewish people. When Herod the Great died in 4 CE the Romans divided his puppet kingdom into three. Herod Antipas, like his father, gained a reputation for ostentatious entrances into cities. These were grand processions "accompanied by bodyguards in gleaming armour of silver and gold", according to the account of Philo. Jerusalem at the time of Jesus was a Herodian city. It is Luke who mentions the presence of Antipas at the Passover festival at which Jesus was executed. These festivals were perfect occasions for great displays of Herodian prestige and power. The entry and appearance of Herodian families during the major festivals was routine. These ostentatious entries may offer us some new insight into the significance of Jesus' entry in Jerusalem.

The entry was a piece of dramatic symbolism very much in the prophetic tradition. It was a public act. At heart it may well have been dramatic ridicule and satire. Was this entry a 'public send-up' of Antipas, ridiculing him as Jesus was greeted with the very palm branches that the puppet king inscribed on his coins? Jesus was opposed to the kind of royal theology that Solomon had created. The very flowers of the field, the wild flowers were more splendid that Solomon in all his glory – a rather biting criticism. Now the kingship of the contemporary ostentatious puppet was being held up to ridicule. The controlling metaphor of the life of Jesus was a radical kingless kingdom.

It was after this piece of public satire that Jesus challenged the temple system in the white-hot temperature of the Passover festival. The temple created a powerful visual impression on everyone who saw it. It was a monument of marble and gold, incense and dramatic ritual. For over-taxed, hard-pressed

Galilean peasants it was a monument of oppression. It was the centre of Jewish economic power, a banking system imposing tithes, offerings and taxes on an already heavily taxed peasantry.

It is against this background of economic oppression that Jesus observed the people making the temple offering. A poor widow put two of the smallest coins into the treasury box. The widow's giving has often been portrayed as a model of sacrificial giving; the giving of her last penny has been held up as virtuous. The opposite is the case. Jesus is not pointing to her sacrificial generosity. It is rather an angry story. Widows were among the most vulnerable of the poor in his world. They were nobodies, without protection and rights. Poor widows were at the very bottom of the social heap. Jesus is angry because a religious system, in the name of God, is taking the very last penny from one of the most vulnerable people in society. Where now her 'daily bread'? She was a victim of an exploitative, oppressive religious system.

Jesus was in conflict with the religion, economics and politics of the temple. It was an institution adding much to the daily grind of peasant lives. The religious institution had become part of the world's domination system. Its ritual of hierarchical holiness, expressing itself in religious and economic oppression, was the complete antithesis of the covenantal vision. This was the great paradox of the temple:

> . . . in order to enshrine the idea of the Covenant directly between the people and God, a huge bureaucratic organisation had arisen at the central cult place, maintained by a vast civil service of scribes, administrators, accountants, service personnel, Temple officers, and high priestly families who were all dependent on the Temple revenues for their support . . . there must have been a question in the minds of many of the People of Israel about which of the Temple's aspects – the covenantal or the oppressive – was the dominant one.

(Richard A Horsley and Neil Asher Silberman, *The Message and the Kingdom*, Grosset/Putnam, 1997, pp 75–6.)

This is the context in which that other piece of dramatic, prophetic symbolism took place. The 'cleansing of the Temple' challenged a whole religious system and in particular its high priests who lived in elegant villas overlooking the temple, built at the expense of poor widows.

Session 4 Plan

Welcome (5 minutes)

Working in small groups (10 minutes)

    What are your views about the role of the church in Northern Ireland?

Feedback (10 minutes)

Overheads (10 minutes)

    Social World of Jesus: Galilee

Read Mark 11:15–19 (5 minutes)

Overheads (10 minutes)

    Perspectives on the temple

Role-play (30 minutes)

    Debate on Jesus' actions in the temple

    Group participants are allocated the following roles and are asked to read the relevant background information: Moneylender and merchant; Sadducee; Pharisee; Follower of Jesus; Bandit; Peasant.

    Reflect on your reaction to Jesus' action in the temple and prepare to explain your thoughts and feelings in an open discussion with those representing the other groups listed.

Debriefing (15 minutes)

    1. How did you feel in your role?

    2. What are the key issues that are emerging?

Small group discussion: (15 minutes)

    What are the practical implications of the action of Jesus in the temple for: (a) churches in our community (b) those who are marginalised by the churches?

Feedback and discussion of points raised (10 minutes)

Overhead 1

Social world of Jesus

Politics

◆ Israel fell under Roman imperial control in 63 BCE and was governed by rulers appointed by Rome.

◆ The combination of Roman rule and Hellenistic cultural influences meant traditional ways and identities were in question.

Economic pressures

◆ The triple system of tax was crippling:

1. Rome demanded land, crop and customs tax;

2. Priesthood and temple tithes required by Torah;

3. Herodian tax for building projects.

35–40% of income went on taxation.

Result – debt, loss of land, increase of landless labourers.

Religion

◆ Jewish monotheism –YHWH only true God, Israel chosen people, therefore what happened to Israel of universal significance.

◆ God would soon act within history to vindicate them and establish justice and peace.

◆ Religion and politics, piety and revolution went hand in hand. Believed when YHWH became King Israel would return from exile, evil would be defeated and YHWH would return to Zion.

Overhead 2

Galilee

◆ Galilee was a place of conflict – political, economic and cultural.

◆ From 4 BCE to 39 CE administered by a tetrarch, Antipas, who maintained the police state created by the tyrant Herod.

◆ Majority of population were peasants who were poorly paid and suffered economic exploitation and oppression.

◆ Greek cities were being built. Galilee was the breadbasket – rural, landless Jewish peasants were supplying food for the Greek urban dwellers.

◆ There was much resentment among peasants as they lived with exploitation and the erosion of their way of life.

◆ Many were forced to live in the Greek cities.

◆ It is described as the most troublesome of the Jewish districts (revolts). A Roman emperor had enslaved up to 30,000 Galilean men.

◆ The rural–urban conflict was political, economic and cultural.

Session 4, Handout 1

Mark 2:1–19

15 Then they came to Jerusalem. And he entered the temple and began to drive out those who were selling and those who were buying in the temple, and he over-turned the tables of the money-changers and the seats of those who sold doves; 16 and he would not allow anyone to carry anything through the temple. 17 He was teaching and saying, 'Is it not written,

"My house shall be called a house of prayer for all the nations"? .

But you have made it a den of robbers.'

18 And when the chief priests and the scribes heard it, they kept looking for a way to kill him; for they were afraid of him, because the whole crowd was spell-bound by his teaching. 19 And when evening came, Jesus and his disciples went out of the city.

NRSV Bible

Overhead 3

Perspectives on the temple

Temple supporters believed the temple was:

- the symbolic heart of Judaism;
- the dwelling place of YHWH;
- the place of sacrifice and atonement for sins;
- a sign of Israel's election;
- a place of protection from harm;
- the financial centre of Judaism.

They made it:
- the centre of Israel's political life;
- the power base of the priestly élite;
- the centre of the purity system.

As the centre of holiness the temple needed to be:
- protected against defilement.

Consequently:
- Gentiles were excluded;
- many Jews, on the margin of society, experienced the temple as a source of corruption and oppression eg the story of the widow's mite.

Session 4, Handout 2

And the walls came tumbling down

Group work

Debate on Jesus' actions in the temple

Group participants are allocated the following roles:
◆ Moneylender and merchant
◆ Sadducee
◆ Pharisee
◆ Follower of Jesus
◆ Bandit
◆ Peasant

Read background notes and reflect on your reaction to Jesus' action in the temple. Prepare to explain your thoughts and feelings in an open discussion with those representing the other groups listed.

Debriefing

1. How did you feel in your role?
2. What are the key issues that are emerging?

Session 4, Handout 3

Critique of temple

Sadducees

◆ A conservative, aristocratic class who believed only the written Torah came from Moses.

◆ They supported the temple and priests and became involved in political affairs. The high priest came from their rank and served as head of state who, together with other leading priests, directed the Sanhedrin.

◆ They protested at the heavy Roman taxation of the Jewish people. It did not occur to them to reduce the taxes paid to the temple and priests, which had been decided when the Jewish state had its own monarchy and was responsible for maintaining a military force and a complete political administration.

◆ They vanished with the destruction of the Jewish state in 70 CE.

Pharisees

◆ A lay movement of scholars. Their name came from Hebrew 'Perushim' – the separated ones. They were also called 'Hakhamim' –scholars of Oral Law.

◆ They attempted to make Israel "a Kingdom of Priests and a Holy Nation" following the same laws of purity that applied to temple priests.

◆ They believed holiness of temple, land and people depended upon careful observance of the Torah. They sought to counter the corrosive effects of Roman political control and Gentile influence.

◆ They were developing the view that the study of Torah and extension of purity laws to every Israelite would count as an equivalent of worshipping in the temple.

Bandits

◆ Committed to the principle that God was on Israel's side and believed redemption from oppression by foreign powers depended on the actions of those prepared to establish God's reign by force.

◆ Refused to acknowledge the lordship of Caesar and pay Roman taxes on the grounds that the produce of the land belonged to YHWH. They did not recognise the high priest, who was not descended from the family of Zadok, and they opposed the exploitation of the Jewish people.

◆ Peasants regarded them as honourable and a symbol of hope that their oppression at the hands of a foreign government was not inevitable. They shared the fundamental values and religion of the peasant society of which they remained a marginal part.

Moneylenders and Merchants

◆ By securing loans to Jewish peasants at high interest rates, merchants could maintain a leisurely lifestyle in Jerusalem.

◆ If peasants were unable to meet the merchants demands for payment of loans, they forfeited their ancestral land to them.

◆ Merchants were often the object of brigand attacks. Many wealthy merchants left their estates in Jewish regions in search of safe surroundings among the Gentiles.

Peasants

◆ A large proportion of their produce was given to the temple priests to satisfy religious tithing laws.

◆ They looked to the temple and priesthood as a positive symbol of the unity of the people and their link with God. They blamed the Romans for their abuse and regarded the heavy tribute Rome imposed as robbery and illegitimate.

◆ They supported the bandits and viewed them as heroic victims of Roman injustice; they offered them protection from the Romans.

Jesus

◆ Compares the money changers and merchants to "a den of robbers". This is a reference to Jeremiah 7:11 where the "violent ones" believed the temple provided them with security against Babylon, despite their violation of the covenant.

◆ Articulated the role of the temple to be "a House of Prayer for all the Nations" referring to Isaiah 56:7.

◆ Recognised the money changers and merchants symbolised the quest for holiness at the centre of temple ideology.

◆ Pointed out that the "quest for holiness" promotes separation from anything considered unclean. It establishes boundaries between the pure/impure, righteous/sinner, male/female, rich/poor, Jew/Gentile.

◆ By his actions confirmed his view that the quest for a holy, separated nation was in error. The temple had become a centre of exclusiveness, resisting other nations instead of welcoming them in.

◆ Presented the people with an alternative socio-political vision of human life in community. He shifted the emphasis from the need for holiness to the challenge to be compassionate as God is.

◆ Lived his vision embracing the just and unjust alike, offering forgiveness and healing to all and practising an open table. In his life and teaching, radically challenged all that the temple had come to signify.

Session 4, Handout 4

Group work exercise 1

What are the practical implications of the action of Jesus in the temple for:

1. churches in our community?

2. those who are marginalised by the churches?

Session 5 Introduction

Fashion me a people
Paul on forming alternative community

Not only Jesus lived in a concrete, historical world – so too did Paul. The bypassing of Paul's social and political location has contributed much to various distortions of him. He has been used to support oppression and maintain a status quo. Women continue to hear Paul's voice as a voice of oppression. "The history of Pauline interpretation is the history of the apostle's ecclesiastical domestications" (Ernest Käsemann quoted in Neil Elliott, *Liberating Paul: The Justice of God and the Politics of the Apostle*, Orbis, 1995). This domestication has led to the justification of slavery, unquestioned obedience to the state, the silencing of women in the church, and the legitimising of anti-Semitism. Paul has been more often misread than read. Something of a rescue operation is needed for Paul. He requires liberation if he is to speak a liberating and challenging word to contemporary Christians. Liberating him will not be easy given the layers of domesticated ecclesial interpretation.

Essential to this is the recovery of Paul's social and political location. The foreground to the Pauline texts is that of Greek-Roman cities, systems of patronage and Roman ideology and imperial propaganda. Paul cannot be understood apart from this world. His vocabulary is often drawn from this imperial and ideological world. He was a communicator par excellence. His original readers or leaders in Corinth, Philippi or Thessoloniki would have understood where he was coming from. They would have recognised his language drawn from the socio-economic and political world of which they were a part. Paul did not invent religious vocabulary; he borrowed key political buzzwords and without abandoning their original meaning, used them to give Christian faith and values highly visible and public meaning.

When Paul uses the expression "peace and security" in I Thessalonians 5:3, the small faith community there would have immediately recognised the language as belonging to the propaganda of imperial Rome. The empire preached "peace and security". When Paul proclaims "destruction" he is seriously undermining the Pax Romana and declaring the empire and its propaganda a lie and a delusion. The Thessalonian Christians knew only of one 'empire', Christ's! Paul is no apolitical Christian advocating a timeless unquestioning obedience to state power. He has exposed and challenged the lie of state propaganda and the empire's spin doctors.

The focus of this session is on his correspondence with the Christian house churches in another great urban centre, Corinth. This Christian community was riddled with multiple problems. Many of the problems had to do with power relations. These power issues were bound up with economic and class issues. The minority wealthy were dominant and dominating. The majority poor were being made to feel inferior, not just economically, but also culturally, educationally and spirituality. Corinth was a church of élites and élitism. This was especially acute at the weekly celebration of the Eucharist. Unlike the not very edifying arguments of the last 500 years, Corinth's eucharistic problem was not about dogmatic theology. The Corinthian problem was economic.

In reality the Corinthian church simply mirrored the conflicts and divisions of the wider Corinthian society. Like Corinthian society the church is diverse, stratified and divided at a number of points. The sharp division between the rich and the poor was reflected in the church. The more middle class, better educated, business people, property owners and artisans, though a minority, maintained the power. They had the problem with attending and hosting dinner parties, essential to maintaining business contacts and contracts, where meat sacrificed to idols was eaten. The poor found this practice deeply offensive and saw it as compromising faith. Were the wealthy to go on offending their poor sisters and brothers or lose their business deals? The deepest inner convictions cannot escape conflicts. Christian faith and values are not lived in a vacuum but in the market place and the public square.

Paul is only too aware of social conflicts and ethical dilemmas in such urban locations as Corinth. At the same time it is not enough for the church to merely be a microcosm of Corinthian society. The divine purpose is to fashion an alternative people. God's alternative society was given expression by Paul in his body of Christ metaphor.

His vocabulary is again drawn from the public place. Not just the Corinthian Christians but any Corinthian would have recognised his 'body' metaphor as one of the key political buzzwords of first-century Corinth. It meant the 'body politic', the citizen body of the state. It was a well-established political metaphor. The Corinthian Christians are to be the body of Christ, the alternative body politic, the contrast citizen body. Paul was not depoliticising the metaphor. He was intentionally taking a political buzzword, with all its political significance, and calling on the Corinthian Christians to embody in their power relations all that God intends a body politic to be.

In 1 Corinthians 12:13–26 Paul is offering a community model. Given his use of political metaphor, this is not confined to church community. It is a model for a healthy body politic. The church is to model such a healthy citizen body.

Following the theme of the temple, this session picks up Paul's use of the metaphor. The Corinthian Christians are being encouraged to see themselves as the "temple of the Holy Spirit". It is a collective image, not an individualistic one. The Corinthian Christian community is a temple of God. It is not the Jewish temple that Paul has in mind: that would have made little sense in a Greco-Roman city. Paul is drawing attention to the obvious. Every Greco-Roman city had a temple which was at the heart of the city's public life. All of this had to do with the emperor cult, which was integral to Roman imperial society. The cult provided cohesion and produced social order across the disparate cities and provinces of the empire. It provided the urban ethos of cities like Corinth and Ephesus and highlights the "closely interrelated role of 'religion' and 'politics' in the structuring of power relations in imperial society." (Richard Horsley, *Paul and Empire: Religion and Power in Roman Imperial Society*, Trinity Press International, 1997, p 20.)

As the imperial cult developed and spread, so too did the proliferation of shrines, temples and festivals in the emperor's honour. The emperor became a god and temples places of emperor worship. The temple often housed a statue of a Greek god which helped to deify the emperor. The latter was in fact called 'god' and the main purpose of the cult was "to cultivate and express 'piety' (eusibia, devotion and socially oriented commitment) towards him" (ibid, p 21). The cult was not merely religious, it was socio-political. In the temple worship, people were committing themselves to live together according to the emperor's values. The temple came to dominate public space. In Corinth this was the case with the temple as a commanding structure dominating the city centre. As citizens of Corinth went about their everyday lives, the temple and the importance of the emperor pervaded the public space. Public life was permeated by the cult. Indeed the town square usually had more than one temple. The imperial cult with its temples formulated the institutions of city life. Civic space was pervaded by the imperial presence and imperial values. The temple was the symbol of the ethos of civic society and public life.

Paul, therefore, used a powerful image when he described the Corinthian community as the "temple of God". In their life together they were to worship the living God, which in itself set them against the gods. That included the gods of empire and emperor worship. It meant also that in public life and civic society the Christians lived by an alternative value system. Power relations were based on radically alternative values, which were certainly not those of domination. The Christian community in Corinth was to embody an alternative ethos for civic society and the public square. By the presence of the Holy Spirit, God was fashioning another kind of civic ethos and public ethic. The Corinthian Christian community was to be an alternative temple at the centre of the city's life.

It's a daring and radical image from Paul. Corinthian texts have been used to legitimise separation and isolationism: "Come out from among them and be separate." In the light of the temple and body metaphors used in these letters by Paul, such texts need to be reread. Paul is not calling for rigid separation in Corinth. The Christians can no more cut themselves off from the public life of the city than they can from the air they breathe. It is at the very heart of civic public life that they live and are to be different – different in their ultimate loyalties, their values and in the way they practice power relations. Like the body metaphor, the temple is a powerful political and civic image. At the very centre of Corinthian civic and public life "you are God's temple and . . . God's Spirit dwells in you".

Session 5 Plan

Welcome (5 minutes)

Group work exercise 1 (15 minutes)

Create an equal number of small groups and divide the following scenarios between them:

1. Northern Ireland has a missile-manufacturing industry. In the light of this, how should the faith community deal with the ethics and economics of weaponry?

2. Eucharist is also described as holy communion. How and in what ways are contemporary eucharists the expression of unholy division?

Feedback (10 minutes)

Overhead (5 minutes)

The temple as a public symbol in the Greek city.

Read 1 Corinthians 3:16–17 (5 minutes)

Group work exercise 2 (10 minutes)

In light of the significance of the imperial temple at the heart of the city of Corinth and its public life, what is Paul saying to Corinthian Christians?

Feedback (10 minutes)

Overhead (10 minutes)

Corinth – the socio-political context

Group work exercise 3 (15 minutes)

See handout 3

Feedback from scenarios (15 minutes)

Overhead (5 minutes)

God's alternative society

Plenary session: (15 minutes)

In the discussion, the following questions will be considered.

1. How does the modern Christian community relate to issues of culture and cultural identity?

2. What does it mean for Christians in Northern Ireland at a time of community building to be God's alternative public society?

Session 5, Handout 1

Group work exercise 1

Create an equal number of small groups and divide the following scenarios between them.

1. Northern Ireland has a missile-manufacturing industry. In the light of this, how should the faith community deal with the ethics and economics of weaponry?

2. Eucharist is also described as holy communion. How and in what ways are contemporary eucharists the expression of unholy division?

Overhead 1

The temple as a public symbol in the Greek city

◆ Temples were built in honour of the emperor.

◆ Images or statues of the emperor were found in and around the temple.

◆ The emperor was sometimes called god. A cult developed that was meant to cultivate piety – ie devotion to the emperor that meant social commitment to the emperor, empire and structures of empire.

◆ A religious cult was practised that involved sacrifices.

◆ The imperial presence permeated the whole of public space and life.

◆ Imperial temples put the emperor at the centre of public life in cities like Corinth and Ephesus.

◆ Everyone participated in public festivals that became obligatory by 90–110 CE. Individuals were obliged to offer a pinch of incense to the emperor yearly (equivalent to the oath of allegiance to a flag) and make a public confession that Caesar was lord. This became law after the time of Paul's letter to Corinth (50–53 CE).

◆ It was cultural tradition in Corinth for married men to have sexual relationships with temple prostitutes. This may even have been expected as part of the cultic practice. First Corinthians 6:12–20 seems to suggest that some men in the church were still involved with this practice. It may have been a cultural norm but Paul was opposed to it.

◆ A major dispute within the Corinthian church was over the issue of participation in Greco-Roman cults. The more wealthy Corinthian Christians were participating in the temple cultic meals and other dinner parties, which were a part of the culture of maintaining status, social and business relationships, and the hope of being elected to public office in Corinthian society. This practice caused offence to the weaker (poor) members of the church who perceived the sacrifices involved as being truly offered to the gods and therefore diluting Christianity.

Session 5, Handout 2

Group work exercise 2

1 Corinthians 3:16–17

[16] Do you not know that you are God's temple and that God's Spirit dwells in you? [17] If anyone destroys God's temple, God will destroy that person. For God's temple is holy, and you are that temple.

NRSV Bible

Task:

Read the above passage and consider the following.

In light of the significance of the imperial temple at the heart of the city of Corinth and its public life, what is Paul saying to Corinthian Christians?

Overhead 2

Corinth – the socio-political context

Social structure of the city

◆ Caesar refounded Corinth in 44 BCE

◆ Settled freedmen – Roman citizens

◆ Eight of 17 Christian names – Latin, Greeks, Jews

◆ Rapid economic upturn:

– handsomely built houses

– resumption of Isthmian games

– wealth based mainly on trade

– great and wealthy city – Greece's commercial centre

– centre of government administration

◆ Sharp division between rich and poor

"Sordidness of the rich and the misery of the poor"

(Contemporary Greek writer)

◆ Corinthian Christians:

– diverse ethnic origins

– different social strata – mainly poor/slaves

– theological/cultural divisions

– Lord's supper

– eating meat sacrificed to idols

– support of itinerant missionaries

– support of Paul

◆ Corinthian church is a microcosm of Corinthian society

◆ Paul's community model – 1 Corinthians 12:13–26:

– one body, many parts – celebrating differences

– caring for the different parts of the body

– the value of everyone's gifts

– the value of cooperation and interdependence

Session 5, Handout 3

Group work exercise 3

Allocate the following scenarios and relevant scripture texts between the groups.

Scenario 1

The cult of temple prostitution was part of Corinthian culture. How does the alternative public Christian community relate to the accepted public norms of the society? If you are a business person in Corinth and if doing business/making profits means involvement in the business dinner parties of those who buy into the temple cult, what is the Christian to do? What is Paul asking of the Christian community in relation to this issue?

Scenario 2

The Corinthian church, like the rest of Corinth, reflects deep socio-economic divisions. The wealthy members of the Corinthian church are a minority. The majority of its members are drawn from the lower socio-economic strata of Corinthian society: "Consider your own call, brothers and sisters: not many of you were wise by human standards, not many were powerful, not many were of noble birth. ' (1 Corinthians1:26)

When the Corinthian Christians met to celebrate the Eucharist, the deep economic divisions became evident. In a setting where Eucharist was a full meal, the wealthy and advantaged, who had plenty of leisure time, were arriving fIrst. When the poor slaves arrived, most of the food had gone and they were deprived of the most substantial meal they would have had in the week. When Paul said in 1 Corinthians 2:29: "For all who eat and drink without discerning the body, eat and drink judgement against themselves" the body he is referring to is the community. The Eucharist at Corinth had become an expression of division and the division was economic.

In what ways is Paul encouraging the Christian community to embody just social and economic relationships?

Session 5, Handout 4

A reading from 1 Corinthians 8:1–13 (Scenario 1)

[1] Now concerning food sacrificed to idols: we know that 'all of us possess knowledge.' Knowledge puffs up, but love builds up. [2] Anyone who claims to know something does not yet have the necessary knowledge; [3] but anyone who loves God is known by him. [4] Hence, as to the eating of food offered to idols, we know that 'no idol in the world really exists', and that 'there is no God but one.' [5] Indeed, even though there may be so-called gods in heaven or on earth – as in fact there are many gods and many lords – [6] yet for us there is one God, the Father, from whom are all things and for whom we exist, and one Lord, Jesus Christ, through whom are all things and through whom we exist. [7] It is not everyone, however, who has this knowledge. Since some have become so accustomed to idols until now, they still think of the food they eat as food offered to an idol; and their conscience, being weak, is defiled. [8] 'Food will not bring us close to God.' 9 We are no worse off if we do not eat, and no better off if we do. [9] But take care that this liberty of yours does not somehow become a stumbling-block to the weak. [10] For if others see you, who possess knowledge, eating in the temple of an idol, might they not, since their conscience is weak, be encouraged to the point of eating food sacrificed to idols? [11] So by your knowledge those weak believers for whom Christ died are destroyed. [12] But when you thus sin against members of your family, and wound their conscience when it is weak, you sin against Christ. [13] Therefore, if food is a cause of their falling I will never eat meat, so that I may not cause one of them to fall.

NRSV Bible

Session 5, Handout 5

A reading from 1 Corinthians 11:17–34 (Scenario 2)

[17] Now in the following instructions I do not commend you, because when you come together it is not for the better but for the worse. [18] For, to begin with, when you come together as a church, I hear that there are divisions among you; and to some extent I believe it. [19] Indeed, there have to be factions among you, for only so will it become clear who among you are genuine. [20] When you come together, it is not really to eat the Lord's supper. [21] For when the time comes to eat, each of you goes ahead with your own supper, and one goes hungry and another becomes drunk. [22] What! Do you not have homes to eat and drink in? Or do you show contempt for the church of God and humiliate those who have nothing? What should I say to you? Should I commend you? In this matter I do not commend you! [23] For I received from the Lord what I also handed on to you, that the Lord Jesus on the night when he was betrayed took a loaf of bread, [24] and when he had given thanks, he broke it and said, 'This is my body that is for you. Do this in remembrance of me.' [25] In the same way he took the cup also, after supper, saying, 'This cup is the new covenant in my blood. Do this, as often as you drink it, in remembrance of me.' [26] For as often as you eat this bread and drink the cup, you proclaim the Lord's death until he comes. [27] Whoever, therefore, eats the bread or drinks the cup of the Lord in an unworthy manner will be answerable for the body and blood of the Lord. [28] Examine your-selves, and only then eat of the bread and drink of the cup. [29] For all who eat and drink without discerning the body, eat and drink judgement against

themselves. [30] For this reason many of you are weak and ill, and some have died. [31] But if we judged ourselves, we would not be judged. [32] But when we are judged by the Lord, we are disciplined so that we may not be condemned along with the world; [33] So then, my brothers and sisters, when you come together to eat, wait for one another. [34] If you are hungry, eat at home, so that when you come together, it will not be for your condemnation. About the other things I will give instructions when I come.

NRSV Bible

Overhead 3

God's alternative society

Corinth

- ◆ Network of cells – spreading into the province of Achaia
- ◆ Social movement
- ◆ Paul urges group solidarity
- ◆ Community of saints – opposed to the 'world'
- ◆ Conduct its life in complete independence of the world
- ◆ Church lives under the radical freedom of the gospel
- ◆ Paul's 'body' metaphor – the body of Christ
- ◆ Well-established political metaphor
- ◆ Citizen body of the city state
- ◆ 'Body politic'

Corinthian Church

- ◆ Independent communities over against dominant society
- ◆ Social-economic solidarity which is international and different from the empire model
- ◆ The language of politics highlights the unity, harmony and mutual cooperation of the faith community
- ◆ Model a community of interdependence
- ◆ Corinthian churches form an alternative society
- ◆ Model God's design for the whole 'body politic'

Session 5, Handout 6

Plenary session

In the discussion, the following questions will be considered.

1. How does the modern Christian community relate to issues of culture and cultural identity?

2. What does it mean for Christians in Northern Ireland at a time of community building to be God's alternative public society?

Session 6 Introduction

A community without a temple!
Can religious institutions survive in the new Northern Ireland?

The sessions to date have explored the tensions between institutional religion and community. Institutional religion, represented by the temple, was about more than spirituality. The temple controlled more than the human relationship with God and did more than provide people with access to God. What developed, perhaps inevitably, was a bureaucratic and hierarchical system, which had to do with the politics of power and the economics of privilege. The temple impinged on every area of people's lives. It became a dominant and controlling factor which ordinary people experienced as oppressive. What ought to have been the means to a divine end became the end itself. The system became its own prison.

In the Bible there is a great deal of ambivalence towards the temple. It is not the only story. Whatever the faults of the temple system, it was in the temple and during its highly dramatic liturgy that Isaiah of Jerusalem was overwhelmed by the holiness or otherness of God and experienced his deep sense of call to be a prophet from within the royal court. It was no easy task to be the spokesperson of God at the very heart of the system. Yet the vocation and empowerment to carry it through came from participation in the liturgy of the temple institution (Isaiah 6). It is also within the temple worship that new songs were sung and subversive acts of praise were offered to God against the gods, eg Psalms 85 and 95.

Yet in all three temple periods the anti-temple theme is heard. The controversial founding of the institution of monarchy was accompanied by the building of the first Jerusalem temple. A centralised political authority was paralleled by a centralised cult. The cult legitimised and helped maintain the power and wealth of the king, who in turn was more than prepared to maintain the power of the cult. Solomon's temple was a symbol of oppression and injustice. Centuries later it was a focus of false security for Jeremiah and Ezekiel. The latter was one of its Zadokite priests and judged it as a place of idolatry.

In the second temple period the exclusive vision of the Zadokites was supported by Haggai and Zechariah. Ezra and Nehemiah built a community around temple, priest and law which included ethnically pure definitions of identity and excluded all those considered less than pure. Ethnic purity was defined in terms of having been in Babylonian exile and returned. The disempowered Levites expressed a more inclusive vision of community in Third Isaiah (chapters 56–66). Their vision of the temple was as "a house of prayer for all peoples" (56:7). This universal and inclusive vision was in opposition to the narrow vision of the pro-Persian movement which rebuilt the temple after the exile.

The centralised cult and the Jerusalem institutionalised religion of the temple was very much alive at the time of Jesus. Yet he was in frequent conflict with the system, being highly critical of its moral and ethical bankruptcy. Mark's theological interpretation of the death of Jesus depicts the veil of the temple being torn in two. This for Mark symbolises the destruction of an unjust and oppressive economic, political and religious institution. The temple was to last for only another 40 years before being totally destroyed by the Romans in 70 CE.

John the Divine was in the anti-temple tradition. His was a radical vision of a new Jerusalem in which there was no temple (Revelation 21:22).

John's writing, which is a classical example of Jewish apocalyptic literature – crisis or resistance literature – was addressed to a cluster of seven churches in Asia Minor. Much of the language and imagery is Jewish and apocalyptic. John was familiar with the Jerusalem temple and the anti-temple tradition. He was also familiar with the imperial cult and the significance of temples at the heart of Greco-Roman cities. One of the cities with a Christian community was Pergamum. It was the capital of Roman Asia and the centre of imperial worship for the whole region. Pergamum had a temple to Augustus and to Rome built in 29 BCE. For John, the Jerusalem temple was:

> . . . no different from the temple of Augustus in Pergamum or the temple of Artemis in Ephesus. All were manifestations of a centralised system that stood against God. Rather than having a priestly class standing above the people, John sees the entire people who resist empire as a nation of priests (1:6). This egalitarian vision saw God and the Lamb as living in the city among the people.

(Wes Howard-Brooke and Anthony Gwyther, *Unveiling Empire: Reading Revelation Then and Now*, Orbis, 1999, p 187.)

Significantly, much of John's vision of the new Jerusalem, the new community, is drawn from Ezekiel's vision. Even more significant, where Ezekiel the priest dreamt of a new temple in the new city, John sees no temple. The life of God's new community knows nothing of religio-economic and social oppression by a religious institution. In the joyful life of the new Jerusalem in the socio-political, socio-economic and socio-cultural spheres, the followers of the Lamb practice a different lifestyle in all three spheres. The vision of the new Jerusalem is an anti-imperial vision pointing to possibilities for an alternative political structure, a more just and equality based economic practice, and a counter-cultural definition of reality.

So the followers of Jesus refused to worship in the imperial temple and to buy meat sacrificed in the temples. This had very real consequences and some Christians paid a price for it economically and politically. Yet their refusal to participate in empire did represent a real shift in the balance of power. Their actions were subversive of imperial power, religion and culture. The very possibility of alternatives destabilised the empire's power over people. Those who were ready to die rather than give their ultimate loyalty to the empire seriously challenged the empire's violence.

Apocalyptic literature stands in the tradition of hope. Whether expressed through this particular literary genre or others, the Bible is strong on hope. In each of the three temple periods there were voices of hope providing alternative visions. In the face of all-pervasive and oppressive institutional religion, the Hebrew prophets, story-tellers, Jesus and apocalyptics like John the Divine offered visions of hope.

The hope they offered was not 'pie in the sky when you die'. Biblical hope is hope earthed in the here and now and in the concrete historical realities of life. The seven churches of Asia Minor were to "come out of Babylon" (18:4), to be communities of active resistance. They were to refuse the seduction of empire and their exodus from the economic and political seduction of empire stamped it as "doomed". Beyond the myth of empire was the counter-myth of the empire of God. Beyond the imperial arrogance and economic exploitation was the empire of "our Lord and of his Messiah" (11:15–18). Through the lens of biblical hope, John already sees Babylon as fallen (chapter 18). Hope exposes the lie, falsehood, illusion of empire, be it economic, political or religious. "Breaking free of empire is, by its very nature, an ongoing task" (Howard-Brooke and Gwyther, p 179). Such hope, therefore, is intended to impinge on, impact and shape how we live and work in the contemporary situation.

The vision of a community without a temple calls for critical living in the world. It creates critical distance between a faith and hope-filled value base and the prevailing culture. The empires of world and society are never ultimate or absolute. The critical vision calls for active community building based on alternative values. The hope is not for another world but for this one. That may well be the main point of John's new Jerusalem without a temple.

Session 6 Plan

Welcome (5 minutes)

Group reflection: (10 minutes)

What insights have we gained from an exploration of the temple theme?

Feedback (15 minutes)

Overhead (10 minutes)

Ambivalence in the Bible towards temple religion

Read Revelation 21:22–27 (5 minutes)

Group work exercise 1 (15 minutes)

Given the role of the temple in religion and the belief that it was the place of the divine presence in the midst of the world; given the suspicion and criticism of the temple in the Bible story, what is the Book of Revelation saying when in its vision of a new heaven and a new earth, in other words a new community, there is no temple?

Feedback (15 minutes)

Overhead (15 minutes)

The tradition of hope

Group work exercise 2 (15 minutes)

Consider the following questions.

1. What kind of community do these visions of hope encourage us to build in our situation?

2. How do our churches become agents of hope, keeping alive God's community vision?

3. What practical steps do we need to take? Where do we go from here?

Feedback and discussion(15 minutes)

Overhead 1

Ambivalence in the Bible towards temple religion

1st temple period

◆ Solomon's temple, which embodied the spirit of Canaanite society and religion, was a symbol of oppression and injustice.

◆ For Jeremiah (7:4) it was a focus of false security.

◆ For Ezekiel (8:5) it was a place of idolatry.

2nd temple period

◆ The tension between the exclusive vision of the Zadokites, supported by Haggai and Zechariah, and the universal inclusive vision of the marginalised, disempowered Levites is expresses in 3rd Isaiah.

◆ Ezra/Nehemiah consolidated life in the new community around temple, priest and law, defining identity in terms of ethnic purity and excluding other groups and identities.

3rd temple period

◆ Jesus was in frequent conflict with the temple system of his day. He was critical of the moral and ethical bankruptcy of the institution, which was religious, political and economic.

◆ Mark interprets the death of Jesus, in his description of tearing the veil of the temple in two, as the destruction of an unjust economic, political and religious institution.

Session 6, Handout 1

Revelation 21:22–7

[22] I saw no temple in the city, for its temple is the Lord God the Almighty and the Lamb. [23] And the city has no need of sun or moon to shine on it, for the glory of God is its light, and its lamp is the Lamb. [24] The nations will walk by its light, and the kings of the earth will bring their glory into it. [25] Its gates will never be shut by day – and there will be no night there. [26] People will bring into it the glory and the honour of the nations. [27] But nothing unclean will enter it, nor anyone who practises abomination or falsehood) but only those who are written in the Lamb's book of life.

NRSV Bible

Group work exercise 1

Given the role of the temple in religion and the belief that it was the place of the divine presence in the midst of the world; given the suspicion and criticism of the temple in the bible story, what is the Book of Revelation saying when in its vision of a new heaven and a new earth, in other words a new community, there is no temple?

Overhead 2

The tradition of hope

1st temple period

◆ In Isaiah, God's future promises a new Davidic king who will reign in justice and righteousness (Isaiah 11:1–5; 32:1).

◆ In Jeremiah, broken covenant shall be replaced by new covenant (Jeremiah 31:31) written upon the heart.

2nd temple period

◆ In this period Ruth and Jonah represent alternative visions of community.

◆ Ruth illustrates how when the marginal and persecuted are brought into the centre and empowered, the community is enriched. Jonah comes to recognise the radical freedom of God who will extend salvation to whomever it pleases him to redeem; even to those perceived as an enemy (Assyrians).

3rd temple period

◆ In the Beatitudes Jesus outlines the relational nature of God's community, where justice and righteousness underpin all relationships and provide the basis for a peace filled, compassionate, healthy community.

Overhead 3

Book of Revelation

◆ The Book of Revelation represents a clash between two powers.

– the power of the empire represented by the emperor;

– the power of the reign of God represented by the lamb who was slain.

◆ This is a clash between imperialistic, dominating power and the suffering power of loving service and compassion.

◆ In the Book of Revelation the Christian community refuses to acknowledge Caesar as Lord and will only give its ultimate loyalty to Christ as Lord who is the suffering lamb.

◆ John the Divine envisions a new community without a temple. He is not only in the biblical tradition of suspicion regarding temple religion, which has become the practice of unjust relationships and structures, but is also offering a radical counter image to the imperial cult and its temple.

◆ Each of the seven churches John the Divine addresses, in Asia Minor, would have had an imperial temple in the city centre. He is offering the suffering communities a vision of hope. Again he stands in the tradition of hope.

◆ Biblical hope is not pie in the sky. It is intended to impinge on, impact and shape how we live and work in the contemporary situation.

Session 6, Handout 2

Group work exercise 2

Consider the following questions.

1. What kind of community do these visions of hope encourage us to build in our situation?

2. How do our churches become agents of hope, keeping alive God's community vision?

3. What practical steps do we need to take? Where do we go from here?

Course Four Outline

Journey towards communities of integrity
Exploring nationalism, identity and violence from a biblical perspective

Course description

In this course we explore issues of nationalism, identities and violence from the perspective of the Bible and engage in the search for a more authentic community, liberated from all that dehumanises and excludes. If we are to build sustainable communities of integrity then we need to deal with the issues outlined in this course.

Course outline

Session 1   National/ethnic identities and injustices

Session 2   Religion and nationalism

Session 3   The underside of globalisation

Session 4   The myth of redemptive violence

Session 5   The alternative story – a culture of non-violence

Session 6   Towards communities of integrity

Session 1 Introduction

National/ethnic identities and injustices

Nationalism is a modern concept. It is not much more than 200 years old. Contrary to popular perception, it has not been around since the beginning of time and it is not part of the construction of the universe. God did not create nationalism! Songs like 'A Nation Once Again' may represent a legitimate modern aspiration but the wishful looking back to a lost national identity in antiquity is an anachronistic and delusory reading of history. The past is always more complex and often elusive. More often we are dealing with a mythological past or an ideological past, ie the past read from the perspective of a contemporary ideology.

Prior to the late eighteenth and early nineteenth centuries, Europe consisted of old empires, dynasties and monarchies. Their demise was replaced by the development of nationalism. National movements arose agitating for national independence.

One of the empires was that of the Habsburgs. In 1781 Marie Therese set about remodelling the Habsburg Empire. She abolished serfdom in Bohemia, Moravia and what was left of Silesia. A peasant rebellion of 1775 played a major part in securing this reform. But the Habsburg Empire was multi-ethnic and little account was taken of this. German was made the official language and Bohemian traditions were curtailed. That stimulated the growth of Czech national consciousness and was the first phase in the formation of the modern Czech nation. What was set in motion continued up to 1870 and is referred to as the national revival. This included the revival of the Czech language and a Czech national culture. By the end of the nineteenth century new Czech political parties emerged and 1907 saw the first elections under universal suffrage. After World War One the new borders of Czechoslovakia were confirmed by the peace treaties which concluded with the Paris Peace Conference in 1920. On 14 November 1918 the Habsburg dynasty was deposed and the new republic was proclaimed.

The Czech story is only one example of the movement towards modern nationalism in which various groups were dreaming of their own nation state, characterised by their own language and culture. In this era Zionism also emerged, as did a strong sense of Irish nationalism.

Much of the new phenomenon of nationalism was emerging in opposition to imperial domination. This has been called the 'bent twig' theory of nationalism, which expostulates that it is a reaction to oppression and humiliation. It has been suggested that the "nationalism of Israelis and Palestinians may be so intractably strong because both are reacting against having been victims" (Irving Berlin quoted in Jonathan Glover, *Humanity: A Moral History of the Twentieth Century*, Jonathan Cape, 1999, p 146).

The nation states that did emerge created flags and national hymns and expected from their peoples ultimate loyalty to the point of laying down one's life for the sake of the nation. Nationalism became absolutist and gave birth to a twentieth century characterised by militarism and war which claimed more lives than all of the other centuries of recorded history put together. The latter part of the twentieth century also saw the brutality of regional and ethnic conflict.

Since national identity has been constructed in part by using a story from the past, this narrative can and has created conflict. Narratives are often either of defeat or victory. Narratives of defeat leave a sense of grievance, which has to be redressed. Narratives of victory stir resentment in those defeated. Such narratives can be identified at the heart of the history of Protestant–Catholic relationships in Northern Ireland, fuelling the spiral of conflict and hostility.

The creation of nation states is not a simple matter either. The problem is often like that of the Russian doll. "Inside one nation is a smaller one wanting to get out, but inside that second one is a yet smaller one wanting to get out" (Glover, pp 133–4). The former Yugoslavia is one example. Inside Yugoslavia, Croatia wants independence but inside Croatia, the Krazina wants independence. Serbia and Kosovo also illustrate the Russian doll problem.

Nationalism and nation states are complex, with minority concerns needing to be addressed. Alternative visions sometimes emerge. A vision of society rooted in liberty, equality and fraternity emerged from the French revolution. Against a model of society controlled by monarchy, privileged élite and powerful clergy, this vision of equality of rights and citizenship was developed. It was a vision for a more democratic order. It was defeated by violence and opposed by the church.

The 1798 Rebellion in Ireland was much influenced by the French Revolution and the American War of Independence. The vision here also was of equality, justice, freedom and parliamentary reform. It was a reaction to Protestant Ascendancy, the domination of the majority by a 10% minority who were the privileged and élite. Sectarian violence and military might ended the Irish alternative vision.

Though concepts of nationalism did not exist during the period of biblical history and cannot be read back into its narratives, there are models of experience dealing with the tensions around group purity. The texts chosen for reflection in this session are drawn from an important period in the history of the Hebrew people.

In 543 BCE the Edict of Cyrus allowed the exiles in Babylon to return to their homeland. Some of the background to this can be read in the notes from the series on 'Building Authentic Community for the 21st Century'.

Much of the tension around the reconstruction of community among the rubble and 'rabble' of Jerusalem was on issues of identity. Nehemiah's rebuilding of walls had to do, not only with security but with boundaries and the maintaining of boundaries. This was why all foreigners were expelled from the city before the beginning of the Sabbath and were not allowed back until the Sabbath ended.

Ezra focussed on the issue of inter-marriage between former Jewish exiles and those who lived in and around Jerusalem but were members of other ethnic groups. The 'holy seed' could not be mixed so legislation was enacted to enforce divorce of foreign wives. This obviously put these women outside the community and therefore left them socially and economically vulnerable. The injustice of that seemed secondary to or even justified by the purity of the identity ideology of Ezra. Some may argue that the serious situation faced by the former exiles made an emphasis on purity of identity inevitable. When backs are to the wall there is a retreat, even a necessary one to survive, to a sense of being pure people. Identity becomes a primary concern. This no doubt is what happens, but the right to identity can and sometimes does impose injustices on others.

The great literary renaissance of the exile and return had produced, among other writings, the final edited text of Deuteronomy. Permanent exclusion orders were declared in this community constitutional document against Ammonites and Moabites. These ancient enemies were never to be included within the boundaries of the pure Jewish people, yet this period also produced the protest literature of Ruth and Jonah. The love story which is Ruth has a more radical layer of meaning. It is a radical challenge to the Deuteronomic exclusion order and the legislation and policy of Ezra and Nehemiah. Ruth is no less than a Moabite who becomes part of great King David's ancestry. David has Moabite blood in his veins! So much for racial and ethnic purity! Ezra and Nehemiah, as well as the Deuteronomic editors, had forgotten parts of the people's narrative. The short story of Ruth is really subversive of the narrow exclusivism at work in post-exilic Judaism.

Alternative visions of identity and community are necessary. The competing visions are often exclusivist–inclusivist. Can they co-exist? Did the people of the return from exile ever resolve the problem?

Session 1 Plan

Welcome and introductions (10 minutes)

Group work exercise 1 (10 minutes)

Either reprographic copies of the following flags will be distributed to the group or they can be shown as separate overheads:

◆ Ulster Loyalist (red hand; crown)

◆ Ulster Provincial (red hand; yellow/red)

◆ Union (red/white/blue)

◆ Irish (green/white/orange)

(Flags from other European countries may be included to situate the theme of identity in a more international context.)

Working in small groups

1. Identify the symbolism of each flag.

2. Consider whose identity is represented by these flags.

Feedback (10 minutes)

Buzz and feedback (5 minutes)

What is nationalism?

Overheads (10 minutes)

The history of nationalism and creation of wars in the twentieth century

The challenge of alternative visions

Group work exercise 2 (15 minutes)

1. Since nationalism can become a defining ideology claiming ultimate loyalty, is there a place within a nation state for an alternative vision?

2. What role can alternative visions play in a nation state?

Feedback (10 minutes)

Biblical Reflection

Background information on texts (5 minutes)

Task:

Read the relevant texts:

Group 1: Ezra 9:1–4, 10:1–5; Nehemiah 13:1–3; Deuteronomy 23:3–5

Group 2: Ruth 1:1–18

Imagine that you are supporters of this community vision. Create a profile of the kind of community in Jerusalem you want and indicate why it should be this way.

Preparation time (10 minutes)

Role-play:

Each group will present and defend its community vision. (15 minutes)

Reflective discussion (10 minutes)

Consider the following questions:

1. How did you feel in your role?

2. What dynamics were operating between the groups?

3. Can you connect the role-play experience with a real life situation?

4. How do we deal with competing visions of identity and community?

Plenary (10 minutes)

An overhead or copy of the following will be shown/distributed to the group:

◆ South African flag

◆ European flag

Question for discussion:

How do we deal with competing visions of identity and community?

Session 1, Handout 5

Group work exercise 1

Working in small groups:

1. Identify the symbolism of each flag.

2. Consider whose identity is represented by these flags.

Overhead 1

History of nationalism and creation of wars in the twentieth century

◆ The late eighteenth century and early nineteenth century saw the demise of old empires and monarchies.

◆ In the nineteenth century various national movements arose in eastern Europe: Poles, Czechs, Slovaks, Serbs, Croatians and Lithuanians began agitating for national independence.

◆ In the nineteenth century Ireland also sought home rule or national independence.

◆ Various groups were dreaming of their own nation state characterised by their own language and culture.

◆ By the end of the nineteenth century political Zionism emerged with the idea of a Jewish state.

◆ Nationalism as we know it today was born in the nineteenth century, giving birth to the nation state where political power was concentrated in the hands of one or more ethnic communities within its boundaries.

◆ Nation states created flags, national anthems and expected from their peoples ultimate loyalty to the point of laying down one's life for the sake of the nation.

◆ Absolute nationalism and national interest gave birth to a twentieth century characterised by militarism and war which claimed more lives than all of the other centuries of recorded history put together.

◆ Nationalism is a collective group identity confined within national boundaries. Nationalism may become the dominant ideology for a group's claims for itself.

◆ A nation state is a structure in which political power is in the hands of one of more ethnic communities within it boundaries. A nation state may contain many nations, ie a multi-ethnic/multi-cultural nation.

Overhead 2

The challenge of alternative visions

◆ The French Revolution took place in 1789 against a society controlled by monarchy, privileged élite and powerful clergy.

◆ The Revolution's vision was expressed in the words 'Liberty, Equality, Fraternity'. It was a vision of equality of rights and citizenship.

◆ In 1798 the Irish Rebellion occurred, influenced by the events and values of the French Revolution and the American War of Independence.

◆ The United Irishmen wanted to create a society characterised by equality, justice and parliamentary reform. It would also unite Protestant, Catholic and Dissenter.

◆ The French and Irish alternative visions were overcome and destroyed by violence.

Session 1, Handout 6

Group work exercise 2

1. Since nationalism can become a defining ideology claiming ultimate loyalty, is there a place within a nation state for an alternative vision?

2. What role can alternative visions play in a nation state?

Session 1, Handout 7

Biblical reflection

Task:

Read the relevant texts:

◆ Group 1:   Ezra 9:1–4, 10:1–5; Nehemiah 13:1–3; Deuteronomy 23:3–5

◆ Group 2:   Ruth 1:1–18

Imagine that you are supporters of this community vision. Create a profile of the kind of community in Jerusalem you want and indicate why it should be this way.

Preparation time (10 minutes)

Role play – each group will present and defend its community vision. (15 minutes)

Reflective Plenary (10 minutes)

Consider the following questions.

1. How did you feel in your role?

2. What dynamics were operating between the groups?

3. Can you connect the role-play experience with a real life situation?

4. How do we deal with competing visions of identity and community?

Session 1, Handout 8

Background information on Ezra/Nehemiah

◆ In 543 BCE the decree of Cyrus allowed the return of exiled Jewish community to Jerusalem and the rebuilding of he temple.

◆ Ezra 1:2–4 is probably the text of Cyrus' proclamation in Hebrew.

◆ In 520 BCE a large group of exilic Jews returned to Jerusalem and began the rebuilding of the temple. It was completed in 515 BCE.

◆ Because Jerusalem remained unfortified and still had no economic or administrative infrastructure, the Persians sent Nehemiah as governor in 445 BCE.

◆ Nehemiah's main task was to rebuild the walls of Jerusalem, repopulate it by transferring people from the rural areas, and reform temple worship.

◆ Sometime after this and before 398 BCE Ezra arrived with 5,000 exilic Jews to Jerusalem.

◆ Ezra was largely concerned with shaping a new identity since the Jewish people had experienced the loss of national identity, independence and the destruction of their state.

◆ Crucial for Ezra and Nehemiah is purity of identity.

◆ Nehemiah's chief concern was with the rebuilding of the walls, which had to do with boundaries and ways in which the identity of the Jews could be maintained – for example, Nehemiah 13:19–22. Foreigners were expelled from Jerusalem before the beginning of Sabbath and were kept outside until it ended.

◆ Ezra is focussed on inter-marriage, which he declares to be a violation of the Torah since it leads to the mixing of the 'holy seed' with the people of "the lands". Foreign wives therefore are to be divorced and put outside the community.

◆ The final text of Deuteronomy was edited and completed around this time. In Deuteronomy 23:3–5 Ammonites and Moabites were to be excluded from the Assembly of the Lord even to the tenth generation because they were ancient enemies of Israel. To the tenth generation means they were to be permanently excluded. This permanent exclusion order against Moabites is radically challenged by the short story of Ruth, a Moabite who is included in King David's ancestry.

◆ For Ezra/Nehemiah the vision of community was one of ethnic purity and exclusion.

Session 1, Handout 9

Background information on Ruth

◆ At one level the book of Ruth is about the wonder of human love, loyalty and affection.

◆ At another level the book is political and is countering an exclusivist vision of community.

◆ Though the book of Ruth has been written during the post-exilic rebuilding of Jerusalem, the story is set in a much earlier period when Israel was a confederation of tribes.

◆ Naomi is a Judean woman driven to Moab by famine. She is widowed in Moab. Her two sons marry Moabite women and then prematurely die. Naomi is now responsible for her two Moabite daughters-in-law. She decides to return to Bethlehem and one of her daughters-in-law, Ruth, pledges loyalty and decides to accompany her.

◆ In Bethlehem, Ruth marries Boaz and becomes the great-grandmother of King David.

◆ The story of Ruth is a piece of protest literature opposing Ezra's ethnic purity policies. It has been described as "a subtle piece of propaganda against the view that one's position within Israel was dependent upon purity of blood or correctness of genealogy. For God's greatest favour was bestowed upon Israel through a mixed marriage – the very thing Nehemiah and Ezra frowned upon!" (Bernhard Anderson, *Understanding the Old Testament*, 4th ed, 1986, p 492).

◆ A charming love story is in reality subversive of the narrow exclusivism at work (ethnic/nationalist) in post-exilic Judaism.

Session 1, Handout 10

Ezra 9:1–4; 10:1–5

[1] After these things had been done, the officials approached me and said, 'The people of Israel, the priests, and the Levites have not separated themselves from the peoples of the lands with their abominations, from the Canaanites, the Hittites, the Perizzites, the Jebusites, the Ammonites, the Moabites, the Egyptians, and the Amorites. [2] For they have taken some of their daughters as wives for themselves and for their sons. Thus the holy seed has mixed itself with the peoples of the lands, and in this faithlessness the officials and leaders have led the way.' [3] When I heard this, tore my garment and my mantle, and pulled hair from my head and beard, and sat appalled. [4] Then all who trembled at the words of the God of Israel, because of the faithlessness of the returned exiles, gathered around me while I sat appalled until the evening sacrifice . . . Chapter 10 While Ezra prayed and made confession, weeping and throwing himself down before the house of God, a very great assembly of men, women, and children gathered to him out of Israel; the people also wept bitterly. [2] Shecaniah son of Jehiel, of the descendants of Elam, addressed Ezra, saying, 'We have broken faith with our God and have married foreign women from the peoples of the Land, but even now there is hope for Israel in spite of this. [3] So now let us make a covenant with our God to send away all these wives and their children, according to the counsel of my lord and of those who tremble at the commandment of our God; and let it be done according to the law. [4] Take action, for it is your duty, and we are with you; be strong, and do it.' [5] Then Ezra stood up and made the leading priests, the Levites, and all Israel swear that they would do as had been said. So they swore.

NRSV Bible

Session 1, Handout 11

Nehemiah 13:1–3

[1] On that day they read from the book of Moses in the hearing of the people; and in it was found written that no Ammonite or Moabite should enter the assembly of God, [2] because they did not meet the Israelites with bread and water, but hired Balaam against them to curse them – yet our God turned the curse into a blessing. [3] When the people heard the law, they separated from Israel all those of foreign descent.

NRSV Bible

Deuteronomy 23:3–5

[3] No Ammonite or Moabite shall be admitted to the assembly of the Lord. Even to the tenth generation, none of their descendants shall be admitted to the assembly of the Lord, [4] because they did not meet you with food and water on your journey out of Egypt, and because they hired against you Baalam son of Beor, from Pethor of Mesopotamia, to curse you. ([5] Yet the Lord your God refused to heed Baalam; the Lord your God turned the curse into a blessing for you, because the Lord your God loved you.)

NRSV Bible

Session 1, Handout 12

Ruth 1:1–18

[1] In the days when the Judges ruled, there was a famine in the land, and a certain man of Bethlehem in Judah went to live in the country of Moab, he and his wife and two sons. [2] The name of the man was Elimelech , the husband of Naomi, and the names of his two sons were Mahlon and Chilion; they were Ephrathites from Bethlehem in Judah. They went into the country of Moab and remained there. [3] But Elimelech, the husband of Naomi, died, and she was left with her two sons. [4] These took Moabite wives; the name of one was Orpah and the name of the other Ruth. When they had lived there for about ten years, [5] both Mahlon and Chilion also died, so that the woman was left without her two sons or her husband.

[6] Then she started to return with her daughters-in-law from the country of Moab, for she had heard in the country of Moab that the Lord had had consideration for his people and given them food. [7] So she set out from the place where she had been living, she and her two daughters-in-law, and they went on their way to go back to the land of Judah. [8] But Naomi said to her two daughters-in-law, 'Go back each of you to your mother's house. May the Lord deal kindly with you, as you have dealt with the dead and with me. [9] The Lord grant that you may find security, each of you in the house of your husband.' Then she kissed them, and they wept aloud. [10] They said to her, 'No, we will return with you to your people.' [11] But Naomi said, 'Turn back, my daughters, why will you go with me? Do I still have sons in my womb that they may become your husbands? [12] Turn back, my daughters; go your way, for I am too old to have a husband. Even if I thought there was hope for me, even if I should have a husband tonight and bear sons, [13] would you then wait until they were grown? Would you then refrain from marrying? No, my daughters, it has been far more bitter for me than for you, because the hand of the Lord has turned against me.' [14] Then they wept aloud again. Orpah kissed her mother-in-law, but Ruth clung to her. [15] So she said, 'See, your sister-in-law has gone back to her people and to her gods; return after your sister-in-law.' [16] But Ruth said, 'Do not press me to leave you or to turn back from following you! Where you go, I will go; where you lodge, I will lodge; your people shall be my people, and your God my God. [17] Where you die, I will die – there will I be buried. May the Lord do thus and so to me, and more as well, if even death parts me from you!' [18] When Naomi saw that she was determined to go with her, she said no more to her.

NRSV Bible

Session 2 Introduction

Religion and nationalism

Today there are more than 50 ethnic conflicts going on in the world. They have a multiplicity of causes, one of which is religion. Indeed religion is involved in most of them. This has been described as the "weakening influence of traditional religion and ideology, coupled with a growth of new religions and fundamentalism" (Theo Tschuy, *Ethnic Conflict and Religion: Challenge to the Churches*, WCC, 1997, p x). The relation between ethnic conflicts and religion is a challenging one. It is easier to attempt denial of the role of religion than to acknowledge how it has legitimised and fuelled ethnic and nationalistic conflicts. A World Council of Churches Working Group on Racism, Indigenous Peoples and Ethnicity recognised in 1996 that while "churches have sometimes provided identity and security to threatened communities, the report of this meeting notes that churches have also given support and legitimation to ethnic and national values and élites which threaten other ethnic groups" (Ibid, pp xiii–xiv). The report claimed that "Churches provide legitimacy for the re-emergence of ethnic nationalism . . . Some churches, while professing conciliatory intervention, are often feeding the very conflicts (frequently violent) which they are supposed to conciliate" (Ibid, p xiv).

All of this happens where religion is a key factor which shapes the identity and ethos of a community. The examples are obvious. When the Serbian forces invaded Croatia, they destroyed many Catholic churches and attacked monasteries. The Serbs were Orthodox. When the Serbs surrounded Sarajevo, they destroyed thousands of Islamic and Jewish manuscripts. Serbs and Croats destroyed Islamic sites in Bosnia which included more than 800 mosques. When Catholic Croatian forces attacked Serbia, villagers were locked in the Orthodox church and burned alive.

The medieval Crusades were fought in the name of religion and have left a legacy to the present between Christians and Muslims. Christian anti-Semitism stretches back centuries and has not gone away. In many of these conflict zones nationalism, ethnic identity and religion are key factors. This is also true in Northern Ireland. The stronger the religious identity, the more intense can be the hostility and conflict.

The British national motto and the preamble to the 1937 Irish constitution are cited in this session as examples of religion being merged with national identities. Other examples could be cited, such as the German constitution and the motto on the back of an American dollar bill. Of course there is a critical question to be asked: who is the God of these mottos and constitutions? Is this a Christian concept of God or a God made in the national image? The Jesus of the Irish constitution seems suspiciously like a 1916 Easter Rising model! The God of 'For God and Ulster' sounds more like a UVF chaplain!

It is not just that religion is used or abused for imperial, political or ideological ends. Religion is sometimes a willing accomplice, either by overt legitimacy or a conspiracy of silence. For religious people and churches there is no neutrality here.

A 1994 consultation in Sri Lanka representing 21 countries faced up to the challenge to the churches.

The church is challenged constantly and critically to search the Scriptures as it seeks to understand ethnicity and nationalism, opening itself to new insights and acknowledging where it has abused Scripture to justify its own understanding of ethnicity and nationalism . . . The church is challenged to reassess critically its own history and evaluate its own involvement in ethnic conflicts and in nationalistic desires for power.

(Report in full in Tschuy pp 150–6, quotation from p 154.)

The biblical focus is in the clash between royal theology and the radical Mosaic covenant theology. The former is embodied by Solomon and the critique of the status quo theology he bequeathed to the people of Israel is from the sixth-century prophet Jeremiah. Background notes to these two theologies can be found in the course 'Being authentic community for the twenty-first century' and in the two sessions 'Solomon's temple: house of cards or household of God?' and 'Delusions of grandeur'.

The texts from 1 Kings provide a profile of the economic, political and religious practice of Solomon and the royal court. His nationalisation of God is particularly significant. His religion was the religion of God's captivity. Solomon developed a model of civil religion and was less a paradigm of wisdom and more a political fool.

Jeremiah's alternative theology is in sharp contrast. Radical conservative that he was, he appealed to the old Mosaic covenant which was a radical socio-economic and political vision for society. In this covenant, God was radically free and was not at the disposal of any system, institution or power arrangement. God was never to be confined or made captive by any economic, religious or political system, nor was any system to be given ultimate allegiance. The covenant invoked by Jeremiah was in fact subversive of any ultimate claims. It is this covenant theology which subverts the claims of nationalism, especially absolute nationalism. It both subverts and critiques the active and passive roles of religion in nationalism.

The core covenant words used by Jeremiah are the essential values for a community of integrity. Covenant is essentially about the horizontal and social relationships. The core covenant values are rooted in the nature of God. As the church is challenged to reassess critically its own history and evaluate its involvement in ethnic conflicts and nationalistic desires and dreams, it may also need to realise that "there will be no new community on earth until there is a fresh articulation of who God is" (Walter Brueggemann, *A Social Reading of the Old Testament: Prophetic Approaches to Israel's Communal Life*, Fortress Press, 1994, p 47).

Session 2 Plan

Welcome (5 minutes)

Small group work on what is nationalism? (5 minutes)

Feedback (5 minutes)

Overhead (5 minutes)

Religion and nationalism

Questions for clarification (5 minutes)

Overhead (15 minutes)

Critiquing Royal Theology

Questions for clarification (5 minutes)

Group work exercise 1 (30 minutes)

You have been given responsibility to govern a nation state. Your model of nation state is to be based on either royal or covenant theology.

Draw a diagram to illustrate how you will organise your nation state. Show how your nation state will be structured economically, politically and religiously and how its relationships and networks will look. Give your nation state a name.

Feedback (15 minutes)

Overhead (5 minutes)

Abuses of Covenant theology

Questions for clarification (5 minutes)

Plenary (20 minutes)

1. How have these covenant theologies abused God?

2. What should the relationship be between religion and nationalism?

Overhead 1

Religion and nationalism

◆ Nationalism as we know it today was born in the nineteenth century, giving birth to the nation state where political power was concentrated in the hands of one or more ethnic communities within its boundaries.

◆ Nation states created flags, national anthems and expected from their peoples ultimate loyalty to the point of laying down one's life for the sake of the nation.

◆ Absolute nationalism and national interest gave birth to a twentieth century characterised by militarism and war which claimed more lives than all of the other centuries of recorded history put together.

◆ British motto:

'For God and the Empire' – enscribed on honours awards for outstanding service.

◆ Preamble to the Constitution of Ireland (1937):

In the Name of the Most Holy Trinity, from Whom is all authority and to Whom, at our final end, all actions both of men and States must be referred. We, the people of Éire, humbly acknowledging all our obligations to our Divine Lord, Jesus Christ, who sustained our fathers through centuries of trial, gratefully remembering their heroic and unremitting struggle to regain the rightful independence of our Nation, and seeking to promote the common good, with due observance of Prudence, Justice and Charity, so that the dignity and freedom of the individual may be assured, true social order attained, the unity of the country restored, and concord established with other nations do hereby adopt, enact, and give ourselves this Constitution.

Questions for consideration

1. Who is the God of the British Motto? Who is the God of the Irish constitution?

2. Is there a place for God in national mottos and constitutions?

Overhead 2

Critiquing royal theology

Jeremiah Chapter 9:23–4

[23] Thus says the Lord: 'Do not let the wise boast in their wisdom, do not let the mighty boast in their might, do not let the wealthy boast in their wealth; [24] but let those who boast boast in this, that they understand and know me, that I am the Lord; I act with steadfast love, justice and righteousness in the earth, for in these things I delight', says the Lord.

NRSV Bible

◆ Jeremiah is critiquing the dominant royal theology by using the Mosaic covenant theology.

◆ In the Hebrew Scriptures these two theologies are in constant tension.

Royal theology

◆ Jeremiah uses three words to describe the Royal theology.

1. Riches – the royal prerogative, gift to the king and mark of a good king.

2. Might – the royal establishment imposing its will no one may challenge. The royal establishment created the myth of its own powerfulness and imposed its power through militarism.

3. Wisdom – is not about discerning good and evil but the capacity to manage and control the people in a self-serving way. All of reality is defined by the Royal court.

◆ This Royal theology began with Solomon (tenth century) and became the dominant theology within Israel until 587 BCE when the kingdom and monarchy were destroyed by the Babylonians.

Session 2, Handout 1

Group work exercise 1

You have been given responsibility to govern a nation state. Your model of nation state is to be based on either royal or covenant theology.

Draw a diagram to illustrate how you will organise your nation state. Show how your nation state will be structured economically, politically and religiously and how its relationships and networks will look. Give your nation state a name.

Reflective questions after feedback

1. What role does God have in your nation state

2. How is God envisioned and why?

Session 2, Handout 2

Solomon's royal theology

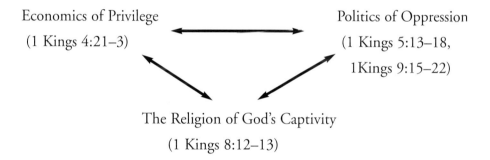

Economics of Privilege
(1 Kings 4:21–3)

Politics of Oppression
(1 Kings 5:13–18,
1Kings 9:15–22)

The Religion of God's Captivity
(1 Kings 8:12–13)

1. Solomon replaced the economics of equality with the economics of privilege.

2. Solomon replaced the politics of justice with the politics of oppression.

3 Solomon replaced the religion of God's radical freedom with the religion of God's captivity.

a) By making God a captive of the temple, Solomon used God to legitimise his economics and politics.

b) By controlling God within the temple, the economically and politically oppressed had no court of divine appeal or voice of protest.

Session 2, Handout 3

Solomon's royal theology

1. Economics of privilege: 1 Kings 4:21–3

[21] Solomon was sovereign over all the kingdoms from the Euphrates to the land of the Philistines, even to the border of Egypt; they brought tribute and served Solomon all the days of his life. [22] Solomon's provision for one day was thirty cors of choice flour, and sixty cors of meal, [23] ten fat oxen, and twenty pasture-fed cattle, one hundred sheep, besides dear, gazelles, roebucks, and fatted fowl . . .

NRSV Bible

2. Politics of oppression: 1 Kings 5:13–18

[13] King Solomon conscripted forced labour out of all Israel; the levy numbered thirty thousand men. [14] He sent them to the Lebanon, ten thousand a month in shifts; they would be a month in the Lebanon and two months at home; Adoniram was in charge of the forced labour. [15] Solomon also had seventy thousand labourers and eighty thousand stonecutters in the hill country, [16] besides Solomon's three thousand three hundred supervisors who were over the work, having charge of the people who did the work. [17] At the king's command, they quarried out great, costly stones in order to lay the foundation of the house with dressed stones. [18] So Solomon's builders and Hiram's builders and the Gebalites did the stonecutting and prepared the timber and the stone to build the house.

NRSV Bible

Session 2, Handout 4

I Kings 9:15–22

[15] This is the account of the forced labour that King Solomon conscripted to build the house of the Lord and his own house, the Millo and the wall of Jerusalem, Hazor, Megiddo, Gezer [16] (Pharaoh king of Egypt had gone up and captured Gezer and burned it down, had killed the Canaanites who lived in the city, and had given it as dowry to his daughter, Solomon's wife; [17] so Solomon rebuilt Gezer), Lower Beth-horon, [18] Baalath, Tamar in the wilderness, within the land, [19] as well as all of Solomon's storage cities, the cities for his chariots, the cities for his cavalry, and whatever Solomon desired to build, in Jerusalem, in Lebanon, and in all the land of his dominion. [20] All the people who were left of the Amorites, the Hittites, the Perizzites, the Hevites, and the Jebusites, who were not of the people of Israel – [21] their descendants who were still left in the land, whom the Israelites were unable to destroy completely – these Solomon conscripted for slave labour, and so they are to this day. [22] But of the Israelites Solomon made no slaves; they were the soldiers, they were his officials, his commanders, his captains, and the commanders of his chariotry and cavalry.

NRSV Bible

3. The religion of God's captivity: 1 Kings 8:12–13

¹² Then Solomon said, 'The Lord has said that he would dwell in thick darkness. ¹³ I have built you an exalted house, a place for you to dwell for ever.'

NRSV Bible

Session 2, Handout 5

Mosaic covenant theology

◆ Jeremiah offers a radical critique of the Royal theology/ideology.

◆ The alternative theology is based on the covenant of Moses at Sinai.

◆ The alternative theology has two reference points.

1. To understand and know Yahweh. In the Mosaic covenant, God is radically free and can never be confined or made captive by any economic, religious or political system.

2. The Mosaic covenant requires ultimate allegiance to God alone and never to any economic, religious or political system.

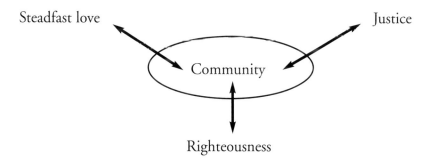

◆ Steadfast love (Hesed) – commitment to total well-being of each person in community; mutual solidarity and compassion.

◆ Justice (Mispat) – not punitive but restorative, distributive and transformative justice; it's about social and political equality.

◆ Righteousness (Sedaqa) – right relations based on justice and compassion.

Overhead 3

Abuses of covenant theology

South Africa

◆ Settler theology was Dutch Reformed theology, with an emphasis on being God's chosen people in the promised land.

◆ This covenant theology produced the doctrine of apartheid which became a system of domination and oppression against the majority black community.

◆ "The white missionaries taught us to pray and when we opened our eyes our land had gone." (Archbishop Desmond Tutu)

USA

◆ In the seventeenth century the Pilgrim Fathers left England and arrived in their new land of freedom and opportunity.

◆ They brought with them a strong covenant theology in which they now perceived themselves as God's chosen people in their promised land.

◆ This covenant theology was closely connected to the new-found economic prosperity which was exclusively identified with white Europeans.

◆ This covenant theology became the basis of the American dream of freedom and prosperity, though in reality equality of opportunity was a myth.

Northern Ireland

◆ The Ulster Plantation of 1609 brought mainly Scottish Presbyterians to the north-east of Ireland. They came with their strong Calvanistic covenantal theology.

◆ Anglicanism, already the established Church in Ireland, was also strongly Calvinistic at that time.

◆ The essence of this theology was a doctrine of predestination, sometimes double predestination, closely associated with being in the promised land.

◆ For an insecure settler people, this theology shaped identity and provided a sense of superiority and dominance.

◆ Hard work and economic prosperity were perceived as signs of being God's chosen people.

◆ Again a theological vision became a social and economic vision based on separation, inequality, superiority and injustice.

Plenary questions

1. How have these covenant theologies abused God?

2. What should the relationship be between religion and nationalism?

Session 2, Handout 6

Plenary questions

1. How have these covenant theologies abused God?

2. What should the relationship be between religion and nationalism?

Session 3 Introduction

The underside of globalisation

Globalisation is a fact of life. It is the inevitable consequence of air travel, satellite communication, the television age, information technology, all of which have helped to 'shrink' the planet. In the twenty-first century, people live in a global city, a global community. Our neighbours are no longer merely those in the same street, but people from once far away places who have now become our 'technological' neighbours.

There are positive sides to this. There is more opportunity than ever to experience a richer diversity of culture. There are opportunities to exchange cultures and information. I can communicate instantly with a business partner or a relative on the other side of the globe.

There are, however, negatives which are becoming all too apparent. The major negative is bound up with economics and capital. Global capitalism is the great reality of our time, yet only 20% of the world's population enjoy the fruits of the global economy. A staggering 80% still struggle to live and are slipping into deeper poverty. Global capitalism has become the new religion. Corporations expanded beyond the borders of their countries looking for new markets and cheap labour. Unregulated access to natural resources have had consequences for the environment, often the environment of those being exploited. Corporations were transformed into multinationals and have now become transnationals. The latter are, in effect, stateless. They transcend the limitations on capital imposed by nation states and pursue the free market. Economic globalisation, in fact, bypasses the sovereignty of nation states. Governments are no longer really in control of economics.

Globalisation is supported by a world financial system: "A few global computer systems located in New York, London, and Belgium allow money to flow freely around the world each day, independent of government regulation or control" (Wes Howard-Brooke and Anthony Gwyther, *Unveiling Empire: Reading Revelation Then and Now*, Orbis, 1999, p 240). Global capital in the shape of the General Agreement on Tariffs and Trade and the World Trade Organisation now control governments while national control bankers are well-nigh powerless in the face of the seemingly absolute power held by corporate bodies.

The vices of global capital are numerous. There is the power of marketing and media to create illusion. There is also the seduction of the economic empire, the attractiveness of material wealth and comfort. The ideology of global capital becomes a substitute for true religion. The worshipping of its idols is the twenty-first-century idolatry.

Globalisation is also marked by homogenisation, the squeezing of everyone into a single global culture of sameness, but based on consumption. The icons of this consumption are well-known: clothing, food and entertainment.

The challenge of globalisation in its negative and destructive forms is to develop an ethics of resistance. Two biblical texts may provide a basis for such an ethic.

The temptations of Jesus (Luke 4:1–13) are well-known but perhaps rarely understood as a model of resistance to the seductive empire of the evil one. In the Gospels they are situated after the baptism of Jesus and just before he begins his public ministry. The desert experience is often read from an individualistic perspective and usually spiritualised. The intensity of the struggle is often missed. Jesus was struggling with the very nature and purpose of his ministry. What kind of leader would he be? Each of the temptations reflect a very real expectation of a Jewish leader in first-century Palestine. In a debt-laden society where 95% of the Galilean population was in economic slavery, it would have been popular to have presented oneself as an economic messiah. Jumping from the temple pinnacle would have been spectacular but would have diverted the people from facing into the real issues of the time. The Romans, after all, could provide bread and circuses. The escapism of entertainment or modern-day sport is a sedative against the pain of where people are and also an opium that does not empower for transformation and change. Power and its use are always crucial. The abuse of power is a way to build the empire, especially through violence and domination.

Jesus faced all of these temptations and rejected them all, drawing his inspiration from Deuteronomy with its insights into authentic community and its rootedness in social justice. Jesus was not unconcerned with bread. The Lord's Prayer prayed in a situation of intense poverty, and hunger was not about a spiritualisation of daily bread. Yet quick fix economic miracles do not deal with the deepest needs of community. All three temptations deal with the use of power, indeed the temptations to abuse power, be it economic, political or cultural power.

The story of Luke does not suggest that Jesus faced these temptations only at the beginning of his ministry: "When the devil had finished every test, he departed from him until an opportune time." The struggle with the use and abuse of power was there until the end.

The Revelation text (chapter 18) may surprise. That part of this otherwise strange book is concerned with the seduction of economic empire is not how it is usually read. Revelation is either treated as a kind of 'Old Moore's Almanac', a happy hunting ground for those who see apocalypse now around the next corner. Or, perhaps most in the faith community have given up on making any sense of the book and have left it to the crystal ball gazers. It is a much more profound book than either approach realises.

Revelation is not a book about the 'end'. It was a book written in the genre of Jewish apocalypse as a pastoral response to a situation in which the seven churches of Asia Minor found themselves. The great dominating power is 'Babylon', the Roman Empire. Each of the seven churches has been challenged in different ways to clarify and work out its relationship with the 'great city'. All except two of the churches are guilty of collusion with imperial power. Only Smyrna and Philadelphia are not called to repent. They are to persevere in their ethic of resistance to empire and embrace more deeply God's alternative way. The nature of the collusion by the other five churches is not only in relation to political power, but to the economic seduction of the empire. The churches had compromised themselves and their faith on the economics of the empire.

Revelation is a book essentially about power and justice. It is a "call to have faith in God rather than empire" (Howard-Brooke and Gwyther, p xxiii). These faith communities are to resist the political domination of Rome and the economic seduction and domination of the same empire. Chapter 13 is about resistance to dominating and absolutist political power. Chapter 18 is about resistance to the economic and commodity exploitation of Babylon. The book as a whole was calling on the faith communities of Asia Minor to resist the political and economic oppression of the Roman Empire (Babylon).

In the important eighteenth chapter, Babylon is depicted as practising economic exploitation. Its affluence is described as opulent. The empire is like a woman clothed in purple and scarlet and gilded with gold and precious stones and pearls (17:4). Its affluence is seductive and the text offers a damming critique of its arrogance and exploitation. A list of luxury goods and ordinary commodities is provided in 18:12–13. The empire controls the market. It not only completely controls the commodity market but also controls the bodies and souls of its consumers. Buying and selling are not only the very essence of being human; bodies and souls are owned by the economic empire. I consume, therefore I am but the consumer becomes enslaved by the seduction of economic empire.

In ancient Rome 'bodies' were slaves. They were not persons but rather commodities. But Babylon also traded in human souls. The economic empire defined the very essence of humanity. The empire's economics had become a system of domination. It 'stamped' the people as it would certify the deeds of sale. They belonged to the empire, were owned and possessed by it.

Within the larger perspectives of reality, the alternative reality of the divine empire, John uses rhetorical style language to see Babylon as already fallen. The political and economic power of empire has within it the seeds of its own destruction. It becomes drunk with its own arrogant and absolutist myth of power (18:10):

Alas, alas, the great city,

Babylon, the mighty city!

For in one hour your judgement has come.

The kings, traders and seafarers, those who have made their economic fortunes, mourn. The faith community is called to come out of Babylon, resist its seductive power and create alternative lifestyles and systems.

Part of the judgement on Babylon is that economic empires cannot be built at the price of social justice. Economic progress and social justice belong together.

Economics, like much religion, is rooted in individualism. The individualism of the Enlightenment was also true of the Protestant Reformation. It was the right of the individual to approach God directly, without the help of clergy or church. Modern economics bought into this and wedded religious insights with those of political science. The individual can pursue her or his own economic interests.

It is the concept of community that has suffered at the hands of individualism. Though human beings live in community such as family, city or nation, the sense of community has broken down. Ironically from a biblical perspective, the Scripture story is strongly communitarian. Modern religious individualism managed to lose its biblical roots. Modernity is characterised by individualism. Margaret Thatcher claimed that there was no such thing as community! What became known as Thatcherism, the economics, was thoroughly individualistic.

Robert Bellah, the American sociologist, claims with justification that "the strong sense of community generated by our early biblical and civic republican traditions no longer functions" (in Sallie McFague, *Life Abundant: Rethinking Theology and Economy for a Planet in Peril*, Fortress Press, 2001, p 82). Bellah is writing from within the American experience, but his insight is recognisable in a European context. What has the phenomenon of the 'Celtic tiger' done to the sense of community and solidarity in Irish society?

It is the recovery of the worth of the individual within community that is needed. If modern economics is often destructive of community and therefore that individual's worth and dignity, then the faith perspective ought to be critical and engage in an ethic of resistance.

Session 3 Plan

Welcome (5 minutes)

Buzz and feedback (10 minutes)

What is globalisation?

Overhead (5 minutes)

Globalisation

Questions of clarification (5 minutes)

Group work exercise 1 on Luke 4 (15 minutes)

Feedback and group discussion (20 minutes)

Overhead (5 minutes)

The economic world view

Questions of clarification (5 minutes)

Read Revelation 18:1–24 (5 minutes)

Overhead (5 minutes)

Revelation – the ethics of resistance

Questions of clarification (5 minutes)

Group work exercise 2 on Creating a Credo (20 minutes)

Feedback and group discussion (15 minutes)

Overhead 1

Globalisation

Characteristics of globalisation:

◆ The increasingly interconnected character of the political, economic and social life of the people on the planet.

◆ Post-1989 allowed for a worldwide expansion of global economy, which ignored national boundaries, moved capital quickly, engaged in short-term projects to maximise the profit margin.

◆ Twenty per cent of the world's population enjoy the fruits of global capitalism. Eighty per cent struggle to live and are slipping into deeper poverty.

◆ Communication technologies mean the instant communication of messages and information around the world.

◆ Homogenisation of global cultures is marked by hyper-culture (dominant overarching culture) based on consumption.

◆ The icons of consumption are clothing, food and entertainment eg denim jeans, McDonald's, Coca-Cola, films/videos etc.

◆ Economic globalisation bypasses the sovereignty of nation states.

Session 3, Handout 1

The underside of globalisation

Luke 4:1–13

[1] Jesus, full of the Holy Spirit, returned from the Jordan and was led by the Spirit in the wilderness, [2] where for forty days he was tempted by the devil. He ate nothing at all during those days, and when they were over, he was famished. [3] The devil said to him, 'If you are the Son of God, command this stone to become a loaf of bread.' [4] Jesus answered him, 'It is written, 'One does not live by bread alone.' [5] Then the devil led him up and showed him in an instant all the kingdoms of the world. [6] And the devil said to him, 'To you I will give their glory and all this authority; for it has been given over to me, and I give it to anyone I please. [7] If you, then, will worship me, it will all be yours.' [8] Jesus answered him, 'It is written, 'Worship the Lord your God, and serve only him.' [9] Then the devil took him to Jerusalem, and placed him on the pinnacle of the temple, saying to him, 'If you are the Son of God, throw yourself down from here, [10] for it is written, 'He will command his angels concerning you to protect you,' [11] and 'On their hands they will bear you up, so that you will not dash your foot against a stone.' [12] Jesus answered him, 'It is said, 'Do not put the Lord your God to the test.' [13] When the devil had finished every test, he departed from him until an opportune time.

NRSV Bible

Session 3, Handout 2

The underside of globalisation

Group work exercise 1

Luke 4:1–13

Task:

Working in four groups read the text.

◆ Group 1 from the perspective of the multinationals.

◆ Group 2 from the perspective of the 20% rich.

◆ Group 3 from the perspective of the 80% poor.

◆ Group 4 from the perspective of the Jesus community.

Feedback

Group discussion:

1. How can we respond to globalisation?

2. What difficulties do we face in responding?

Feedback

Overhead 2

The underside of globalisation

The economic world view:

◆ Human beings are self-interested individuals.

◆ Will create a machine (global) capable of benefiting all eventually.

◆ As long as economy grows, all individuals in society will eventually participate.

◆ Human nature is individualistic and the goal is growth.

◆ View comes from Enlightenment and Reformation (individualism).

◆ Religious contribution to economics – sacredness of individual and sinfulness of all before God, ie greed, selfishness.

◆ Political science contribution – 'rights of man' – life, liberty and the pursuit of happiness.

◆ Economics combined these to create a new person – one who has the freedom to pursue his or her own personal economic interests.

◆ Twenty-first-century economic individual exists outside community.

◆ Strong biblical sense of community has been lost.

◆ Biblical covenant model balances individual rights with responsibilities for larger good.

◆ Assumptions about human life, rights and responsibilities no longer begin with the strong sense of solidarity towards others.

◆ We live in communities, cities, countries, but the image we have of human life is not fundamentally relational.

Session 3, Handout 3

The underside of globalisation

Revelation 18:1–24

[1] After this I saw another angel coming down from heaven, having great authority; and the earth was made bright with his splendour. [2] He called out with a mighty voice, 'Fallen, fallen is Babylon the great! It has become a dwelling place of demons, a haunt of every foul spirit, a haunt of every foul bird, a haunt of every foul and hateful beast. [3] For all the nations have drunk of the wine of the wrath of her fornication, and the kings of the earth have committed fornication with her, and the merchants of the earth have grown rich from the power of her luxury.' [4] Then I heard another voice from heaven saying, 'Come out of her, my people, so that you do not take part in her sins, and so that you do not share in her plagues; [5] for her sins are heaped high as heaven, and God has remembered her iniquities. [6] Render to her as she herself has rendered, and repay her double for her deeds; mix a double draught for her in the cup she mixed. [7] As she glorified herself and lived luxuriously, so give her a like measure of torment and grief', [8] therefore her plagues will come in a single day – pestilence and mourning and famine – and she will be burned with a fire; for mighty is the Lord God who judges her.' [9] And the kings of the earth, who committed fornication and lived in luxury with her, will weep and wail over her when they see the smoke of her burning; [10] they will stand far off, in fear of her torment, and say, 'Alas, alas, the great city, Babylon, the mighty city! For in one hour your judgement has come.' [11] And the merchants of the earth weep and mourn for her, since no one buys their cargo any more, [12] cargo of gold, silver, jewels and pearls, fine linen, purple, silk and scarlet, all kinds of scented wood, all articles of ivory, all articles of costly wood, bronze, iron and marble, [13] cinnamon, spice, incense, myrrh, frankincense, wine, olive oil, choice flour and wheat, cattle and sheep, horses and chariots, slaves – and human lives. [14] 'The fruit for which your soul longed has gone from you, and all your dainties and your splendour are lost to you, never to be found again?' [15] The merchants of these wares, who gained wealth from her, will stand far off, in fear of her torment, weeping and

mourning aloud, [16] 'Alas, alas, the great city, clothed in fine linen, in purple and scarlet, adorned with gold, with jewels, and with pearls! [17] For in one hour all this wealth has been laid waste!' And all shipmasters and seafarers, sailors and all whose trade is on the sea, stood far off [18] and cried out as they saw the smoke of her burning, 'What city was like the great city?' [19] And they threw dust on their heads, as they wept and mourned, crying out, 'Alas, alas, the great city, where all who had ships at sea grew rich by her wealth! For in one hour she has been laid waste!' [20] Rejoice over her, O heaven, you saints and apostles and prophets! For God has given judgement for you against her. [21] Then a mighty angel took up a stone like a great millstone and threw it into the sea, saying, 'With such violence, Babylon the great city will be thrown down, and will be found no more; [22] and the sound of harpists and minstrels and of flautists and trumpeters will be heard in you no more; [23] and the light of a lamp will shine in you no more; and the voice of bridegroom and bride will be heard in you no more; for your merchants were the magnates of the earth, and all nations were deceived by your sorcery. [24] And in you was found the blood of prophets and of saints, and of all who have been slaughtered on earth.'

NRSV Bible

Overhead 3

The underside of globalisation

Revelation 18 – the ethics of resistance

◆ A book calling for resistance to the political and economic oppression of the Roman Empire (Babylon).

◆ Revelation 18 – Babylon as economic exploiter.

　1. Seductive affluence of Babylon.

　2. Critique of economic arrogance and exploitation.

◆ Revelation 18:12–13 – list of luxury goods and ordinary commodities.

　1. Imperial economy has grasped everything.

　2. Trading in bodies and human souls.

◆ Bodies = slaves – not human but commodities.

◆ Human souls – buying and selling the very essence of humanity.

◆ Bodies and souls are owned by the economic empire – I consume, therefore I am.

◆ Babylon is fallen – mourned by kings, traders and seafarers.

◆ Revelation 18:4–5 – come out of Babylon.

　1. Faith community is to resist the seduction of oppressive economic empire.

　2. Refuse to participate – create alternatives.

　3. Five of the seven churches had compromised their social justice integrity and were seduced by the

economy of the empire

◆ Economic progress will not be bought at the price of social justice.

◆ Economic progress and social justice belong together.

Session 3, Handout 4

The underside of globalisation

Group work exercise 2

A credo is an expression of one's core values, the values that really matter.

Task:

Working in small groups, compose a shared credo that expresses agreed core values on ethical economics.

Feedback

Plenary question:

How can our credos become action points?

Session 4 — Introduction

The myth of redemptive violence

Myths are to be found in every culture. The popular notion of a myth as a fairy tale or an unbelievable story is wide of the mark. A myth is a profound piece of storytelling. To ask if it is literally true is to miss the point. An Indian chieftain, before he begins telling his tribal creation myth, says, "I don't know if it happened this way or not, but its true." What is true is not confined to the literal, historical or scientifically verifiable. Poetry, metaphors and myths can all be vehicles of what is true.

A myth, therefore, is a story explaining the way things are. It is a story justifying the way we behave. A myth is attempting to say, 'this is how things are, this is the reality, the truth of the matter'. It may not be morally true; it may be suggesting that the way things are are evil and violent. Yet it is trying to say this is how it is. It requires a critical response from us.

Walter Wink has suggested in his writings that the great dominant myth of our human existence is the myth of redemptive violence. It is the all-pervasive myth of our culture. We may have long since forgotten the original myth or may even never have heard it in its original form, but what it says and claims is deeply ingrained in popular culture, mindsets and psyches.

The origins of the myth are in the ancient city states of Babylon and can be dated to 3000 BCE. There is little evidence prior to this of armies, war heroes and war gods. All of this emerges from the development of city states. The known version of the myth is dated around 1250 BCE, though it undoubtedly was created much earlier. It attempted to explain the way things are and justify human behaviour. Violence is how it is and is in the very nature of the gods. Indeed the gods legitimise violence.

The violence that emerged with the Babylonian city states was not only the violence of war in which people were massacred. It was also about violence against women. Women were sexually subjugated. The myth also attempted to say that this is how it is.

The myth is called the 'Enuma Elish' and is outlined in the session handout. The implications are also outlined in a handout. Paul Ricoeur, the French philosopher, has provided an insightful commentary summarised by Wink.

He points out that in the Babylonian myth, creation is an act of violence. Tiamat, 'mother of all', is murdered and dismembered; from her cadaver the world is formed. Order is established by means of disorder. Creation is a violent victory over an enemy older than creation. The origin of evil precedes the origin of things. Chaos (symbolised by Tiamat) is prior to order (represented by Marduk, god of Babylon). Evil is prior to good. Violence ushers in the godhead. Evil is an ineradicable constituent of ultimate reality, and possesses ontological priority over good.

(Walter Wink, *Engaging the Powers: Discernment and Resistance in a World of Domination*, Fortress Press, 1992, p 14.)

The myth stays with its violent theme. After the creation of the world, the gods imprisoned by Marduk for being on the side of Tiamat complain of the poor meal service. Marduk and Ea then execute one of the captive gods, and from his blood, Ea creates human beings to be servants to the gods.

As humans we are created from the blood of a murdered god. These are our origins, killing is part of who we are. We are incapable of living in peace. This is the natural way of things.

This myth of redemptive violence in which religion legitimises power and privilege as well as male violence and supremacy over women and the use of violence as the way to establish order, peace and security, was re-enacted annually at the Babylonian New Year Festival. Each year it was affirmed that violence is the natural fate of humanity; the violence of war and violence against women.

The original myth is re-enacted in the contemporary world in a variety of ways. Children's cartoons educate children in the myth, again suggesting that this is how it is. Nationalism also articulates the myth through the practice of patriotic religion, national anthems which are often a worship of the state god or a glorification of violence, through to national security policies as the state theology.

The myth lives on in many forms, developing societies characterised by many levels of unjust relations and the use of violence to maintain all of these relations. The myth has many modern forms and remains all-pervasive in popular culture. Many live uncritically out of the view that violence achieves, pays, defends, liberates and is justified.

There are Bible stories that reflect the practice of the myth. The next session will explore the alternative myth created by the Hebrews in exile in Babylon. At the same time life is portrayed in the biblical narratives as it is in all its brutality at times. There are texts of terror and the Tamar story from 2 Samuel 13 is one of them. The story can speak for itself. It is a brutal story of violence against a woman who is loathed and discarded once male sexual lust has been 'satisfied'. Most damning of all, apart from the perpetrators' abuse, is the conspiracy of silence by the other men in the story.

The Eve story appears not to be so overtly violent. But critical attention needs to be given to the traditional interpretation. The latter has perpetuated the subordination of women as a divine mandate, which is more in keeping with the Babylonian myth and has justified verbal, emotional and physical violence against women. A more careful and contextual re-reading of the Genesis texts is required if we are to liberate a Scripture text from interpretation through Babylonian lens.

This is not an easy session. It may raise sensitive issues and even deep hurts. But it is necessary and through sensitive handling can contribute towards a process of healing as well as the demythologising of an ancient all-pervasive myth.

Session 4 Plan

Welcome (5 minutes)

Small group discussion (10 minutes)

What is violence and is there such a thing as 'good' violence?

Feedback (5 minutes)

Overheads (15 minutes)

The nature of violence (5 minutes)

The myth of redemptive violence (5 minutes)

Enuma Elish (5 minutes)

Group work exercise 1 (10 minutes)

1. What is the story saying?

2. What kind of society does this story promote?

Feedback (5 minutes)

Overheads (10 minutes)

The implications of the Enuma Elish (5 minutes)

Characteristics of a violent society (5 minutes)

Discuss in twos or threes (5 minutes)

What are the modern expressions of the myth of redemptive violence?

Feedback (5 minutes)

Overhead (5 minutes)

The modern myths of redemptive violence

Group work exercise 2

Read story of Tamar (2 Samuel 13:1–22) or story of Adam and Eve (Genesis 3:16–19) in groups and answer questions.

Preparation time (15 minutes)

Feedback from groups (20 minutes)

Plenary question (10 minutes)

To what extent has the myth of redemptive violence shaped our thinking and actions?

Overhead 1

The nature of violence

Violence is:

◆ physical or emotional force to injure or abuse someone;

◆ structural, when people are hurt by being unable to break out or rise above harmful societal influences, eg poverty.

Redemptive violence is the belief that:

◆ violence redeems, liberates, frees;

◆ violence saves or defends;

◆ violence conquers, dominates;

◆ violence achieves;

◆ might is right;

◆ victory goes to the strong;

◆ only peace through war.

◆ only security through strength.

'Good' violence is:

◆ sometimes thought necessary to counteract bad violence;

◆ sometimes thought necessary to correct matters that have gone wrong;

◆ deeply ingrained in popular culture.

Overhead 2

The myth of redemptive violence

A myth is:

◆ a story explaining the way things are;

◆ a story justifying why we behave the way we do;

- a worldview out of which we live;
- a description of the deepest reality of the world and life.

The Babylonian myth

- In 3000 BCE Babylonian city states emerge where violence was central to life.
- The city states were characterised by
  - standing armies;
  - new bronze weaponry;
  - rigid hierarchy;
  - patriarchy;
  - worship of war gods;
  - massacre of male victims;
  - sexual subjugation of women.
- Out of Babylon comes the great myth of redemptive violence – the Enuma Elish.

Overhead 3

Babylonian myth - Enuma Elish

- Apsu and Tiamat
- Birth of the younger gods
- Elder gods cannot sleep because of noise – resolve to kill
- Plot is discovered and Apsu is killed
- Tiamat pledges revenge
- Younger gods turn to the youngest, Marduk, for protection
- Marduk's undisputed power in the assembly is the price
- Marduk catches Tiamat in a net
- Drives an evil wind down her throat
- Bursts her distended belly and pierces her heart
- Splits her skull
- Scatters her blood
- Creates the cosmos from her corpse

Session 4, Handout 1

Group work exercise 1

1. What is the story saying?

2. What kind of society does the story promote?

Overhead 4

Implications of Enuma Elish

◆ Creation out of violence

◆ Order established by disorder

◆ Evil is prior to good

◆ Violence is in the nature of gods

◆ Religion legitimises power and privilege

◆ Male violence and supremacy over woman

◆ Woman's subordination is a natural fate

Overhead 5

Characteristics of a violent society

◆ Unjust economic relations

◆ Oppressive political relations

◆ Biased race relations

◆ Patriarchal gender relations

◆ Hierarchical power relations

◆ Use of violence to maintain all relations

Overhead 6

Modern myths of redemptive violence

1. Popeye

◆ Bluto violently abducts a screaming and kicking Olive Oyl.

◆ Popeye tries to rescue her.

◆ Bluto beats the little Popeye to pulp.

◆ Popeye is down and out – violently hammered into the ground.

◆ Bluto is trying to rape Olive Oyl.

◆ Popeye discovers his can of spinach.

◆ Popeye demolishes the hated Bluto and rescues his sweetheart.

◆ Story always the same.

◆ Bluto never learns from violence to respect Olive's humanity.

◆ Popeye learns nothing either.

◆ Cartoon re-enacts the Babylonian myth.

2. Nationalisms marked by:

◆ absolute sovereignty;

◆ patriotic religion;

◆ national anthems – worship of state god;

◆ flags – symbols of absolute allegiance;

◆ militarism as national spirituality;

◆ national security policies as state theology.

3. Nationalism as the highest loyalty

To be nationalist is to be always ready to give up any doctrine, any theory, any ideology, feelings, passions, ideals and values, as soon as they appear as incompatible with the supreme loyalty which is due to the nation above everything else.

A Brazilian general

The myth of redemptive violence is absolute nationalism with God or gods invoked to bless, legitimise and be on its side.

Session 4, Handout 2

Group work exercise 2

Story of Tamar

Group 1: key text 2 Samuel 13:1–22

1. What dynamics of violence are at work in this story?

2. What alternative to violence does Tamar offer?

3. Does the story of Tamar have any relevance in our contemporary context?

Group 2: key text 2 Samuel 13:1–22

Imagine you are Tamar; prepare to tell your story creatively (reflecting on your thoughts, feelings, experiences). Be prepared to have a conversation with Eve.

Group 3: key text Genesis 3:16–19

1. How has this text been traditionally understood? How do you feel about this interpretation?

2. What are the implications of this interpretation for relationships between women and men?

3. In the light of Genesis 1:26–7 and in the context of all of chapter 3, is another interpretation of the text possible?

Group 4: key text Genesis 3:16–19

Imagine you are Eve; prepare to tell your story creatively (reflecting on your thoughts, feelings, experiences). Be prepared to have a conversation with Tamar.

Session 4, Handout 3

Myth of redemptive violence

Groups 1 and 2

2 Samuel 13:1–22

¹ David's son Absalom had a beautiful sister whose name was Tamar; and David's son Amnon fell in love with her. ² Amnon was so tormented that he made himself ill because of his sister Tamar, for she was a virgin and it seemed impossible to Amnon to do anything to her. ³ But Amnon had a friend whose name was Jonadab, the son of David's brother, Shimeah; and Jonadab was a very crafty man. ⁴ He said to him, 'O son of the king, why are you so haggard morning after morning? Will you not tell me?' Amnon said to him, 'I love Tamar my brother Absalom's sister.' ⁵ Jonadab said to him, 'Lie down on your bed, and pretend to be ill; and when your father comes to see you, say to him, 'Let my sister Tamar come and give me something to eat, and prepare the food in my sight, so that I may see it and eat it from her hand.' ⁶ So Amnon lay down, and pretended to be ill; and when the king came to see him, Amnon said to the king, 'Please let my sister Tamar come and make a couple of cakes in my sight, so that I may eat from her hand.'

[7] Then David sent home to Tamar, saying, 'Go to your brother Amnon's house, and prepare food for him.' [8] So Tamar went to her brother Amnon's house, where he was lying down. She took dough kneaded it, made cakes in his sight, and baked the cakes. [9] Then she took the pan and set them out before him, but he refused to eat. Amnon said, 'Send out everyone from me.' So everyone went out from him. [10] Then Amnon said to Tamar, 'Bring the food into the chamber, so that I may eat from your hand .' So Tamar took the cakes she had made, and brought them into the chamber to Amnon her brother. [11] But when she brought them near to him, he took hold of her, and said to her, 'Come, lie with me, my sister.' [12] She answered him, 'No, my brother, do not force me; for such a thing is not done in Israel; do not do anything so vile! [13] As for me, where could I carry my shame? And as for you, you would be as one of the scoundrels in Israel. Now therefore, I beg you, speak to the king; for he will not withhold me from you.' [14] But he would not listen to her; and being stronger than she was, he forced her and lay with her.

[15] The Amnon was seized with a very great loathing for her; indeed, his loathing was even greater than the lust he had felt for her. Amnon said to her, 'Get out!' [16] But she said to him, 'No, my brother; for this wrong in sending me away is greater than the other that you did to me.' But he would not listen to her. [17] He called the young man who served him and said, 'Put this woman out of my presence and bolt the door after her.' [18] (Now she was wearing a long robe with sleeves; for this is how the virgin daughters of the king were clothed in earlier times.) So his servant put her out, and bolted the door after her. [19] But Tamar put ashes on her head, and tore the long robe that she was wearing; she put her hand on her head, and went away, crying aloud as she went.

[20] Her brother Absalom said to her, 'Has Amnon your brother been with you? Be quiet for now, my sister; he is your brother; do not take this to heart.' So Tamar remained, a desolate woman, in her brother Absalom's house. [21] When king David heard of all these things, he became very angry, but he would not punish his son Amnon, because he loved him, for he was his firstborn. [22] But Absalom spoke to Amnon neither good nor bad; for Absalom hated Amnon, because he had raped his sister Tamar.

NRSV Bible

Session 4, Handout 4

Groups 3 and 4

Genesis 3:16–19

[16] To the woman he said, 'I will greatly increase your pangs in childbearing; in pain you shall bring forth children, yet your desire shall be for your husband, and he shall rule over you.' [17] And to the man he said, 'Because you have listened to the voice of your wife, and have eaten of the tree about which I commanded you, "You shall not eat of it", cursed is the ground because of you; in toil you shall eat of it all the days of your life; [18] thorns and thistles it shall bring forth for you; and you shall eat the plants of the field. [19] By the sweat of your face you shall eat bread until you return to the ground, for out of it you were taken; you are dust, and to dust you shall return.

NRSV Bible

Session 5 Introduction

The alternative story – a culture of non-violence

Is the myth of redemptive violence true? Is this how it really is or is there an alternative? History says yes. Historically violence just as often fails as it seems to achieve. What is considered achievement needs to be questioned. The myth may well be the great lie or delusion.

Europe was the centre of two world wars, the bloodiest ever in human history. The first was declared to be the war to end all wars. The Treaty of Versailles was more about crushing the already defeated Germans; Britain and France seeking punitive retribution rather than a peace treaty. It made World War Two inevitable. Nazism was a terrible evil but so too was the 'victorious' outcome. Half of Europe was enslaved and the other half, including Germany, became the rich, with a tendency towards a 'fortress Europe' (western). For all the rhetoric about freedom, the war left a brutal and unjust legacy. Europe is still in a process of conflict transformation but a uniting Europe is a witness to the failure of war and the possibility of peaceful resolution. It may well be that eastern and central Europeans are more aware of this than those in the west.

Non-violence, therefore, is a real option, which people have chosen and which does work. The handout on 'A culture of non-violence' gives a number of concrete historical examples, which show that the culture is possible and effective.

Despite the many stories of violence found in the Bible, there is also a culture of non-violence. Perhaps in this sense the Bible reflects the ambivalence found in much of human life and relationships. The literalistic approach to Scripture or the simplistic belief that everything is the revelation of God, obscures the human dimension and the ability to recognise the human will being confused with divine purpose. The latter confusion not only happened in parts of the biblical story but still happens. Our human desire for revenge can be projected on to God. Punitive concepts of God may have more to do with human vengeance and violence than with divine revelation.

To the Babylonian myth of redemptive violence the Bible does offer an alternative. During their time in Babylonian exile the Hebrews heard the myth. Marduk was the primary Babylonian god, the violent hero of the myth. The exile had been a social, economic, political and theological crisis. Yahweh seemed weaker and inferior to Marduk. How could they sing the Lord's song in a strange land? Yahweh was defeated and powerless among the ruins of Jerusalem. Marduk was the conquering god and his earthly representative, the Babylonian king, was obviously superior to the shattered monarchy of Judah.

Thanks to a pre-exilic prophet like Jeremiah and great prophets of the exile itself, Ezekiel and 2nd Isaiah (chapters 40–55), the exiles did find their voice and did learn to sing again. Second Isaiah in particular was the prophet who helped them interpret their experience, discover meaning in it, obtain a new vision of God and reshape the Hebrew sense of identity and purpose. As a result of this major, poetic piece of theological reflection, Isaiah chapters 40–55 is one of the most creative and significant texts of the Bible. "Comfort, O comfort my people, says your God" (40:1) must have been a hugely transforming and comforting word to a traumatised, voiceless people. Second Isaiah helped them to publicly name their pain, which in turn enabled those who eventually returned to Jerusalem to envisage a new future and community. By interpreting their traumatic experience and publicly naming the pain, the prophet enabled the release of imagination necessary for a new and alternative vision. The poetic visions of the future are found in the later 3rd Isaiah (chapter 56–66).

There were others engaged in theological reflection as well as creative editorial work. It was from these unnamed poets and theologians that the counter story to the Babylonian myth was written. When they found a voice again they created the Hebrew myth. Like much of 2nd Isaiah's material, it was poetic and it was written out of the creative theological thought world of the exile. The counter myth was Genesis 1, a profound piece of poetic theological reflection. Unlike Marduk, the God of Genesis 1 is a good God who creates a good creation. Good is prior to evil. Original sin is not the first word but original blessing. Evil and violence are intrusions into creation and they are problems requiring a solution. There is the mystery of evil and the Bible does not speculate about its origins. For all that, the Hebrews do not pose an absolute dualism. Order overcomes chaos and goodness is both prior and primary.

In contrast to the Babylonian myth where women are inferior, subordinate and victims of violence, the Hebrew myth affirms the equality of the sexes, with women and men created equally in God's image. Creation does not emerge from murder and violence but from the goodness of God, and the God of the Hebrew myth, unlike Marduk, is non-violent.

This is not how Genesis 1 has traditionally been read. The text has more often been the victim of a public dispute between science and religion, evolution versus creationism. This dispute and the literalistic reading of the text has been diversionary, with serious consequences. It avoids the challenge of non-violence by asking the wrong questions of the text and by ignoring the context. Genesis 1 needs to be read in the Babylonian context and as a contrast text to that of the Babylonian myth, the Enuma Elish.

It is also in this context that the royal language of the poem is best understood. To "have dominion" has been heard as domination, which has been the cause of much violence, not only towards other human beings, but also against creation. "Subdue" has also been heard as conquest, another form of violence against animate and inanimate creation. These readings fail to see that this 'kingly' language was reinterpreted in exile by 2nd Isaiah. The prophet took the language of monarchy which had been used of God but was shattered by the exile experience, and connected it with the image of the shepherd. In 2nd Isaiah a key image of God is of the shepherd-king. Chapter 40:9–11 is the classic text where "the Lord God comes with might and his arm rules for him". He is also the God who "will feed his flock like a shepherd; he will gather the lambs in his arms, and carry them in his bosom, and gently lead the mother sheep".

The Genesis poem comes out of this context and this vision of God. The imagery is not of domination and conquest but of gentleness, nurture and tender care. It is the language of non-violence and opens up the possibility for a very different kind of relationship between humans and humans and creation. Out of the violent Babylonian exile from the encounter there with the myth of redemptive violence came the Hebrew counter myth with its culture of non-violence.

Context is also important when dealing with the Gospels. Though written for faith communities in particular situations, the Gospel stories are originally set in first-century Roman Palestine. There is a

Galilean context and a Jerusalem context and the context was situated in violence. There was the violence of the Romans who treated people brutally in order to secure submission. "Repeatedly, the Roman armies burned and completely destroyed towns and either slaughtered, crucified, or enslaved their entire populations" (Richard Horsley with John S Hanson, *Bandits, Prophets and Messiahs: Popular Movements in the Time of Jesus*, Trinity Press International, 1999 edition, p 31). The Romans thought nothing in one situation of rebellion of making 30,000 Galilean men slaves. After capturing Sepphoris they sold its inhabitants as slaves and fired the city. The rebels who were caught during this rebellion were crucified – about 2,000 men.

Economically the people were also oppressed with a triple taxation rate, which added up to 40% of income. Roman, Herodian and temple taxes forced many of the peasant farmers into debt and eventually off their land to become in many cases slaves on the very land they once had owned.

Inevitably there were resistance movements and Messianic pretenders. Bandits and dagger men resorted to the way of violence. Many others took a non-violent form of resistance such as an agricultural strike by Galilean peasants.

This is the foreground to the ministry and teaching of Jesus and it makes his sayings and parables radical and subversive.

Session 5 Plan

Welcome (5 minutes)

Summary of the myth of redemptive violence (5 minutes)

Overheads (10 minutes)

Babylonian myth, Enuma Elish

Implications of the Enuma Elish

Group work exercise 1 (10 minutes)

1. What do you understand by non-violence?

2. Identify examples of the practice of non-violence in our time.

Overhead (5 minutes)

Towards an alternative culture

Group work exercise 2 (15 minutes)

1. What is the effect of violence on relationships (national/international)?

2. Is non-violence a viable alternative? Feedback (10 minutes)

Overhead (5 minutes)

Genesis poem (Genesis 1)

Plenary questions (10 minutes)

Did the Hebrews really believe their own alternative story? Do we?

Group work exercise 3 or role-play

The Jesus community and non-violence

Group work exercise 3 – preparation time (20minutes), feedback (15 minutes)

Role play – preparation time (15 minutes), role-play and debriefing (20 minutes)

Overhead (5 minutes)

Historical examples of non-violence

Plenary discussion (5 minutes)

How can we live out a culture of non-violence in the contemporary world?

Overhead 1 (Overhead 3 from Course 4, Session 4)

Babylonian myth Enuma Elish

◆ Apsu and Tiamat

◆ Birth of the younger gods

◆ Elder gods cannot sleep because of noise – resolve to kill

◆ Plot is discovered and Apsu is killed

◆ Tiamat pledges revenge

◆ Younger gods turn to the youngest, Marduk, for protection

◆ Marduk's undisputed power in the assembly is the price

◆ Marduk catches Tiamat in a net

◆ Drives an evil wind down her throat

◆ Bursts her distended belly and pierces her heart

◆ Splits her skull

◆ Scatters her blood

◆ Creates the cosmos from her corpse

Overhead 2 (Overhead 4 from Course 4, Session 4)

Implications of Enuma Elish

◆ Creation out of violence

◆ Order established by disorder

◆ Evil is prior to good

◆ Violence is in the nature of gods

◆ Religion legitimises power and privilege

◆ Male violence and supremacy over woman

◆ Woman's subordination is a natural fate

Session 5, Handout 1

Group work exercise 1

Working in small groups, consider the following questions:

1. What do you understand by non-violence?

2. Identify examples of the practice of non-violence in our time.

Overhead 3

Towards an alternative culture

If the myth of redemptive violence seems true to life, historically violence just as often fails.

◆ Uniting Europe – witness to failure of war and the possibility of peaceful resolution.

◆ Lithuanians fought a guerrilla war against Soviets until 1952. An estimated total of 50,000 died; 400,000 sent to Siberia.

◆ "After the deportations and the might of our genocide, our people realised that armed struggle was not the way. We needed to rely on patience and non violence." (Lithuanian)

◆ Chicago Police Department resolved 96 consecutive hostage situations without using violence. They patiently talked 96 dangerous people into giving up without violence.

◆ Ghandi achieved the independence and liberation of India through non-violent strategies.

◆ Martin Luther King achieved one of the greatest triumphs for civil rights in the twentieth century through the principle of non-violent resistance:

The ultimate weakness of violence is that it is a descending spiral, begetting the very thing it seeks to destroy. Instead of diminishing evil, it multiplies it. Darkness cannot drive out darkness; only light can do that. Hate cannot drive out hate; only love can do that.

Enough examples in history suggest that:

◆ the spiral of violence can be broken;

◆ people can and do chose non-violence;

◆ the practice of non-violence does work;

◆ the myth can be replaced by possibility.

Session 5, Handout 2

Group work exercise 2

Working in small groups, consider the following questions.

1. What is the effect of violence on relationships (national/international)?

2. Is non-violence a viable alternative?

Overhead 4

Hebrew myth: Genesis poem

◆ Genesis 1 written in Babylon

◆ The poem is a counter myth

◆ A good God creates a good creation

◆ Order overcomes chaos

◆ Good is prior to evil

◆ Neither evil nor violence is part of creation

◆ Women and men created equally in the divine image

◆ Human equality is God's purpose

- ◆ Goodness is corrupted by free human decisions
- ◆ Evil is a problem requiring solution
- ◆ God is non-violent
- ◆ Creation is essentially good

Session 5, Handout 3

The Jesus community and non-violence

Text – Matthew 5:43–8

[43] 'You have heard that it was said, "You shall love your neighbour and hate your enemy." [44] But I say to you, love your enemies and pray for those who persecute you, [45] so that you may be children of your Father in heaven; for he makes his sun rise on the evil and on the good, and sends rain on the righteous and on the unrighteous. [46] For if you love those who love you, what reward do you have? [47] And if you greet only your brothers and sisters, what more are you doing than others? Do not even the Gentiles do the same? [48] Be perfect, therefore, as your heavenly Father is perfect.'

NRSV Bible

Read Matthew 5:38–48, taking into account the background information on its political context. Complete either group work exercise 3 or the role-play exercise.

Group work exercise 3

1. Identify the key points of Jesus' teaching regarding violence and relating to the enemy.

2. What do they say to us in our context?

Or

Role-play

Scenario

A Roman soldier in Nazareth has compelled a bandit to carry his pack to the next village. The bandit has refused. Some of his friends emerge from the shadows, knife the soldier and disappear again.

The Roman response is to surround Nazareth and go from house to house in search of the offenders, destroying and brutalising the village population.

Some of the villagers are followers of Jesus. They are suspect, as is everyone. The Romans fail to find those responsible and call a public meeting with the threat that if the offenders are not found a number of Jewish men will be crucified by the state as an example.

The following groups will be present at the meeting:

◆ Roman soldiers

◆ Galilean peasants

◆ Jesus community

◆ Bandits

Taking into account the political context, prepare to participate in the public meeting. At the meeting the Romans will deliver an ultimatum. Each of the groups will have an opportunity to make a response.

Session 5, Handout 4

Background reading for group work exercise 3 or role-play

The Gospel in political space

First-century Roman Palestine

◆ Jewish Palestine became subject to the Romans in 63 BCE.

◆ After brief Parthian occupation in 40 BCE, the Romans regained control in 37 BCE and appointed Herod the Great as client king.

◆ In 37 BCE began the long and brutal reign of Herod.

◆ Herod's death in 4 BCE provoked popular uprisings.

◆ After Herod's death the Romans divided his territory into three tetrarchies.

◆ Revolts and risings continued and the Romans imposed direct rule in 44 CE.

◆ The Roman governor (Pilate) had the power to appoint and depose the high priest at will.

◆ Rome had exclusive authority over foreign policy and serious domestic dissent, eg capital punishment – crucifixion.

◆ Roman legions were barracked beside the Jerusalem temple.

◆ The imperial power could and did brutally crush any signs of insurrection.

Resistance to Rome

◆ Some Pharisees refused to swear an oath to the emperor.

◆ Pharisees removed the Roman golden eagle from the temple gate.

◆ Mass outcry was provoked by Pilate allowing Roman standards into Jerusalem, violating the prohibition of images.

◆ The Emperor Gaius Caligula (37–41 CE) attempted to place a statue of himself in the Jerusalem temple.

◆ This caused widespread protest and an agricultural strike in Galilee (Jesus' province where he mainly worked).

◆ Most of the Galilean population were peasants, often in poverty and economic debt/slavery from triple taxation.

◆ Social bandits were a persistent problem for the Romans.

◆ They opposed exploitative landowners and imperial power.

◆ Bandits engaged in subversive activity, supported by local peasants and protected by them.

◆ Bandits were Robin Hood-types, ie outlaws.

◆ Sicarri or dagger men specialised in urban political assassination.

◆ These attacks were usually against fellow Jews. There were three main tactics.

    1. Selective, symbolic assignations.

    2. General assassinations, with plundering of property belonging to wealthy and powerful.

    3. Kidnapping for ransom.

◆ Mark's Gospel appears to portray Barabbas as a sicarius terrorist.

Non-violent resistance

◆ Jewish protesters bared their necks to soldiers rather than give in when Pilate tried to introduce Roman standards into Jerusalem.

◆ Tens of thousands of Jews were prepared to die rather than have Caligula's image in the Jerusalem temple. Their protest went on for 40 days.

◆ The agricultural strike by Galilean peasants, refusing to sow next year's crops, caused great Roman concern.

Overhead 5

A culture of non-violence

◆ 1350 BCE – Hebrew midwives carried out the first recorded act of civil disobedience by refusing to carry out Pharaoh's order to kill all Hebrew male babies.

◆ 550 BCE – Hebrew exiles in Babylon on hearing the Babylonian Enuma Elish myth created an alternative myth – Genesis 1:

– creation is good

– work of a good God

– evil does not come before goodness

– evil nor violence is part of creation

– God is non-violent

◆ 167 BCE – Daniel rejected the violent militarism of the Maccabees.

◆ 30 CE – Jesus practiced and taught non-violence in a Roman-occupied and dominated land and was crucified for it.

◆ 1850 – Hungarian nationalists provide non-violent resistance to Austrian rule and win self-governance for Hungary within an Austro-Hungarian federation.

◆ 1901–05 – Finns non-violently resist Russian oppression and force a repeal of conscription laws.

◆ 1957 – Ghana wins independence after a ten-year non-violent struggle.

◆ 1980–89 – Solidarity in Poland brought about the end of repressive communist rule without committing a single violent act.

◆ 1989 – Hungary, Poland, Czechoslovakia, Bulgaria and East Germany win freedom from Soviet control by non-violent means.

◆ Non-violent independence movements begin and eventually succeed in Latvia, Lithuania, Estonia, Georgia, Armenia, Moldova, Ukraine, Albania and Mongolia.

◆ Non-violent demonstrations bring about the end of the Ceausescu regime in Romania.

◆ 1990 – Pro-democracy non-violent protests topple the government of King Birendra of Nepal and end three decades of absolutism.

These are only some examples of non-violence at work in history achieving political freedoms, democracy and justice.

Session 6 Introduction

Towards communities of integrity

Building communities of integrity is one of the major tasks of our time. This is especially true where the process is one of reconstruction after experiences of epochal change or traumatic crisis. This is the situation in many eastern and central European countries following the collapse of the communist system. The 'Velvet Revolution' occurred in the Czech Republic, then Czechoslovakia, in 1989. More than a decade on there is a long way still to go. The Czech Republic has moved further than some other countries emerging from a similar experience. Ukraine and Bulgaria have not moved so quickly. The Czech Republic and Hungary will probably be the next new members of the European Community. Membership for the Ukraine and Bulgaria is still a long way off. That may say as much about the fortress mentality of western European countries as it does about the rebuilding process of some eastern and central European countries.

These are communities in transition and the process will take decades. Northern Ireland is another example of a community in transition with a decades-long process still ahead. The goal in all of these situations is to build communities of integrity.

This is not just about building a new community infrastructure. New political structures are needed and they take time to develop. Economic and social structures need to be put in place, as do educational systems. Transformation takes place at all of these levels.

Crucial to the building process is the development and nurturing of ethical and moral values. How do we nurture the politics of morality, the ethics of economics and compassion of relationships? A community of integrity needs a value base, the public ethics which will provide the social cement holding a society together.

One of the great challenges of the present is how to speak of faith and values in the public place. How do we speak of these in the place where new legal, social, economic, political and community relations are to be built?

One of the great moral and political leaders of our time is Vaclav Havel, the president of the Czech Republic. One of Havel's key themes is 'politics as morality in practice'. Speaking for the first time as president to his people on 1 January 1990 he said: "Our main enemy today is our own worst nature: our indifference to the common good: pride, personal ambition; selfishness and rivalry. The main struggle will have to be fought on this field" (Vaclav Havel, *The Act of the Impossible: Politics as Morality in Practice*, Knoff, 1997, p 8).

Havel bases his political vision on that of the first president of Czechoslovakia, Thomas Masaryk, who based his politics on morality. In the same address, Havel said:

The worst thing is that we live in a contaminated moral environment. We feel morally ill because we got used to saying something different from what we thought. We learned not to believe in anything, to ignore each other, to care only for ourselves. Concepts such as love, friendship, compassion, humility, and forgiveness lost their depth and dimensions . . .

(Ibid, p 4.)

Havel is pinpointing the values, which are essential if a new community is to be rooted in morality and public ethics. He is also highlighting the extent to which a society can become morally ill and the reality of the struggle in a morally contaminated environment.

The key text for this final session is Psalm 85. The particular focus is on verse 10:

Steadfast love and faithfulness will meet;

righteousness and peace will kiss each other.

The Hebrew poet is using key covenant vocabulary to articulate a vision of community. The words used in the group exercise and handout are from a Spanish translation of the Psalm. Core community values are justice, mercy, peace and truth. The four values are interrelated. Meeting and kissing each other are strong metaphors for intimacy. In this Hebrew vision authentic community is where:

◆ we are committed in solidarity to each other – everybody matters;

◆ we live with integrity towards each other;

◆ we live in right relationships based on justice where everyone's humanity is respected; there is equality of dignity and opportunity;

◆ there is shalom (peace) which is central and which is about the personal, social, economic and political well-being of all without exception.

Not only is shalom about the total well-being and harmony of all humanity, it is also about the well-being and harmony of the whole world of nature.

This is the biblical concept of shalom, peace, well-being and all of this is the Hebrew poet's dream for community. She or he dreams of being a community around these core values.

Session 6 Plan

Welcome (5 minutes)

Group work exercise 1 (15 minutes)

Create four groups:

A – Justice

B – Mercy

C – Peace

D – Truth

Invite each group to spend approximately five minutes defining the quality they represent. A spokesperson from each group will then personify that quality for the whole group.

Group work exercise 2 (20 minutes)

Outline the following scenario for each group.

Unless community relations are improved in Northern Ireland, the building of a community of integrity will be impossible. To build a community of integrity requires core values. At this conference Justice, Mercy, Peace and Truth will be asked to state what each requires for a community of integrity to be shaped.

Plenary (20 minutes)

Spokesperson from each group will report back.

Integrated group work exercise 3 (25 minutes)

Round-table talks will take place between each of the groups eg Justice and Peace groups; Mercy and Truth groups; then Justice and Mercy and Peace and Truth etc.

1. How can the particular needs of each quality be met in the building of a community of integrity?

2. What give and take might be required?

Feedback from groups (15 minutes)

Reflection questions for large group: (15 minutes)

1. What were the difficulties?

2. Is it possible to give equal weight to the requirements of justice, mercy, peace and truth?

Reading of Psalm 85:8–13 (5 minutes)

Session 6, Handout 1

Psalm 85:8–13

[8] Let me hear what God the Lord will speak, for he will speak peace to his people, to his faithful, to those who turn to him in their hearts. [9] Surely his salvation is at hand for those who fear him, that his glory may dwell in our land. [10] Steadfast love and faithfulness will meet; righteousness and peace will kiss each other. [11] Faithfulness will spring up from the ground, and righteousness will look down from the sky. [12] The Lord will give what is good, and our land will yield its increase. [13] Righteousness will go before him, and will make a path for his steps.

NRSV Bible

Session 6, Handout 2

Group work exercise 1 (15 minutes)

Create four groups

A – Justice, B – Mercy, C – Peace, D – Truth

Invite each group to spend approximately five minutes defining the quality they represent. A spokesperson from each group will represent the quality to the whole group.

Group work exercise 2 (20 minutes)

Outline the scenario for each group.

Unless community relations are improved in Northern Ireland, the building of a community of integrity will be impossible. To build a community of integrity requires core values. At this conference Justice, Mercy, Peace and Truth will be asked to state what each requires for a community of integrity to be shaped.

Group work exercise 3 (25 minutes)

Round-table talks will take place between each of the groups eg Justice and Peace groups; Mercy and Truth groups; then Justice and Mercy and Peace and Truth etc.

1. How can the particular needs of each quality be met in the building of a community of integrity?

2. What give and take might be required?

Reflection questions (15 minutes)

1. What were the difficulties?

2. Is it possible to give equal weight to the requirements of justice, mercy, peace and truth?

Course Five Outline

The politics of faith
Exploring the Bible as a political text

Course description

Beginning with people's experiences, this course will provide participants with the opportunity to relate biblical insights to public, social, political and community issues. A key consideration of the course is to apply biblical insights to issues of public and community reconciliation and using biblical texts, develop public ethics.

Course outline

Session 1   Reading the Bible in the public place

                Exploring how to connect the Bible with public issues

Session 2   The politics of the Covenant

                Critiquing the Ulster Covenant in the light of the biblical covenant

Session 3   A theology of community relations

                Connecting biblical insights to community

Session 4   Contrast – culture Gospel

                Exploring whether Gospel values can shape an alternative culture

Session 5   The politics of memory

                Exploring biblical insights on remembering that liberates

Session 6   Living economically, living ethically

                Connecting biblical ethics to the market place

Session 1 Introduction

Reading the Bible in the public place
Exploring how to connect the Bible with public issues

To connect the Bible with public issues will require a method of reading quite different from the traditional and popular approaches. There is a reluctance to accept that we are always interpreting Scripture. The Bible never simply says. There is even more reluctance to accept that our reading of Scripture is never innocent. We all bring presuppositions to the text, including bias. The Bible is always read through our lens. These are tinted by our political, social and cultural situation. Gender too plays its part in the approach to the text. The reality is that our reading lenses are heavily tinted.

It is important to recognise this even though it may disturb our cherished readings and challenge our often simplistic views on the authority of Scripture. It may not be easy to realise that there is always a difference between the authority of Scripture and the authority of our interpretation of Scripture. They are not the same! The word of the Lord and our proclaimed or taught word may not be identical.

Reading the Bible in the public place, then, is a critical task. Part of the task is to be critically aware of the reader's bias, not least one's socio-economic place in society and one's political preferences. Every reading, therefore, must be open to alternative insights and changing perspectives.

Two modern ways of interpreting Scripture are not only deeply rooted in the church community but are inadequate as methods of reading in the public place.

The scholastic approach is heavily confessional. Many Christian traditions have developed their theological systems, their distinctive confessional emphases. The scholastic model is highly intellectual, propositional and doctrinal. There is much concern with the church's dogma and its formulations of truth. Such an approach tends to work with timeless and universal theological principles. These truths cross the boundaries of time and are applicable in every time and place. This approach ignores context, situation and any historical and social particularities. Luther's doctrine of justification by faith for example, does not belong to any time or context and furthermore, it becomes the key by which the rest of Scripture is interpreted.

The theological dogmas, formulated and systematised become the lens through which Scripture is read. The bible becomes a book of theological doctrine and is read doctrinally. It is soon explored for proof texts in order to give substance to the doctrine. It is not often recognised that a proof-text approach not only ignores the textual context, it is often reading the doctrinal formulation back into the text.

The old docetic heresy said that Christ only seemed to be human. The divinity of Jesus was emphasised at the expense of his humanity. He only seemed to suffer, but in essence did not. The scholastic practice of reading Scripture is docetic in the sense that the text is read as if it only seemed to have a historical, human, concrete context. Such a reading isolates the text from the contemporary human, concrete and public life situation.

The pietistic approach tends to privatism and an over-emphasis on the vertical. The approach is shared by fundamentalists and existentialists. Much conservative evangelicalism, as distinct from fundamentalism, also tends to a pietistic reading of Scripture.

The vertical relationship with God is primary, with faith being individualistic. Salvation becomes an individualistic experience and the search for holiness of life is also individualistic. Holiness is often confined to issues of personal morality, usually defined in fairly narrow terms. Christ-centred pietism proclaims Jesus as Lord but often as Lord of the individual heart rather than Lord of the world.

The existentialists are also centred on the individualistic. The individual is searching for authentic existence and personal wholeness. All of this tends to a reading of the Scripture text in terms of the individual's relationship with God. The community emphasis of Scripture, which is central, is overlooked and in many cases has been lost. Both the scholastic and the pietistic bypass the crucial horizontal relationships. They do not offer a reading method for the public place.

Culture-bound readings or politicised readings also distort the text. Politicised readings are not the same as a political reading. The former is a reading of the text from a partisan or ideological political perspective and is therefore heavily biased and usually oppressive. The Exodus story has been read in different ways. The examples from South Africa and Northern Ireland are good examples of different readings. Yet, which is the more authentic? The Northern Ireland reading may be seen as sectarian, an example of insecure settler theology and ultimately a theology of domination. At the same time the South African reading, though it may reflect on authentic justice, glosses over an inescapable part of the Exodus story. All liberation theology readings of the story are partial in that they ignore the displacement or extermination of the Canaanites by the religious fervour of the Israelites with God on their side. There is a problem with the exodus model, which arises from a literalist reading.

Having acknowledged all of this, there is no neutral reading of the Bible. Even when churches remain silent in the face of abuses of political or economic power, they are taking the side of the abuser. How we read the Bible always has social and political implications.

Reading the Bible in the public place requires a public reading of the Bible. This means taking seriously the public or socio-political, economic and cultural context of the biblical texts and the contemporary context. A socio-political reading of the Scripture text is suggested by the interpretative circle. This method of reading is dealt with more fully in the introductory material to the manual. It is the method that underlies the Scripture focus in all of the courses.

The exercise in applying the circle is based on a Jeremiah text. The book is located in the period just before and just after the destruction of Jerusalem in 587 BCE. The dominant power was that of the expanding Babylonian empire. Jeremiah's key insight was that the threat to Jerusalem and its destruction was the judgement of God against the city. The city was to be destroyed and then built again. The theme is about end and new beginning. Such an emphasis put Jeremiah at odds with the leaders of the religious establishment. Royal theology or the theology of the monarchy believed in the indestructibility of Jerusalem. Jeremiah had no such illusions. The covenant had been broken, ie the community was constructed on injustice and oppression which was political and economic. As a prophet, Jeremiah announced the judgement of God and perceived the Babylonians as the agents of that judgement. But this prophetic task was not just to pull down but to build up: "His task is to help his community to face the loss of the old world of king and temple and to receive a new world defined by Yahweh" (Walter Brueggemann, *Hopeful Imagination: Prophetic Voices in Exile*, SCM Press, 1986, p 12).

The key text, chapter 1:4–19, gives expression to the prophetic call of Jeremiah. His ministry is a ministry of 'over against'. The holy city and its temple are to be dismantled: "The call is precisely against the royal ideology of the day. Yahweh and Yahweh's prophet stand profoundly against the deceptively constructed world of king and temple" (Ibid, p 13).

Jeremiah was called to conflict and the only ultimate comfort he had in the heat of conflict with the royal establishment was the divine promise, "I will be with you" (verses 8 and 19). A false ideology and theology is to be deconstructed and in this role: "Jeremiah is set for such conflict because he is summoned by God to tell the truth about the fundamentally false organisation of life in Jerusalem" (Ibid, p 14).

Session 1 Plan

Welcome (5 minutes)

Group work exercise 1 (10 minutes)

Discuss in groups the following questions.

1. What is the Bible?

2. What do we mean by the authority of the Bible?

3. How do we interpret Scripture?

Overhead (5 minutes)

Two modern ways of interpreting Scripture

Questions of clarification (5 minutes)

Overhead (5 minutes)

Culture-bound readings (5 minutes)

Questions of clarification (5 minutes)

Group work exercise 2 (20 minutes)

Read Exodus 14 – the story of the exodus of the Hebrews from Egypt and consider the following.

1. What was the significance of the Exodus for the Hebrews?

2. How do you understand the Exodus story in our contemporary world?

Feedback (10 minutes)

Overhead (5 minutes)

The basic principles of interpretation

Questions of clarification (5 minutes)

Overhead (5 minutes)

A social, political reading of Scripture

Questions of clarification (5 minutes)

Group work exercise 3 (20 minutes)

Applying the circle

Read Jeremiah 1:4–19 and the background information provided and consider the following questions.

1. What is the text saying?

2. What is the text saying in context?

3. How do we hear the text in our contemporary context?

Feedback (15 minutes)

Session 1, Handout 1

Reading the Bible in the public place

Group work exercise 1

Discuss in small groups the following questions.

1. What is the Bible?

2. What do we mean by the authority of the Bible?

3. How do we interpret Scripture?

Overhead 1

Two modern ways of interpreting Scripture

1. Scholastic

◆ Timeless and universal theological principles

◆ Church dogma

◆ Ignoring historical and social particularities

◆ The docetic heresy

2. Pietistic/privatism:

(a) Fundamentalists

◆ Individual search for holiness

◆ Vertical relationship

◆ Lord of our hearts rather than the world

(b) Existentialists

◆ Individual search for authentic existence

◆ Individual search for personal wholeness

Overhead 2

Culture-bound readings

Interpretations of the Exodus story

South Africa	Northern Ireland
Liberation of black community from slavery of apartheid.	Protestant deliverance from Romanism. Chosen people, Promised Land.

◆ There is no neutral reading of the Bible.

Nazi Germany	Northern Ireland
Scholastic reading of the Bible failed to challenge the rise of national socialism. The churches had no critical voice.	Pietistic Protestant reading of the Bible failed to challenge abuses of power. The churches had no critical voice.

◆ Scholastic or pietistic readings of the text can leave the socio-political world unchallenged.

◆ How we read the Bible always has social and political implications.

Session 1, Handout 2

Reading the Bible in the public place

Group work exercise 2

Read Exodus 14 – the story of the exodus of the Hebrews from Egypt and consider:

1. What was the significance of the Exodus for the Hebrews?

2. How do you understand the Exodus story in our contemporary world?

Session 1, Handout 3

Exodus 14:1–31

[1] Then the Lord said to Moses: [2] Tell the Israelites to turn back and camp in front of Pi-hahiroth, between Migdol and the sea, in front of Baalzephon; you shall camp opposite it, by the sea. [3] Pharaoh will say of the Israelites, ' They are wandering aimlessly in the land; the wilderness has closed in on them.' [4] I will harden Pharaoh's heart, and he will pursue them, so that I will gain glory for myself over Pharaoh and all his army; and the Egyptians shall know that I am the Lord. And they did so.

[5] When the king of Egypt was told that the people had fled, the minds of Pharaoh and his officials were changed towards the people, and they said, 'What have we done, letting Israel leave our service?' [6] So he had his chariot made ready, and took his army with him; [7] he took six hundred picked chariots and all the other chariots of Egypt with officers over all of them. [8] The Lord hardened the heart of Pharaoh king of Egypt and he pursued the Israelites, who were going out boldly. [9] The Egyptians pursued them, all Pharaoh's horses and chariots, his chariot drivers and his army; they overtook them camped by the sea, by Pi-hahiroth, in front of Baalzephon.

[10] As Pharaoh drew near, the Israelites looked back, and there were the Egyptians advancing on them. In great fear the Israelites called out to the Lord. [11] They said to Moses, 'Was it because there were no graves in Egypt that you have taken us away to die in the wilderness? What have you done to us, bringing us out of Egypt? [12] Is this not the very thing we told you in Egypt, "Let us alone and let us serve the Egyptians" For it would have been better for us to serve the Egyptians than to die in the wilderness.' [13] But Moses said to the people, 'Do not be afraid, stand firm, and see the deliverance that the Lord will accomplish for you today; for the Egyptians whom you see today you shall never see again. [14] The Lord will fight for you, and you have only to keep still.'

[15] Then the Lord said to Moses, 'Why do you cry out to me? Tell the Israelites to go forward. [16] But you lift up your staff and stretch out your hand over the sea and divide it, that the Israelites may go into the sea on dry ground. [17] Then I will harden the hearts of the Egyptians so that they will go in after them; and so I will gain glory for myself over Pharaoh and all his army, his chariots, and his chariot drivers. [18] And the Egyptians shall know that I am the Lord, when I have gained glory for myself over Pharaoh, his chariots, and his chariot drivers.'

[19] The angel of God who was going before the Israelite army moved and went behind them; and the pillar of cloud moved from in front of them and took its place behind them. [20] It came between the army of Egypt and the army of Israel. And so the cloud was there with the darkness, and it lit up the night; one did not come near the other all night.

[21] Then Moses stretched out his hand over the sea. The Lord drove the sea back by a strong east wind all night, and turned the sea into dry land; and the waters were divided. [22] The Israelites went into the sea on dry ground, the waters forming a wall for them on their right and on their left. [23] The Egyptians pursued, and went into the sea after them, all of Pharaoh's horses, chariots, and chariot drivers. [24] At the morning watch the Lord in the pillar of fire and cloud looked down upon the Egyptian army, and threw the Egyptian army into panic. [25] He clogged their chariot wheels so that they turned with difficulty. The Egyptians said, 'Let us flee from the Israelites, for the Lord is fighting for them against Egypt.'

[26] Then the Lord said to Moses, 'Stretch out your hand over the sea, so that the water may come back upon the Egyptians, upon their chariots, and chariot drivers.' [27] So Moses stretched out his hand over the sea, and at dawn

the sea returned to its normal depth. As the Egyptians fled before it, the Lord tossed the Egyptians into the sea. [28] The waters returned and covered the chariots and the chariot drivers, the entire army of Pharaoh that had followed them into the sea; not one of them remained. [29] But the Israelites walked on dry ground through the sea, the waters forming a wall for them on their right and on their left.

[30] Thus the Lord saved Israel that day from the Egyptians; and Israel saw the Egyptians dead on the seashore. [31] Israel saw the great work that the Lord did against the Egyptians. So the People feared the Lord and believed in the Lord and in his servant Moses.

NRSV Bible

Overhead 3

Basic principles of interpretation

◆ We need to try and enter into the world of the text.

◆ We need to attempt to understand the original audience to which the text was addressed.

◆ Our life situation and experience will shape the questions we bring to the text.

◆ Genuine listening to the text will allow it to shape our understanding and action within our situation.

Overhead 4

A social-political circle

Session 1, Handout 6

Group work exercise 3

Applying the circle

Read Jeremiah 1:4–19 and the background information provided and consider the following questions.

1. What is the text saying?

2. What is the text saying in context?

3. How do we hear the text in our contemporary context?

Session 1, Handout 7

Jeremiah 1:4–19

[4] Now the word of the Lord came to me saying, [5] 'Before I formed you in the womb I knew you, and before you were born I consecrated you; I appointed you a prophet to the nations.' [6] Then I said, 'Ah, Lord God! Truly I do not know how to speak, for I am only a boy.' [7] But the Lord said to me, 'Do not say "I am only a boy"; for you shall go to all to whom I send you, and you shall speak whatever I command you. [8] Do not be afraid of them, for I am with you to deliver you, says the Lord.' [9] Then the Lord put out his hand and touched my mouth; and the Lord said to me, 'Now I have put my words in your mouth. [10] See, today I appoint you over nations and over kingdoms, to pluck up and to pull down, to destroy and to overthrow, to build and to plant.' [11] The word of the Lord came to me, saying, 'Jeremiah, what do you see?' And I said I see a branch of an almond tree.' [12] Then the Lord said to me, 'You have seen well, for I am watching over my word to perform it.' [13] The word of the Lord came to me a second time, saying, 'What do you see?' And I said, 'I see a boiling pot, tilted away from the north.' [14] Then the Lord said to me: Out of the north disaster shall break out on all the inhabitants of the land. [15] For now I am calling all the tribes of the kingdoms of the north, says the Lord; and they shall come and all of them shall set their thrones at the entrance of the gates of Jerusalem, against all its surrounding walls and against all the cities of Judah. [16] And I will utter my judgements against them, for all their wickedness in forsaking me; they have made offerings to other gods, and worshipped the works of their own hands. [17] But you, gird up your loins; stand up and tell them everything that I command you. Do not break down before them, or I will break you before them. [18] And I for my part have made you today a fortified city, an iron pillar, and a bronze wall, against the whole land – against the kings of Judah, its princes, its priests, and the people of the land. [19] They will fight against you; but they shall not prevail against you, for I am with you, says the Lord, to deliver you.

NRSV Bible

Background notes on Jeremiah

◆ Jeremiah early sixth century BCE.

◆ Believed threat to Jerusalem and its destruction by the Babylonians was the judgement of God.

◆ Jeremiah's theme 'End and New Beginning'.

◆ Royal theology believed in the indestructibility of Jerusalem.

◆ Covenant had been broken ie politically/economically by unjust/oppressive society.

◆ Jeremiah's task:

  1. To help his community face the loss of the old world.

  2. To receive a new world defined by Yahweh.

Session 2 Introduction

The politics of the Covenant
Critiquing the Ulster Covenant in the light of the biblical covenant

Covenant has a very long history. The Hebrews were not the first to develop the idea. Their near-eastern neighbours had long used the concept of covenant and always as a political treaty. Covenant was essentially a political idea involving a religious dimension and rituals. The political dimension to covenant has often been overlooked. The scholastic and pietistic readings of Scripture have spiritualised the idea and confined it to the vertical relationship with God. Even the annual Methodist Covenant Service, for all its strength and emphases at one point on relationships and reconciliation, does not connect with the political reality. The pietism of the service gets in the way.

Why should the Hebrew people have depoliticised covenant and spiritualised it? They didn't, but we did. However, while they reinterpreted covenant from a Yahwistic perspective, they retained its essential political nature. Covenant had to do with a way of organising society.

In the biblical tradition the roots of covenant were at Sinai. Moses was the key player in the covenant with Yahweh, which drew its primary inspiration from the Exodus experience. The God of the covenant was the God who liberated the brickworkers/slaves from Egyptian political, economic and cultural oppression. At Sinai the liberator God entered into pledged relationships with the people and they with God and each other. Sinai was about the beginning of community formation. The ten commandments given as part of the Sinai covenant were not mere laws or a legalistic code. They were the basis of the community constitution. The covenant community relationships were to be shaped by justice, solidarity, compassion and right relations. This community in the making had been liberated from an élitist system of political and economic power, which was oppressive and dominating. Out of Egypt and in a new country, they were surrounded by Canaanite city states, which were also oppressive and unjust models of political and economic organisation. Covenant was the vocation to shape an alternative society. Covenant was a radical socio-economic vision, egalitarian and essentially about a community of equals. The later monarchy with its power structures, especially with Solomon, destroyed the covenant ideal of community. It was the prophets who kept the covenant vision alive, with Jeremiah as an example of a radical conservative, calling for a renewed covenant. Over against the royal ideology and theology, he called for a return to the radical covenantal society. The old organisation of society, which in its economic and political injustice was anti-covenant, was to be destroyed and a new covenantal society was to be built.

The key text, Jeremiah 31:31–34, has often been read out of its socio-political context. The text has suffered from spiritualisation and an individualistic perspective. Its key words have been distorted by such readings. Forgiveness and the knowledge of God have long since become the victims of pietistic readings.

In the Jubilee tradition forgiveness is release from debt and socio-economic slavery and the overcoming of social inequality by a just redistribution of power and resources. This is far removed from the long-standing sacramental and pietistic captivities of the word. The key covenant words underlined by Jeremiah are all about social and human relationships. The knowledge of God is not intellectual knowledge or scholastic knowledge. It has nothing to do with correct formulations of theological doctrines. It is knowledge that pays attention and gives priority to the economically vulnerable, oppressed, exploited and marginalised. To know God, for Jeremiah, was to do justice. The practice of just economic and political relationships was the practical knowledge of God. Knowledge is a doing word in the Hebrew tradition and is about the transformation of social relations and public institutions for justice. It is also egalitarian because in the covenant vision such knowledge is available from the least to the greatest. There is an abolition of social rank and distinction.

This is the radical vision of the Mosaic covenant applied by Jeremiah to his sixth-century society in its injustice and domination of the weak. This 'new covenant' language is rooted in the Mosaic/Sinai covenant and is the basis of the covenant language used by Jesus. The Hebrew roots are communal and are about a radically different socio-political and economic ordering of society. Jeremiah did not spiritualise the idea nor make it apolitical; neither did Jesus. The reign of God, which was the covenantal dream, was no less social, economic and political. Whilst no political system, economic structure or social ideology can ever be identified with the reign of God, the dynamic presence and activity of God is political in that God is involved in historical processes and has always been profoundly concerned with the organisation of society and the practice of social justice for all. Covenant is about community formation, which is inclusive and justly so.

Covenant has continued to be a political word, though frequently far removed from the biblical vision. The history of covenants are largely Scottish and Presbyterian, drawing on concepts of election and promised land. The use of covenant at different times in Scottish history has always to be contextualised. The issues then may not be the issues now, yet very often covenant has suffered from politicisation. There is an anti-Catholic history and often those within the covenant are asserting ascendancy and even domination in religion and politics. This was always about exclusivism. Not all were to be included within the covenantal society – some were enemies and objects of vitriolic language and actions.

It was on these Scottish covenants, especially that of 1643, that the Ulster Covenant of 1912 was based. As two Unionists sat in Westminster rooms discussing the Home Rule crisis, one of them recalled the Scottish covenant of 1643 and from that there developed the idea of an Ulster Covenant which was approved by the larger Protestant churches and signed in solemn ceremony following religious services. The key person in the construction of the covenant text, and present on that night in Westminster when the idea was conceived, was Thomas Sinclair, a Presbyterian elder and MP.

The signing of the Covenant by thousands, including the three larger Protestant church leaders, is deeply embedded in the unionist/Protestant historical memory. The Ulster Covenant was a religio-political document, yet how reflective in it sentiments was it of the biblical covenant? Was it radically egalitarian, concerned with justice for all in the north-eastern part of Ireland, or was it partisan, about the holding of privileges by a section, a minority within Irish society? Was it also an expression of violence, a pledging to use means of violence to achieve a political goal? Did it legitimise the use of the gun in twentieth-century politics? This is not just about a past best forgotten. It was only in 1912 and Irish memory is nearly always contemporary! In a few years the centenary will be reached. How will that be marked in what will be a very different Northern Ireland? If there are commemorations, what role will the Protestant churches play? Will there be a Jeremiah calling for a renewed biblical covenant with its radical implications for all the people within society? The second question in the final group work exercise is very significant. The final plenary question may even be about future vision. The biblical covenant is a very public idea.

Session 2 Plan

Welcome (5 minutes)

Group work exercise 1 (15 minutes)

Discussion on the following questions.

1. What do you understand by a covenant?

2. Can you think of an example of a covenant?

3. How are covenants used?

Feedback (10 minutes)

Overhead (5 minutes)

The history of covenants

Questions of clarification (5 minutes)

Group work exercise 2 (10 minutes)

Discussion on the following questions.

1. What are these covenants really saying?

2. What do they have in common?

Feedback (5 minutes)

Reading of Jeremiah 31:31–4 (5 minutes)

Buzz and feedback (10 minutes)

What does Jeremiah mean by covenant?'

Overhead (5 minutes)

The new covenant vision of Jeremiah

Questions of clarification (5 minutes)

Group work exercise 3 (20 minutes)

Read the text of the Ulster Covenant and consider the following questions.

1. What is the Ulster Covenant saying?

2. Imagine you are Jeremiah reading the Ulster Covenant. Prepare a response to the Ulster people.

Feedback (10 minutes)

Plenary reflection (10 minutes)

Consider the following question.

In a new Northern Ireland context do we need another covenant?

Session 2, Handout 1

Group work exercise 1

In your group consider the following questions:

1. What do you understand by a covenant?

2. Can you think of an example of a covenant?

3. How are covenants used?

Overhead 1

The history of covenants

First Scottish Covenant – 1557

John Knox and Reformers covenanted between themselves and God to make the Reformed Church the established religion in Scotland.

King's Covenant – 1581

Political – bound King James to uphold true Presbyterian religion and political liberty.

Solemn League and Covenant – 1643

Signed by Scottish Presbyterians and English Parliament – pledged to preserve reformed religion in Scotland and introduce it to England and Ireland.

Westminster Confession of Faith – 1649

Definitive statement of Presbyterian covenantal theology and politics.

General Synod of Ulster – 1715

Purpose of the Westminster Confession was to "extirpate Popery, prelacy, schism and prophaness; to maintain the privileges of Parliament and the rights and prerogatives of the King."

Solemn League and Covenant – 1643

"To root out of the empire all heretics and enemies of the true worship of God."

Pope was the "Roman anti-Christ".

Catholic worship was described as the Pope's "five bastard sacraments, his devilish mass, his blasphemous priesthood".

Westminster Confession – 1649

Pope was "that anti-Christ, that man of sin and son of perdition, who glorifies himself as opposed to Christ".

Session 2, Handout 2

Group work exercise 2

In small groups, discuss the following questions:

1. What are these covenants really saying?

2. What do they have in common?

Session 2, Handout 3

Jeremiah 31:31–4

[31] The days are surely coming says the Lord, when I will make a new covenant with the house of Israel and the house of Judah. [32] It will not be like the covenant that I made with their ancestors when I took them by the hand to bring them out of the land of Egypt – a covenant that they broke, though I was their husband, says the Lord. [33] But this is the covenant that I will make with the house of Israel after these days, says the Lord: I will put my law within them, and I will write it on their hearts; and I will be their God, and they shall be my people. [34] No longer shall they teach one another, or say to each other, 'Know the Lord', for they shall all know me, from the least of them to the greatest, says the Lord; for I will forgive their iniquity, and remember their sin no more.'

NRSV Bible

Discussion question

1. What does Jeremiah mean by covenant?

Overhead 2

The new covenant vision

Jeremiah 31:31–4

1. Rooted in forgiveness
◆ God's forgiveness – social and human relationships

◆ Forgiveness of debts

◆ End of slavery

◆ Overcoming social inequality

2. Totally committed to right relations
◆ Justice, mercy, compassion and righteousness characterise all relationships

3. Marked by knowledge of God
◆ To know God is to do justice

◆ Knowledge = attention to poor and needy

◆ Knowledge = transformation of social relations and public institutions for justice

4. An egalitarian community
◆ Knowledge from the least to the greatest

◆ No social rank or distinction

Session 2, Handout 4

The Ulster Covenant

Being convinced in our consciences that Home Rule would be disastrous to the material well-being of Ulster, as well as of the whole of Ireland, subversive of our civil and religious freedom, destructive of our citizenship and perilous to the unity of the Empire, we, whose names are underwritten, men of Ulster, loyal subjects of His Gracious Majesty King George V, humbly relying on the God whom our fathers in days of stress and trial confidently trusted, do hereby pledge ourselves in solemn covenant throughout this our time of threatened calamity to stand by one another in defending for ourselves and our children our cherished position of equal citizenship in the United Kingdom and in using all means which may be found necessary to defeat the present conspiracy to set up a Home Rule parliament in Ireland. And in the event of such a parliament being forced upon us, we further solemnly and mutually pledge ourselves to refuse to recognise its authority. In sure confidence that God will defend the right we hereto subscribe our name. God save the King.

Group work exercise 3

Read the text of the Ulster Covenant and consider the following questions.

1. What is the Ulster Covenant saying?

2. Imagine you are Jeremiah reading the Ulster Covenant. Prepare a response to the Ulster people.

Session 3 Introduction

A theology of community relations
Connecting biblical insights to community

Exodus was the foundational event for the Hebrew people. The liberation from Egyptian oppression shaped identity and community. It also gave the Hebrew people their core vision of God. The annual Passover festival is the Exodus celebration, which renews the experience as foundational and definitional. It remains the defining narrative for Jewish people wherever in the world. The narrative has also provided a paradigm for liberation in many contemporary situations of political and economic oppression.

The Exodus paradigm is not without its problems. Critics have pointed out that contemporary liberation theology has edited out part of the narrative, which speaks of the destruction of the pursuing Egyptians and the Canaanites who were somewhat in the way of the liberated slaves arriving in the promised land. At other times in history the narrative has been used to justify the elimination of indigenous people by Western colonising people. Puritan preachers in North America easily referred to Native Americans as Amalekites and Canaanites. That was enough to justify extermination. Colonial plunder has read this narrative as a text of terror.

Within the Jewish tradition there has been some unease about the narrative. One rabbinic tradition has God saying; "The work of my hands has drowned in the sea and shall you chant songs?" Also God does not "rejoice in the downfall of the wicked" (Michael Prior, *The Bible and Colonialism: A Moral Critique*, Sheffield Academic Press, 1997, p 283). A case is made for rehabilitating the Exodus, which, in the face of suffering and oppression, can still inspire hope and action. Michael Prior wishes to reinterpret the promised land motif within the context of reinterpretation, which has already taken place in 2nd Isaiah (55:2–13) and by Jesus.

The issue cannot be ignored given the use of the Exodus narrative to justify oppression in Latin America, Africa and Palestine. At the same time the narrative does provide a defining experience of community. Whilst the text we now have was written centuries later and is more theological reflection than a literal or historical account of an event, it does contrast two opposed models of community which were part of Hebrew memory and experience. The God of Exodus was opposed to the gods of Pharaoh, not as a religious or doctrinal conflict, but as two diametrically opposed models of organising society. The nature of the gods shaped the nature of community. The vision of the gods translated into community structures. This was also true of Yahweh.

Egyptian model of Community

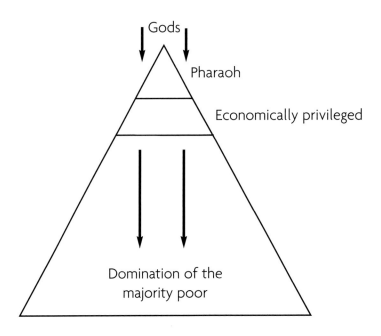

Hebrew model of Community

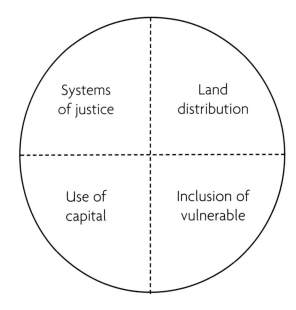

The Egyptian model of community was based on a hierarchical structure and was a domination system, which was oppressive of the majority poor.

The Hebrew model was a participatory, partnership and egalitarian model basing its relationships and structures on the nature of the Exodus God. It was the covenantal model of community in which relationships were those of committed solidarity and the structures were based on distributive justice.

The Exodus qualities of community are expressed in Exodus 15. The style is hymnic, a song of Miriam in the freedom tradition which is also encountered in the songs of Deborah, Hannah, Judith and Mary. As with all songs of worship, they are a response to God's grace. Israel's life is centred on worship of the God who is the source of life and freedom.

In the Hebrew tradition worship was not just towards God but also against the gods. In the act of worship, all earthly power was relativised. There was no other God and all other gods were put in their place or put into proper perspective. The gods of Egypt and Canaan could never be absolutised in the context of worship of the Exodus God. Whatever power the gods had to shape society and its structures was never ultimate. Alternative power relations and structures were always possible, as was transformation. This radically free God could not be monopolised by the liberated slaves either and if they paid more attention to the Canaanite Baals, constructing a hierarchical and dominating system, then they too came under the judgement of God. Worship was a radical, social and political act!

The righteousness of God was the norm for community action. Righteousness has the sense of right relations, but right relations in particular based on justice. God was the God who was against, and took decisive action against, all forms of injustice. The liberating and gracious activity of God was to establish right or just relations. The justice was distributive and restorative. People's dignity and humanity mattered to God and both were diminished by oppressive politics and exploitative economics. The social and business ethics articulated by the Holiness Code of Leviticus 19:35–6 have their source in the righteous God of the Exodus experience.

At the heart of God and community relations for the Hebrews was compassion. The core covenant word CHESED is essentially about loyal love and compassion. It is a norm for all relationships. Compassion is the ability to suffer alongside. The compassionate One is:

Father of the fatherless and protector of widows . . .

God gives the desolate a home to dwell in;

He leads out the prisoners to prosperity;

Psalm 68:5–6

And if he cries to me, I shall hear, for I am compassionate.

Exodus 22:26

The divine nature was to be reflected in the nature of community and this nature was disclosed in the Exodus:

Here we have the explicit naming of a concept central to the notion of community structure in early Israel, divine compassion . . . The quality of divine compassion as the model for the community implied openness to the excluded, a point of access for the disenfranchised. In fact, taken in its most fundamental and original meaning, the compassion of the Deliverer God Yahweh implied that this community was present in the world precisely as a home for the enslaved, the poor, the bereaved.

(Paul D Hanson, *The People Called: The Growth of Community in the Bible*, Harper and Row, 1986, p 49.)

Session 3 plan

Welcome (5 minutes)

Group work exercise 1 (10 minutes)

Discussion on the following questions.

1. What do you understand by community?

2. Share a meaningful experience of community?

Feedback (10 minutes)

Overhead (5 minutes)

Exodus – A defining experience of community

Questions of clarification (5 minutes)

Group work exercise 2 (25 minutes)

Imagine you are liberated Hebrew slaves. Draw a diagram representing the Egyptian model of community as you experienced it.

Reflect on your experience of living out of this model.

Feedback (15 minutes)

Role-play (45 minutes)

'Competing visions of community'

Preparation (10 minutes)

Role play (20 minutes)

Reflection (15 minutes)

Session 3, Handout 1

A theology of community relations

Connecting biblical insights to community

Group work exercise 1

Small group discussion on the questions:

1. What do you understand by community?

2. Share a meaningful experience of community?

Group work exercise 2

1. Imagine you are liberated Hebrew slaves. Draw a diagram representing the Egyptian model of community as you experienced it.

2. Reflect on your experience of living out of this model.

Overhead 1

Exodus – A defining experience of community

1. Egyptian understanding of community

◆ The God of Exodus was opposed to the gods of the Pharaoh. Ancient empires/city states were built on the assumption that the divine/god's intention was that some humans were created to enjoy:

1. greater esteem;

2. privilege;

3. material comforts.

The vision of the gods translated into:

1. hierarchical structure;

2. domination;

3. special privilege;

4. caste system.

2. Hebrew understanding of community

◆ Exodus revealed the nature of God.

◆ Exodus revealed the nature of community modelled on the nature of God.

◆ Exodus resulted in the creating of community structures related to:

1. systems of justice;

2. land distribution;

3. use of capital;

4. treatment of vulnerable classes.

◆ Israel's socio-economic and political structures were to have their ultimate source in the nature of the Exodus God.

Session 3, Handout 2

Competing visions of community

Role-play

Groups:

Miriam/Moses group

Hebrew Tribal Elders

Canaanite Leaders

Read Exodus 15 and the handout on Exodus qualities of community.

Scenario:

You have just arrived in the promised land and the task is to build a community based on Exodus qualities.

The Canaanite leaders are opposed to your presence and the model of community you want to create. It is a threat to the privileged position they hold in their community.

The tribal leaders recognise from their Egyptian experience the Canaanite model of community. They are even attracted to it because in an agricultural society the Canaanite fertility gods seem to be quite successful.

Miriam and Moses are totally committed to the Exodus, God's vision of community.

A meeting will be held in the public square at which all of the groups will be present and concerns will be expressed.

– The Canaanites are opposed to the Exodus model.

– The tribal leaders are unsure.

– Miriam and Moses are committed.

Prepare for the public discussion.

Session 3, Handout 3

Exodus 15:1–18

[1] Then Moses and the Israelites sang this song to the Lord: 'I will sing to the Lord, for he has triumphed gloriously; horse and rider he has thrown into the sea. [2] The Lord is my strength and my might, and he has become my salvation; this is my God, and I will praise him, my father's God, and I will exalt him. [3] The Lord is warrior; the Lord is his name. [4] Pharaoh's chariots and his army he cast into the sea; his picked officers were sunk in the Red Sea. [5] The floods covered them; they went down into the depths like a stone. [6] Your right hand, O Lord, glorious in power – your right hand, O Lord, shattered the enemy. [7] In the greatness of your majesty you overthrew your adversaries; you sent out your fury, it consumed them like stubble. [8] At the blast of you nostrils the waters piled up, the floods stood up in a heap; the deeps congealed in the heart of the sea. [9] The enemy said, "I will pursue, I will overtake, I will divide the spoil, my desire shall have its fill of them. I will draw my sword, my hand shall destroy them." [10] You blew with your wind, the sea covered them; they sank like lead in the mighty waters. [11] Who is like you, O Lord, among the gods? Who is like you, majestic in holiness, awesome in splendour, doing wonders? [12] You stretched out your right hand, the earth swallowed them. [13] In your steadfast love you led the people whom you redeemed; you guided them by your strength to your holy abode. [14] The peoples heard, they trembled; pangs seized the inhabitants of Philistia. [15] Then the chiefs of Edom were dismayed; trembling seized the leaders of Moab; all the inhabitants of Canaan melted away. [16] Terror and dread fell upon them; by the might of your arm, they became still as a stone until your people whom you acquired passed by. [17] You brought them in and planted them on the mountain of your own possession, the place, O Lord, that you made your abode, the sanctuary, O Lord, that your hands have established. [18] The Lord will reign for ever and ever.'

NRSV Bible

Session 3, Handout 4

Exodus qualities of community – Exodus 15

1. Worship as response to God's grace

◆ Exodus 15 – Song of Miriam – hymnic form.

◆ Worship was the primary quality of community.

◆ Worship is focused on the source and centre of life and freedom.

◆ Focus on liberating God relativises all earthly power.

◆ The gracious, saving God is the ultimate reality.

◆ Worship acknowledges the sole lordship of God.

2. God's righteousness as norm for community action: Exodus 15:11–12

◆ At the heart of Hebrew community was a norm that relativised all other authorities.

◆ A new standard of righteousness was experienced.

◆ God took incisive action against injustice.

◆ God acted to establish right or just relations.

◆ Example of God's righteousness or justice – Leviticus 19:35–6.

◆ Sedeq – just measures important in a society where the weak and the poor are most harmed by dishonesty/injustice.

◆ God's quality of justice is a relational quality.

◆ The norm for Israel's laws and social structures.

3. God's heart of compassion as the heart of community relations: Exodus 15:13

◆ Hesed = goodness, kindness, mercy, compassion, steadfast love.

◆ Hesed is covenant love – utterly trustworthy – a norm for all relationships.

◆ God liberated and sustained community out of compassion.

◆ Community requires justice and justice needs to be infused with compassion.

◆ Liberation from a heartless social order (Egypt) is liberation into a social order with heart, which is compassion.

◆ Order by itself can be oppressive – justice can be an abstraction.

◆ Compassion = a heart reaching out to embrace all – especially the weak, poor and the stranger.

Session 3, Handout 5

A theology of community relations: competing models of community

Reflection on role-play

Consider the following questions.

1. How did you feel in your role?

2. What tensions were experienced?

3. Was the Exodus model of community a realistic possibility?

4. What are its essential qualities?

5. Does it offer a model of community relations for a divided society?

Session 4   Introduction

Contrast – culture gospel
Exploring whether gospel values can shape an alternative culture

In 1951 H Richard Niebuhr, an American theologian and ethicist, published a highly influential book, *Christ and Culture*. The book became Niebuhr's best-seller and has shaped the theological consciousness of many who wrestle with authentic Christian witness in the public place.

Niebuhr surveyed five different ways in which Christians in the past have attempted to resolve the problem of Christ and culture. For Niebuhr, this was the basic moral issue and the enduring problem. Over half a century later the issue and the problem remain and will never go away. "The problem is involved in relations between loyalties to Christ and culture, church and state, faith and reason, and Christian discipleship in secular society" (Stassen, Yeager and Yoder, *Authentic Transformation: A New Vision of Christ and Culture*, Abington Press, 1996, p10). Paul faced the same issue in his letter to the Roman Christians with his imperative not to be "conformed to this world, but to be transformed by the renewing of your minds" (Romans 12:2).

Niebuhr's five typologies were:

◆ Christ against culture – radical tension;

◆ Christ of culture – accommodation and assimilation;

◆ Christ above culture – two sets of values on different lines;

◆ Christ and culture in paradox – moving between both worlds;

◆ Christ transforming culture – conversion.

Put more simply, Christian responses to society have tended to:

◆ withdraw from society;

◆ compromise with society;

◆ selectively affirm and reject in society;

◆ transform society.

For Niebuhr the answer lies in transformation or conversion of culture. The Mennonite theologian John Howard Yoder is critical of Niebuhr's position, believing that his "favouring the 'transformation' vision correlates with a low estimate of the power of evil". Yoder appeals to an older Reformation theology which described culture as fallen. Yoder would be closer to the 'Christ against culture' typology and see the Christian response as living in radical tension with culture.

All of this underlines the demanding and perennial challenge before the Christian community. Niebuhr defined culture as everything which people do.

> Far from being limited to that narrow realm of the arts to which the word refers in some other contexts, the term 'culture' points for Niebuhr to every realm of human creative behaviour, and especially to those points at which we may observe inhuman experience certain kinds of continuity in this world. The State, the economy, the family, the arts are all samples of the great world of culture.

(Yoder in Strassen et al, p33.)

Since all of these embody their own set of cultural values, how are they challenged by the radical demands of Jesus? What does it mean, therefore, to proclaim by word and action a 'contrast culture' gospel? Can gospel values shape an alternative society?

How we answer these questions will depend a great deal on how we envision Jesus. In the Christian Scriptures Christianity is represented as a way of life by which we follow Jesus (Acts 9:2, 22:4). But the Jesus we follow is often a Jesus without a context.

> In the most un-Jewish of all possible moves, the Jew Jesus became a 'detached' Jesus at the hands of the great ecumenical councils. He was detached from his own historic community and its way, and found himself metaphysically fused to God alone. So one searches in vain in the classic creeds, those pure distillations of the faith, for anything at all about Jesus as the way in any moral sense, or of his community's way.

(Larry Rasmussen quoted in Strassen et al, p 227.)

Reconnecting Jesus with his community and world is an essential task for the Christian response to culture. Without such a reconnection there will be little moral critique of all that is defined as culture. The Christian community will have difficulty embodying an alternative culture with contrast values. In this session, therefore, there is an attempt to enter the world of Jesus and especially the Galilee in which he spent most of his time. There is no avoiding the Jewishness of his world, culture and of himself. Background notes and information on overheads/handouts dealing with the world of Jesus are found in the session 'And the walls came tumbling down' from the course 'Being authentic community for the twenty-first century'.

The core metaphor for Jesus' teaching and ministry was the reign of God. The overhead presentations are based on a book by the Asian theologian CS Song. From his Asian experience Song offers perceptive insights on this primary gospel metaphor. Especially pertinent is the quotation from an Orthodox Jew on the Beatitudes. If the Sermon on the Mount is the heart of what Jesus meant by the reign of God, then the Beatitudes are the essence of the essence of what he perceived the reign of God to be. They do reverse the dominant values and call for a radical discipleship. Attempts have been made to project them into a future or to spiritualise them or to apply them only to private discipleship. None of these approaches takes the Beatitudes seriously. They each represent in their own way the domestication of Jesus, not least by detaching Jesus and his teaching from his real life Jewish community and Roman occupied world. The overhead on 'Kingdom lifestyle' is a reading of the Beatitudes from, and for, the social world of relationships and community. They are offered as a reflective reading at the end of the session after the group has engaged in an important exercise of rewriting the Beatitudes in the local group context. The earlier plenary question regarding tensions between the reign of God and existing contemporary culture needs to be probing and sharp in its focus.

Session 4 Plan

Welcome (5 minutes)

Buzz and feedback (5 minutes)

What is culture?

Buzz and feedback (5 minutes)

What is the relationship of the church to culture?

Overhead (5 minutes)

The world of Jesus – text

Overhead (5 minutes)

The world of Jesus – diagram

Questions of clarification (5 minutes)

Role-play (30 minutes)

Preparation (15 minutes)

Feedback and dialogue (15 minutes)

Overheads (10 minutes)

The reign of God

Questions of clarification (5 minutes)

Open plenary (10 minutes)

Consider the following question.

What are the tensions between the reign of God and the existing culture of our time?

Group work exercise 1 (20 minutes)

Read Matthew 5:1–12 and rewrite the beatitudes in your own local context.

Feedback (10 minutes)

Reflective reading of overhead Kingdom lifestyle (5 minutes)

Overhead 1

The world of Jesus

◆ Occupation and domination by imperial power

◆ Oppressed by the burden of heavy taxation

◆ Overwhelmed by economic debt

◆ Controlled and exploited by temple system

◆ Frequent nationalistic insurrections

Overhead 2

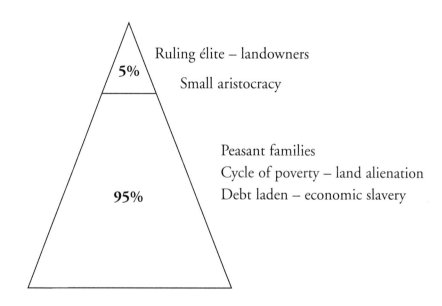

5% Ruling élite – landowners

Small aristocracy

95% Peasant families
Cycle of poverty – land alienation
Debt laden – economic slavery

Session 4, Handout 1

Contrast – Culture Gospel

Role-play

Characters in role-play:

• Roman governor – Pilate

• Jewish high priests

• Galilean peasants

Scenario:

Imaginatively enter into your character role from within the world of Jesus as portrayed in the presentation.

From your perspective address the following questions.

1. What is your experience from within this first-century culture?

2. What challenges do you face within the cultural context? What are your fears?

3. What are your hopes for your Palestinian society ten years from now and how might they be realised?

Feedback

The groups will share their various responses to these questions, then enter into a conversation addressing the issues raised.

Session 4, Handout 2

Roman governor – Pilate

◆ Pilate finds himself serving in a particularly thankless and difficult post. He is a no-nonsense Roman colonial official who knows that riots or rebellions will damage his career.

◆ Pilate's office has two responsibilities.

1. To tame and Romanise the late Herod's kingdom.

2. To enrich his own coffers and Romanise his public persona.

◆ Pilate's ambition is to be back in the Roman forum and to rise to greater glory. He, therefore, keeps one eye on public order in Judea and his ears and eyes open for potentially significant changes in the power relations of Rome.

◆ Pilate aggressively promotes Roman power and the imperial cult. He sent troops into Jerusalem, and the Jewish temple, with battle standards proudly raised and with golden eagles, and other imperial insignia, glinting brightly in the sun. All his predecessors had avoided this display, out of sensitivity to the Jewish prohibition on idolatrous images, but Pilate made no special concessions.

◆ Angry Jewish people had descended on Pilate's headquarters at Caesarea and were prepared to die rather than allow graven images to be brought into the holy city and the temple. Pilate was forced to back down.

◆ Later Pilate sent soldiers into the temple to take funds from the treasury to help pay for the construction of a water aqueduct. Crowds gathered in protest. Pilate had soldiers, disguised as civilians and armed with clubs, at a prearranged signal, violently and bloodily deal with the crowds.

◆ During the festivals Jerusalem is the most dangerous potential source of political embarrassment. The tens of thousands who gather for each of the major festivals are a source of disorder and violence. Pilate wastes no time in calling out troops to take care of troublemakers, "mingling their blood with their sacrifices" (Luke 13:1).

Jewish high priest

◆ The Jewish high priests and their families have been exalted to their position of power by Herod the Great.

◆ They are caught in a dangerous position between the Jewish population and the cold officials of Rome eg Pilate.

◆ The high priestly families are in charge of the temple treasury, workshops and storerooms and have amassed large fortunes. Their responsibilities, privileges and wealth they will hand on to sons.

◆ They are permanent residents of Jerusalem and have an elegant lifestyle, living in large mansions. They are buried in elaborate family tombs.

◆ Their wealth and political fortunes are dependent on the Roman authorities. Their main concerns are not with piety but with representing the Judean people to the Roman authorities in making sure that order is maintained in Jerusalem. The Roman officials could and did appoint them to office or dispose of them at will.

◆ The high priests are held hostage by the people during the festivals, hoping that the explosive mix of God and freedom will not destroy the brittle veneer of public order.

Galilean peasants

◆ The peasants are a grass roots Galilean protest movement, involving thousands of nameless people, whose lives, hopes and fears for the future are not recorded. These are the people whom Jesus knew and grew up with and who are the vast marginal majority.

◆ They live in an agrarian culture as small communities of farmers and herders. Their primary aim is family survival on the land of their ancestors, preserving ancient customs and social institutions and faithfully passing them on.

◆ They live in an embattled situation as threatened communities, struggling to hold on to threatened and diminishing autonomy.

◆ They are oppressed by both the Romans and temple system, both of which impose heavy taxation, reducing the peasants to poverty, landlessness and economic slavery.

◆ A large portion of their produce is given to the temple priests to satisfy religious tithing laws. They look to the temple and priesthood as a positive symbol of the unity of the people and their link with God.

◆ They blame the Romans for their abuse and regard the heavy tribute Rome imposes as robbery and illegitimate.

◆ They support the dissident movements within their community, viewing them as heroic victims of Roman injustice, and offer them protection from the Romans.

Overhead 3

The reign of God

◆ Enabling people "to perceive social, political and economic contradictions" – this constitutes the essential part of Jesus' ministry of God's reign.

◆ He envisions a human community in which power does not corrupt, wealth does not create poverty, justice for some does not become injustice for others, and love is not charity of the rich and indignity of the poor but the power that binds people in a bond of communion regardless of colour, sex or creed.

◆ Empowerment, in Jesus' view, must be part of what the reign of God means. Empowering people to fight the root causes that make them poor and hungry (Luke 6:20–21).

◆ "These Beatitudes offer neither congratulations nor consolation with promises for the next world; they are the good news that the God of our forebears, who demands a reversal of our own thinking, will reassess all earthly values here below."

(An Orthodox Jew)

(CS Song, *Quotations from Jesus and the Reign of God*, Fortress Press, 1993)

Overhead 4

The reign Of God

◆ In the reign of God, Jesus envisions a culture of love and compassion to replace the old culture of power, conflict and greed. The culture of love for the neighbour as well as for God is the culture of God's reign.

◆ God's reign, rooted thus in God's creation, cannot be monopolised by a particular nation. As it is based on God's creating activity, which spans the whole of creation and embraces the whole of humanity, the reign of God cannot be restricted within a particular religious tradition.

◆ All human beings are endowed with inviolable humanity.

◆ The society that keeps the poor forever poor is opposed to the reign of God. A nation that discriminates against certain people because of the colour of their skin contradicts the reign of God.

◆ A world that perpetuates patriarchal control over women is hostile to the reign of God.

◆ The religious community that has no room for people of other religious communities is far from being the reign of God.

◆ It testifies to a confident God, the God who is big enough, gracious enough, and large hearted enough to take human beings into God's confidence and make them God's co-workers.

(CS Song, *Quotations from Jesus and the Reign of God*, Fortress Press, 1993)

Session 4, Handout 3

Matthew 5:1–12

[1] When Jesus saw the crowds, he went up the mountain; and after he sat down, his disciples came to him. [2] Then he began to speak, and taught them, saying:

[3] 'Blessed are the poor in spirit, for theirs is the kingdom of heaven. [4] Blessed are those who mourn, for they will be comforted. [5] Blessed are the meek, for they will inherit the earth. [6] Blessed are those who hunger and thirst for righteousness, for they will be filled. [7] Blessed are the merciful, for they will receive mercy. [8] Blessed are the pure in heart, for they will see God. [9] Blessed are the peacemakers, for they will be called children of God. [10] Blessed are those who are persecuted for righteousness' sake, for theirs is the kingdom of heaven. [11] Blessed are you when people revile you and persecute you and utter all kinds of evil against you falsely on my account. [12] Rejoice and be glad, for your reward is great in heaven, for in the same way they persecuted the prophets who were before you.'

NRSV Bible

Group work exercise 1

Read Matthew 5:1–12 and rewrite the Beatitudes in your own local context.

Overhead 5

Kingdom lifestyle

Kingdom of relationships and community

Beatitudes – Matthew 5:1–12 – essence of the kingdom

◆ Recognising the poor (Luke)
◆ Recognising the poverty of our relationships (Matthew)
◆ Feeling and entering into the pain of community brokenness
◆ The practice of mutual tolerance
◆ The passion for justice in society
◆ The spirit of understanding and forgiveness
◆ The single-minded pursuit of healthy community
◆ Active peacemaking and bridge-building
◆ Conflict with injustice

Session 5 **Introduction**

The politics of memory
Exploring biblical insights on remembering that liberates

Every society, community, church and nation has a memory. Without memory, the story of the past, there is an impaired identity, a lack of roots or an absence of a sense of continuity. The story of the past needs to be told often to make sense of the present and to provide a depth dimension to belonging. It is necessary to remember.

Memory, however, can be abused, denied, repressed or be used in a highly selective way. It can also become captive to an ideology or nationalistic and often partisan interpretation. What is being remembered and how?

Memory is frequently invoked in Ireland. Irish people have been accused of having long memories and refusing to let go of the past. Sometimes this point is made by those from other contexts, who have denied painful parts of their own national or collective memory, which is hardly honest! Yet historical memory can be used for sectarian and exclusive purposes. The memory can be an ideological or mythologised re-telling, far removed from what may have happened. The person or hero involved from the past may have little resemblance to historical reality. Cuchullain is invoked by both republicans and loyalists in Ireland as though he was a historical figure and not a creative invention of rich Celtic mythology. Nevertheless he is used to legitimise violent actions against the perceived enemy in the present.

Memory also involved the chosen traumas. Across centuries of Irish conflict each section of the divided community can recall its atrocities suffered and its traumatic experiences. The sufferings and traumas of the other community are ignored or even counted as inferior. The memory of the Catholic Rebellion of 1641 has burned its way deeply into the Protestant psyche. The response of Cromwell in 1649 remains alive in the Catholic psyche. One section of the community remembers 1690 while the other remembers 1916. Each event became a deepening myth based on perceived facts, which in reality had more to do with an ideologically conditioned interpretation.

We have deluded ourselves for a long time that history is based on facts. The only real fact is that history is based on interpretation and interpretation is shaped by social, class, gender, religious and political location. Our socio-political preferences will shape the telling of the story and colour the collective memory.

A key issue, then, is how we use memory. How do we remember? Remembering is an important biblical theme. At the heart of the Jewish faith is the memory of Exodus. At the heart of the Christian faith is the memory of the Jesus story. The former is remembered in the celebration of the Passover while the latter is remembered in the celebration of the Eucharist. Both faith traditions are historical or rooted in memory. Yet the remembering is not merely the recalling of a dim and distant past event. It is remembering in the present in that the Exodus or Christ event is brought into the present and the faithful enter into the story and experience as contemporary. The here and now participation in the stories become present experiences of liberation and hope. In the remembering and active use of historical imagination the present and the future become filled with the potential for liberation and newness.

Remembering, therefore, can either be destructive or redemptive, imprisonment in the past or liberation to a new future. Redemptive remembering has the power to create fresh imagined alternatives. Redemptive remembering can enable people to think, act, speak and even sing differently. Key to redemptive memory is imagination. Through the power of imagination the past is not a closed record or a prison. It produces an energy that offers possibilities for newness and transformation.

The biblical texts offer models of redemptive memory. It is a significant theme for 2nd Isaiah (chapters 40–55). This unknown prophet has a socio-historical location in the Babylonian exile. Reading the words of the prophet in the socio-political context is important for an appreciation of the emphasis on memory.

The trauma of the exile experience is probably beyond even our most imaginative and empathetic grasp. It was a shattering experience for the citizens of Judah. Their social, cultural, political, economic and theological world had collapsed. They wept when they remembered Zion and found it impossible to sing the Lord's song in a strange land (Psalm 137). They were a totally displaced and alienated people dominated by the imperial power, which defined all of reality and made the ultimate claims upon their lives.

Into their Babylonian dominated lives came the first rays of hope. The empire had feet of clay after all. It was neither absolute nor ultimate. Its truth and reality claims were very fallible and utterly finite. Much later in their history the apocalyptic literature of Daniel was to provide a theological perspective on all imperial power and deified empires. The only lasting sovereignty is that of the Most High (Daniel 4:34). The kingdom as strong as iron that crushes and smashes everything has feet of clay and whatever its strength or brutal might, it is essentially brittle (Daniel 2:40–2). This subversive theology of empire and imperial power points to the inherent seeds of destruction at the heart of all superpowers and empires.

Second Isaiah's metaphors are different from Daniel's but introduce the same subversive and relativising perspective on empire: "The grass withers, the flower fades, when the breath of the Lord blows upon it; surely the people are grass. The grass withers, the flower fades; but the word of our God will stand forever" (Isaiah 40:7–8).

The Babylonian empire is withering and fading. The Persian empire is in the ascendancy, though its day of destruction will also come. There is hope for liberation from exile; hope that life can be defined within an alternative reality and that a people can sing again. In this context 2nd Isaiah invokes historical memory and does so as a subversive activity. As a community they are to remember Moses, remember Sarah and Abraham, remember God's blessings as they "look to the rock from which you were hewn, and to the quarry from which you were dug" (Isaiah 51:1). Remembering becomes subversive and transformative in the present. The praise and worship of God alone were subversive of Babylon. Memory becomes liberative, redemptive and opens up new possibilities. A redemptive remembering of the past redefines the present and the future.

At the heart of what 2nd Isaiah offers the exiles is poetic imagination within which is the "potential of unleashing a community of power and action that finally will not be contained by any imperial restrictions and definitions of reality" (Walter Brueggemann, *Hopeful Imagination: Prophetic Voices in Exile*, SCM Press, 1986, p 96).

Language and story become agents of transformation, even community transformation. '… the poet appeals to old memories and affirmations in an astonishing way to jar the perceptual field of Israel and to cause a wholly new discernment of reality' (Brueggemann, p 96). By returning to memory the prophet/poet reads the ancient story for the contemporary moment. Such remembering is as a new gift. Israel's memories contain a future and require a decision.

Session 5 Plan

Welcome (5 minutes)

Buzz and feedback (10 minutes)

1. What is personal memory?

2. What is collective memory?

Buzz and feedback (15 minutes)

How does memory work in Ireland? (eg 'Remember 1690', '1916' etc)

Overhead (5 minutes)

2nd Isaiah on memory

Questions of clarification (5 minutes)

Group work exercise 1 (30 minutes)

2nd Isaiah

Feedback (20 minutes)

Overhead (5 minutes)

The power of memory to liberate

Questions of clarification (5 minutes)

Plenary discussion (20 minutes)

How can we use memory to liberate in our contemporary situation?

Overhead 1

The politics of memory

2nd Isaiah on memory

◆ Social historical setting in exile

◆ Words directed to an alienated community

◆ Hope of release for a displaced community

◆ Life is defined in terms of Babylonian reality

◆ Babylon is imperial power – absolute and ultimate

◆ Reality and loyalty are defined by Babylon

◆ 2nd Isaiah invokes memory as subversive activity

◆ Memory is an act of hope and subversion

◆ Reality is not defined by the dominant power

◆ 2nd Isaiah – poetic imagination – radical, alternative reality

Session 5, Handout 1

Group work exercise 1

2nd Isaiah

In your group, read the relevant biblical text and background notes, then answer the following questions.

1. How is the prophet using memory in your text?

2. How do you think the people in exile heard this text?

3. In what way is the text subversive and liberating?

Group 1 – Remember Moses

Isaiah 43:18–19

[18] Do not remember the former things, or consider the things of old. [19] I am about to do a new thing; now it springs forth, do you not perceive it? I will make a way in the wilderness and rivers in the desert.

NRSV Bible

◆ Text remembers the Exodus event led by Moses.

◆ Exodus and Sinai are about protest and demand.

◆ Each new generation must engage with the radical demands of God – Isaiah 43:8–19.

◆ Memory becomes immediately present in contemporary experience.

◆ Memory is not merely in the past but points to the 'new thing'.

Group 2 – Remember Sarah and Abraham

Isaiah 54:1–4

¹ Sing, O barren one who did not bear; burst into song and shout, you who have not been in labour! For the child of the desolate woman will be more than the child of her that is married, says the Lord. ² Enlarge the site of your tent, and let the curtains of your habitations be stretched out; do not hold back; lengthen your cords and strengthen your stakes. ³ For you will spread out to the right and to the left, and your descendants will possess the nations and will settle the desolate towns. ⁴ Do not fear, for you will not be ashamed; do not be discouraged, for you will not suffer disgrace; for you will forget the shame of your youth, and the disgrace of your widowhood you will remember no more.

NRSV Bible

◆ Memory opens up possibility.

◆ Isaiah text is a reflection on Genesis 18:9–14.

Genesis 18:9–14

⁹ They said to him, 'Where is your wife Sarah?' And he said, 'There, in the tent.' ¹⁰ Then one said, 'I will surely return to you in due season, and your wife Sarah shall have a son.' And Sarah was listening at the tent entrance behind him. ¹¹ Now Abraham and Sarah were old, advanced in age; it had ceased to be with Sarah after the manner of women. ¹² So Sarah laughed to herself, saying, 'After I have grown old, and my husband is old, shall I have pleasure?' ¹³ The Lord said to Abraham, 'Why did Sarah laugh, and say,

'Shall I indeed bear a child, now that I am old?' ¹⁴ Is anything too wonderful for the Lord? At that set time I will return to you, in due season, and Sarah shall have a son.'

NRSV Bible

◆ Genesis:14 – is anything impossible for God?

◆ What is possible for God that the world considers impossible?

◆ The empire says impossible – the empire defines what is and what is not possible.

◆ Babylon defines ultimate reality.

◆ Remembering Sarah and Abraham becomes transformative and subversive in the present.

◆ The act of praise is subversive against Babylon.

Group 3 – Remember God's blessings

Isaiah 51:1–3

[1] Listen to me, you that pursue righteousness, you that seek the Lord. Look to the rock from which you were hewn, and to the quarry from which you were dug. [2] Look to Abraham your father and to Sarah who bore you; for he was but one when I called him, but I blessed him and made him many. [3] For the Lord will comfort Zion; he will comfort all her waste places, and will make her wilderness like Eden, her desert like the garden of the Lord; joy and gladness will be found in her, thanksgiving and the voice of song.

NRSV Bible

◆ 'Listen' is addressed to those who are deeply serious about faith.

◆ Israel is invited to recall the Abraham/Sarah stories. They are the true ancestors of the community of exiles.

◆ Exiles are to recall the ancestors in order to connect with the memory that God gives blessing to this people in the most unlikely circumstance.

◆ What Yahweh did of old for a hopeless people, Yahweh will do again in this present generation of exiles.

Overhead 2

Power of memory to liberate

◆ **Fresh imagined alternatives liberate exiles to:**
  – think differently;
  – act differently;
  – speak differently;
  – sing differently.

◆ Imagination is a liberated return to memory.

◆ The past is not a closed record but an energy that offers possibilities.

Session 6 Introduction

Living economically, living ethically
Connecting biblical ethics to the market place

God does not appear in the modern market. For most economists this is as it should be. It is in no way necessary, according to modern economic theory, to consider God when thinking about economy. Indeed, the absence of God in economic matters is viewed as necessary to the great advances in modern economy.

(M Douglas Meeks, *God the Economist: The Doctrine of God and Political Economy*, Fortress Press, 1989, p xi.)

If God does not appear in the modern market then one of a number of complex reasons may be that the church finds difficulty in relating faith to economic life. If faith has lost its communitarian dimension then this may not be surprising. The individualisation of faith has itself removed God from the market place.

Yet money matters dominate human lives and relationships. Money is soul and therefore shapes and impacts every person. It ultimately matters. Like politics, money is never morally neutral. Economics are not value free. Economic systems can become oppressive and dehumanising. Indeed, most of the world's population is excluded from the market square. Poverty is the greatest expression of violence in any society. Economics, therefore, cannot be divorced from ethics. If money makes the world go round then the money dynamic requires ethical norms and values.

The Bible has little difficulty connecting ethics to the market place because it is a communitarian book and envisions a God whose presence and action always goes far beyond temple, synagogue and church. This session explains three biblical models of experience providing a significant ethical vision.

1. Joseph – Pharaoh's economist

We may not be used to reading the Joseph story from an economic perspective. Yet the key Exodus story has the Egyptian experience as its foreground, with economic oppression in the Egyptian brickworks as central to Hebrew memory. There was an experience of slavery to the Egyptian economic system and a supreme irony was that Pharaoh's great economist was a Hebrew. The great architect of the Egyptian economy was Joseph. Joseph devised an economic and food supply strategy that rescued the nation from economic disaster and chronic starvation. His strategy was an economic success story, which not only made Joseph a national hero but also made international headlines.

The ironic but not unfamiliar twist to the story is that economic success turned to economic oppression and became an inhumane system. Economic power and political power merged. Joseph's economic power became almost absolute. The dynamics of power and the building of an economic system are vividly charted in Genesis chapter 47, especially verses 19–22. The state became all-powerful, disempowering and enslaving people. The economic oppressive system even had religious justification (47:22).

Joseph's economic success was created at the cost of people's humanity and dignity. Wealth and power were in the hands of Pharaoh and the rest experienced poverty, economic exploitation, oppression and exclusion from the household of authentic life. Joseph is the story of the injustice of economic success. It is a story of an economic miracle without ethics and of political power without morality. God did not appear in the Egyptian market place. Yet beyond the inhumane economics of Egypt lay the Exodus, the great economic act of God and liberation to an alternative economic and political community rooted in social justice. God the economist and economic ethics are inseparable.

2. Israel's legal codes

There are three legal codes within the Hebrew Scriptures:

◆ Covenant Code – Exodus 20:22–23:33;

◆ Deuteronomic Code – Deuteronomy 12–26;

◆ Holiness Code – Leviticus 17–26.

The Exodus text reflects the earliest Hebrew law code with the Holiness Code a much later development. All three codes have a primary emphasis on economic ethics. They contain an applied theology of liberating economics. All are in defence of the weak and the poor and protect their endangered economic livelihood. Such legislation in Israel was an attempt to preserve political and economic equality as the basis of order and justice in society. The law codes provide ethics for the market place.

The codes legislate for no interest on loans. Israel's near-eastern neighbours had legal codes allowing high interest rates. Only Israel seems to have prohibited interest because it led to poverty and forms of economic slavery (Deuteronomy 23:19–20). The abuse of loans was destructive of a person's access to livelihood and existence.

Gleaning rights did not allow a farmer to harvest the whole crop. The edges of the field were left for the poor because they had a right to share in the harvest (Deuteronomy 24:19–22). The poor could legally enter a field or vineyard before harvest. God is against poverty and intends those who experience economic slavery to have the right to the means of life.

The law of the tithe has often been misunderstood. Far from being a means of support for a religious institution or church work, the tithe was for the sake of the poor (Deuteronomy 14:22–29). It was for the benefit of the powerless, poor, resident aliens, orphans and widows. The latter were the most vulnerable people in near-eastern society. Tithing was a structural economic response to poverty which was believed to be a violation of any human person and destructive of community.

Hospitality for the poor and stranger was expressed through the Hebrew festivals. Passover, Booths and Tabernacles were commemorations of liberation and abundance. These feasts of abundance were all-inclusive, even going beyond the legal codes in the totality of embrace. The community festivals of abundance were to be shared with the widow, orphan, slave and stranger (Deuteronomy 15:7–11). None were to be excluded from the feasts.

Jubilee was to be expressed through three institutions: fallow year, Sabbath year and Jubilee year. The purpose of these was to ensure that disharmony of class and the accumulation of wealth by a few was not possible.

The Jubilee Year, profiled by Leviticus 25, and part of the Holiness Code, was for every 49th year. Four essential things were to happen.

◆ Slaves were to be liberated.

◆ Debts were to be cancelled.

◆ Land was to be fallow.

◆ Land was to be redistributed to original owners.

Jubilee was about economic rehabilitation and offered the possibility for a transformed, just economy. Justice was to be the basis of a new economic beginning. Essentially the legal codes guaranteed structural protection for the weak, powerless and vulnerable.

3 James and economic justice

The Letter of James still suffers from the marginal status assigned it by one wing of the Protestant Reformation . . . Influential critics of the nineteenth century, however, forcefully adopted Luther's position, interpreting this letter as part of the historical dialectic between Pauline and Judaizing movements in early Christianity (of Gal 2:12; Acts 15:1).

(Luke T Johnson, *The Writings of the New Testament: An Interpretation*, SCM Press, 1999, p 507.)

Luther's verdict was that James was a "right strawy epistle" and this has led to the letter being downplayed and dismissed. Or it has been domesticated and spiritualised. Few would admit to selective reading of Scripture and to developing a 'canon within the canon'. Yet James may rarely be read in a worship context and established scholarship has often consigned it to secondary status. Despite Calvin's appreciative commentary on James, Luther's judgement and dismissal has predominated.

Writing from her Latin American context, Elsa Tamez believes that the neglect of James is due to "the privileged place given to abstract thought in our Western societies. The reasonableness of faith is valued more than the practice of faith" (Elsa Tamez in Gottwald and Horsley, editors, *The Bible and Liberation: Political and Social Hermeneutics*, Orbis/SPCK, 1993, pp 531–2).

Tamez entitles her essay 'The Scandalous Message of James' and knows of "churches where the letter is skipped over in the liturgies because there are many rich members in the congregation, and it is very uncomfortable to speak against them when they are sitting in the front seats" (Ibid, p 532).

The problem with James, far from being over a perceived contradiction of Paul's teaching on faith and righteousness, has more to do with James's radical critique of the rich and their exploitation of the poor. James offers an uncomfortable ethic for the economically comfortable and advantaged.

The critique may well be based on the Holiness Code of Leviticus and a commentary on it. For the biblical tradition, holiness is concerned with economic justice and just relations. James writes to a community where the wealthy are exploiting the poor in at least three ways.

◆ The rich are dragging the poor before the courts.

◆ Wealthy farmers are accumulating wealth at the expense of workers salaries.

◆ The carefree rich merchants have no concern for the poor.

Against this kind of unjust community praxis, the letter is an uncompromising call for the practice of economic justice.

The key themes of the letter are all found in chapter 1. When James calls for the poor to "have patience", it is not a passive and submissive patience he calls for. The most frequently used word is HYPOMONE, which is a military word. "This is a militant patience that arises from the roots of oppression; it is an active, working patience" (Tamez, op cit, p 533).

Again James does not advocate passivity on the part of those suffering at the hands of the rich. James has no theology of endurance in the hope of some reward when death comes. Their suffering is defiant suffering. They do not succumb to pain and oppression, but resist and overcome.

The power of prayer for James is prayer with integrity. It is not platitudinal or otherworldly. Prayer is contextual in that it is concretely set in the experience of economic injustice. It is prayer, which does not live two different lives, one in the church and another different life in the market place. It is not two-faced prayer. We either make friends with God or with the economically unjust world.

Integrity is living with economic transparency and consistency between words, beliefs and deeds. It is living out of God's wisdom, which is the practice of giving without reservation, sincerely, generously and without second thoughts. Integrity is showing faith through works, demonstrating the integrity of Christian life through the practice of economic justice.

It is in the economic context or market place that faith and practice are to be held together. Faith without works is dead (James 2:26). Faith is only 'live' if expressed by good works and good works for James is doing justice. For James also, justice is more than creating right economic structures. It is compassionate justice, which is found in the wisdom of God. Prayer again seeks "the wisdom that comes from above and such wisdom is peaceable, gentle, willing to yield, full of mercy (or compassion) and good fruits, without a trace of partiality or hypocrisy" (James 3:17).

In living economically and living ethically, in connecting biblical ethics to the market place, James has an indispensable place and not least a scandalous message for the powerful and wealthy. Perhaps the Bible is a challenging text book on economic ethics.

Session 6 Plan

Welcome (5 minutes)

Group work exercise 1 (10 minutes)

Consider the following questions.

1. What are your reactions to these sound bites?

2. How true are they?

'Money makes the world go around.'

'If I were a rich man!'

'Money is the root of all evil.'

'You cannot worship God and mammon.'

Feedback (10 minutes)

Overhead (5 minutes)

Joseph – Pharaoh's economist

Questions of clarification (5 minutes)

Role-play (40 minutes)

Preparation time (10 minutes)

Role-play (20 minutes)

Reflection (10 minutes)

Overhead (5 minutes)

Israel's legal codes

Group work exercise 2 (10 minutes)

Consider the following question.

Do these legal codes offer any ethical insights into the practice of economics?

Feedback (5 minutes)

Read James1:1–27 (5 minutes)

Overhead (5 minutes)

James and economic justice

Plenary discussion (15 minutes)

The following questions will be considered in an open discussion.

'Poverty is a test from God.'

'Patient endurance will be rewarded in the next life.'

1. In the light of James chapter 1, is this a Christian response?

2. If poverty is one of the main forms of violence, how can it be challenged in a non-violent way (eg James militant patience and defiant suffering)?

3. What is the church's role in the promotion of living economically, living ethically?

Session 6, Handout 1

Group work exercise 1

Working in small groups, consider the following.

1. What are your reactions to these sound bites?

2. How true are they?

'Money makes the world go around.'

'If I were a rich man!'

'Money is the root of all evil.'

'You cannot worship God and mammon.'

Overhead 1

Joseph – Pharaoh's economist

Genesis 44–47

◆ Exodus was an economic liberation

◆ Managing the food stores successfully

◆ Economic miracle became inhumane

◆ Joseph bought all the land for Pharaoh

◆ Majority suffered economic oppression

◆ Economic oppression had religious justification

◆ Joseph's economic success became inhumane and unjust

◆ Hebrews became an underclass of exploited workers in Pharaoh's profitable brickworks

◆ Exodus was an economic act of God and liberation to alternative economic community rooted in justice

Session 6, Handout 2

Role-play

Scenario:

Twenty years after the famine Joseph dies and Pharaoh's department of economic affairs proposes erecting a memorial to Joseph and designating an annual public holiday in his honour. This requires public support and public subscription.

In a local community a public meeting is called to forward the ideas. At this meeting there will be government department representatives, local peasants, some of whom are slaves, and members of Joseph's family.

Each group will be invited to make representation. Read the background material and prepare your response. Be ready to engage in debate.

Reflection questions

1. How did you feel in your role?
2. What tensions were created by the government department's proposal?
3. What was the government department trying to do?
4. How far is life dominated by economics?

Session 6, Handout 3

Israel's legal codes

◆ Covenant Code – Exodus 20:22–23:33
◆ Deuteronomic Code – Deuteronomy 12–26
◆ Holiness Code – Leviticus 17–26
◆ The code describes the structures and forms of community
◆ God's economy and economic ethos of community includes the following:

1. No interest on loans
2. Gleaning rights, eg story of Ruth
3. Law of tithe – 10% produce given for benefit of poor
4. Hospitality – festivals inclusive, shared hospitality
5. Jubilee – release from debt, return to land, end to slavery

◆ All of these provided the basis for a new economic beginning based on justice:

1. For defence of the poor and weak in society

2. For economic and political equality

Group work exercise 2

1. Do these legal codes offer any ethical insights into the practice of economics?

Session 6, Handout 4

James 1:1–27

[1] James, a servant of God and of the Lord Jesus Christ, To the twelve tribes in the Dispersion: Greetings. [2] My brothers and sisters, whenever you face trials of any kind, consider it nothing but joy, [3] because you know that the testing of your faith produces endurance; [4] and let endurance have its full effect, so that you may be mature and complete, lacking nothing. [5] If any of you is lacking in wisdom, ask God, who gives to all generously and ungrudgingly, and it will be given you. [6] But ask in faith, never doubting, for the one who doubts is like a wave of the sea, driven and tossed by the wind; [7,8] for the doubter, being double-minded and unstable in every way, must not expect to receive anything from the Lord. [9] Let the believer who is lowly boast in being raised up, [10] and the rich in being brought low, because the rich will disappear like a flower in the field. [11] For the sun rises with its scorching heat and withers the field; its flower falls, and its beauty perishes. It is the same with the rich; in the midst of a busy life, they will wither away. [12] Blessed is anyone who endures temptation. Such a one has stood the test and will receive the crown of life that the Lord has promised to those who love him. [13] No one, when tempted, should say, 'I am being tempted by God'; for God cannot be tempted by evil and he himself tempts no one. [14] But one is tempted by one's own desire, being lured and enticed by it; [15] then, when that desire has conceived, it gives birth to sin, and that sin, when it is fully grown, gives birth to death. [16] Do not be deceived, my beloved. [17] Every generous act of giving, with every perfect gift, is from above, coming down from the Father of lights, with whom there is no variation or shadow due to change. [18] In fulfilment of his own purpose he gave us birth by the word of truth, so that we would become a kind of first fruits of his creatures. [19] You must understand this, my beloved: let everyone be quick to listen, slow to speak, slow to anger; [20] for your anger does not produce God's righteousness. [21] Therefore rid yourselves of all sordidness and rank growth of wickedness, and welcome with meekness the implanted word that has the power to save your souls. [22] But be doers of the word, and not merely hearers who deceive themselves. [23] For if any are hearers of the word and not doers, they are like those who look at themselves in a mirror; [24] for they look at themselves and, on going away, immediately forget what they were like. [25] But those who look into the perfect law, the law of liberty, and persevere, being not hearers who forget but doers who act – they will be blessed in their doing.

[26] If any think they are religious, and do not bridle their tongues but deceive their hearts, their religion is worthless. [27] Religion that is pure and undefiled before God, the Father, is this: to care for orphans and widows in their distress, and to keep oneself unstained by the world.

NRSV Bible

Session 6, Handout 5

James and economic justice

◆ Luther describes James as a "right strawy epistle".

◆ Luther's attitude has subsequently led to the letter being downplayed, dismissed, domesticated or spiritualised.

◆ James may be a commentary on the Holiness Code of Leviticus chapters 17–26.

◆ James is a sharp critique of exploitation of poor by wealthy.

   1. Rich dragging poor before courts.

   2. Wealthy farmers accumulating wealth at expense of workers' salaries.

   3. Carefree rich merchants with no concern for poor.

◆ James is an uncompromising call for practice of economic justice.

◆ Themes in James chapter 1 are the following.

   1. Judgement against the rich

   2. Militant patience

   3. Contextual prayer

   4. Defiant suffering

   5. Integrity

◆ James calls for faith and practice.

◆ James calls for compassionate justice.

Session 6, Handout 6

Open plenary session

Task:

After reading James 1:1–27, consider the following questions in an open discussion:

'Poverty is a test from God.'

'Patient endurance will be rewarded in the next life.'

1. In the light of James chapter 1, is this a Christian response?

2. If poverty is one of the main forms of violence, how can it be challenged in a non-violent way (eg James militant patience and defiant suffering)?

3. What is the church's role in the promotion of living economically, living ethically?

Bibliography

Bauckham, Richard, *The Bible in Politics: How to Read the Bible Politically*, SPCK, 1989

Berlin, Irving, in Glover, Jonathan, *Humanity: A Moral History of the Twentieth Century*, Jonathan Cape, 1999

Birch, Brueggemann, Fretheim and Peterson, *A Theological Introduction to the Old Testament*, Abingdon, 1999

Birch, Bruce C, *Let Justice Roll Down: The Old Testament, Ethics and Christian Life*, Westminster/John Knox Press, 1991

Brueggemann, Walter, *A Social Reading of the Old Testament: Prophetic Approaches to Israel's Communal Life*, Fortress, 1994

— *Hopeful Imagination: Prophetic Voices in Exile*, SCM Press, 1986

— *Peace*, Chalice Press, 2001

— *Theology of the Old Testament: Testimony, Dispute, Advocacy*, Fortress, 1997

Ceresho, Anthony R, *Introduction to the Old Testament: A Liberation Perspective*, Orbis, 1992

Fowler, James W, *Faithful Change: The Personal and Public Challenges of Postmodern Life*, Abingdon, 1996

Galloway (ed), Kathy, *Pushing The Boat Out*, Wild Goose Publications, 1995

Hanson, Paul D, *The People Called: The Growth of Community in the Bible*, Harper and Row, 1986

Harris, Maria, *Fashion Me a People: Curriculum in the Church*, Westminster/John Knox Press, 1989

Havel, Vaclav, *The Art of the Impossible: Politics as Morality in Practice*, Knoff, 1997

Himes, Michael J, and Himes, Kenneth R, *Fullness of Faith: The Public Significance of Theology*, Paulist Press, 1993

Horsley, Richard, with Hanson, John S, *Bandits, Prophets and Messiahs: Popular Movements in the Time of Jesus*, Trinity Press International, 1999 ed

Horsley, Richard, *Paul and Empire: Religion and Power in Roman Imperial Society*, Trinity Press International, 1997

Horsley, Richard A, and Silberman, Neil Asher, *The Message and the Kingdom*, Grosset/Putnam, 1997

Howard-Brooke, Wes, and Gwyther, Anthony, *Unveiling Empire: Reading Revelation Then and Now*, Orbis, 1999

Johnson, Luke T, *The Writings of the New Testament: An Interpretation*, SCM Press, 1999

Käsemann, Ernest in Elliott, Neil, *Liberating Paul: The Justice of God and the Politics of the Apostle*, Orbis, 1995

Lockhead David, in Gottwald, Norman K, and Horsley, Richard A (editors), *The Bible and Liberation*, Orbis, SPCK, 1993

McFague, Sallie, *Life Abundant: Rethinking Theology and Economy for a Planet in Peril*, Fortress Press, 2001

McMaster, Johnston and Higgins, Cathy, *Churches Working Together: A Practical Resource*, Community Relations Council, 2000

Meeks, M Douglas, *God the Economist: The Doctrine of God and Political Economy*, Fortress Press, 1989

Moltmann, Jurgen, *Creating a Just Future*, SCM Press, 1989

— *The Power of the Powerless*, SCM Press, 1983

Myers, Ched, *Binding the Strong Man: A Political Reading of Mark's Story of Jesus*, Orbis, 1995 ed

O Murchu, Diarmuid, in *Spiritual Questions for the 21st Century: Essays in Honour of Joan D Chittister*, Orbis Books, 2001

O'Connell Killen, Patricia, and De Beer, John, *The Art of Theological Reflection*, Crossroad, 1998

Prior, Michael, *The Bible and Colonialism: A Moral Critique*, Sheffield Academic Press, 1997

Reich, Robert, quoted in Himes and Himes, *Fullness of Faith: The Public Significance of Theology*, Paulist Press, 1993

Schreiter, Robert J, *The New Catholicity: Theology Between the Global and the Local*, Orbis Books, 1997

Stassen, Yeager and Yoder, *Authentic Transformation: A New Vision of Christ and Culture*, Abington Press, 1996

Tamez, Elsa, in Gottwald and Horsley (editors), *The Bible and Liberation: Political and Social Hermeneutics*, Orbis/SPCK, 1993

Theissen, Gerd, *Social Reality and the Early Christians: Theology, Ethics, and the World of the New Testament*, T and T Clarke, 1993

— and Merz, Annette, *The Historical Jesus*, SCM Press, 1998

Tschuy, Theo, *Ethnic Conflict and Religion: Challenge to the Churches*, WCC, 1997

Vogel, Linda J, *Teaching And Learning In Communities Of Faith: Empowering Adults Through Religious Education*, Jossey-Bass Publishers, 1991

Wiefel in Jewett, Robert, *Christian Tolerance: Paul's Message to the Modern Church*, The Westminster Press, 1982

Wink, Walter, *Engaging the Powers: Discernment and Resistance in a World of Domination*, Fortress Press, 1992